ArtScroll Tanach Series®

A traditional commentary on the Books of the Bible

Rabbis Nosson Scherman/Meir Zlotowitz
General Editors

THE
meGILLaH

THE BOOK OF ESTHER / A NEW TRANSLATION
WITH A COMMENTARY ANTHOLOGIZED FROM
TALMUDIC, MIDRASHIC AND RABBINIC SOURCES.

Published by

Mesorah Publications, ltd

Translated and compiled by
Rabbi Meir Zlotowitz

'An Overview/The Period and the Miracle'
by
Rabbi Nosson Scherman

FIRST EDITION
First Impression ... February, 1976
Second Impression ... March, 1976
Third Impression ... March, 1976
SECOND EDITION
Revised and Corrected
First Impression ... December, 1976
Second Impression ... July, 1977
Third Impression ... January, 1978
Fourth Impression ... April, 1979
Fifth Impression ... July, 1980
Sixth Impression ... December, 1981
Seventh Impression ... January, 1984
Eighth Impression ... December, 1984
Ninth Impression ... January, 1986
Tenth Impression ... June, 1987

Published and Distributed by
MESORAH PUBLICATIONS, Ltd.
Brooklyn, New York 11223

Distributed in Israel by
MESORAH MAFITZIM / J. GROSSMAN
Rechov Harav Uziel 117
Jerusalem, Israel

Distributed in Europe by
J. LEHMANN HEBREW BOOKSELLERS
20 Cambridge Terrace / Gateshead
Tyne and Wear / England NE8 1RP

THE ARTSCROLL TANACH SERIES®
THE MEGILLAH / THE BOOK OF ESTHER
© Copyright 1976, 1978, 1979, 1980, 1981, 1984
by MESORAH PUBLICATIONS, Ltd.
1969 Coney Island Avenue / Brooklyn, N.Y. 11223 / (718) 339-1700

סדר במסטרבת
חברת ארטסקרול בע״מ

Typography by CompuScribe at ArtScroll Studios, Ltd.
1969 Coney Island Avenue / Brooklyn, N.Y. 11223 / (718) 339-1700

Printed in the United States of America by Moriah Offset, Brooklyn, N.Y.
Bound by SEFERCRAFT, Inc., Brooklyn, N.Y.

הסכמת הגאון האמיתי שר התורה ועמוד ההוראה
מורנו ורבנו מרן ר' משה פיינשטיין שליט"א

RABBI MOSES FEINSTEIN
455 F. D. R. DRIVE
NEW YORK, N. Y. 10002

OREgon 7-1222

משה פיינשטיין
ר"מ תפארת ירושלים
בנוא יארק

בע"ה

הנה ידידי הרב הנכבד מאד מוהר"ר מאיר יעקב בן ידידי הרב הגאון ר' אהרן
זלאטאוויץ שליט"א, אשר היה תלמיד חשוב אצלינו בהישיבה, בן תורה וירא
שמים באמת ובתמים, ומכירו אני כל העת בשמו הטוב בכל העינים בהנהגה
ישרה ונכונה כראוי לבני תורה ויראי השי"ת, חבר ספר חשוב בשפת האנגלית
המדוברת ביותר במדינה זו, וקבץ דברים יקרים ופנינים נחמדים מספרי רבותינו
נ"ע על מגלת אסתר אשר הם מעוררים לאהבת התורה וקיום המצות ולחזוק
האמונה בהשי"ת, והוא ראוי לסמוך עליו במה שלקט וקבץ ואשר יסבירם
בדברים נעימים להמשיך את הלב לתורה ולתעודה, וטוב גם לחנוך התלמידים
שיביא להם הרבה תועלת, אשר לכן טוב הדבר שהוא מדפיס ספרו זה להגדיל
אהבת השי"ת ותורתו הקדושה וע"ז באתי עה"ח בתשעה לשבט תשל"ו

נאום משה פיינשטיין

Haskamah   [iv]

בעזהשי"ת

הרב אהרן זלאטאוויץ
Rabbi Aron Zlotowitz

CONGREGATION ETZ CHAIM ANSHEI LUBIN
EXECUTIVE DIRECTOR BOARD OF ORTHODOX RABBIS OF BROOKLYN

RESIDENCE:
1134 EAST 9 STREET
BROOKLYN, N.Y. 11230
(212) 252-9188

Preface to the Second Edition

When the first edition of the ArtScroll Megillas Esther was written, the enthusiastic reception it was to receive was not anticipated and there was surely no expectation of a second edition. The response of the Torah public was such that this memorial to a dear friend became the first publication in a series that will אי״ה embrace the Prophets and Writings as well as other of our holy books. To have gained entree into thousands of Jewish homes and to have become a conduit of Torah wisdom to tens of thousands of Jews is a privilege, of course — but it also imposes an awesome responsibility to be worthy of the trust and expectations of those who have given this series such wide acceptance.

As in the prefaces to Eichah and Koheles, in addition to setting forth what the series attempts to do, we feel that it is essential to make clear what it is not designed to do.

Much of our Torah knowledge is afflicted with a malady — rather than examine the Torah anew, with fresh eyes and more maturity as we grow older, we unfortunately remain with the simplified versions presented to us when we were children.

In this series, an attempt is made to cull the enormous treasury of Torah thought that has been untapped by most people and, by so doing, reveal some of Torah's riches to those for whom it is Israel's most precious possession. At the same time, we are quick to point out that whatever has been offered is but a sampler. We urge our readers to use both the Overview and the Commentary as source material and as springboards to further and deeper study of their own.

גַּל עֵינַי וְאַבִּיטָה נִפְלָאוֹת מִתּוֹרָתֶךְ
Open my eyes that I may behold wonders
from Your Torah (Psalms 119:17)

The wonders are in Torah. We deem ourselves privileged to have helped open eyes to behold them.

The Editors

Table of Contents

Preface

I t is with mixed feelings of joy and sadness that this volume is presented to the public.

☐ Sadness — *because it was undertaken* לעילוי נשמת הרב מאיר ב״ר יחזקאל צדוק ע״ה *in memory of my very intimate and dear friend* Rabbi Mair Fogel ע״ה, *who was tragically cut off from this world on* א יום ג טבת, תשל״ו, *December 7, 1975 — leaving his dear wife* ח״יבל״ *Pearl, and beloved mother Anna as his only surviving immediate family.*

I wanted desperately to perpetuate his noble memory in some meaningful form, and, on the night following his funeral, I undertook to compile this anthology of commentaries on Megillas Esther. My hope was to embark on a work which could be completed within the "sh'loshim," and at the same time make a serious and needed contribution to the Torah public. There was absolutely nothing of this scope available on the Book of Esther for the tradition-seeking reader, *and with around-the-clock-work, the task could be completed within the thirty day-"shloshim" goal.*

☐ Joy — *because it has become evident that a significant contribution has been made to the English-speaking audience: A lucid, literate anthology of commentaries, based entirely on Talmudic, Midrashic, and Rabbinic sources, on what is probably the most familiar book of the Bible — but is nevertheless little understood in the light of our Sages who dwelt upon every letter of the text and elucidated its innermost meanings. Working through many nights, my goal was to delve deep enough to fathom the true meaning of Megillas Esther as understood by our Sages, and to attempt to present it to the English-reading audience in a palatable and readable manner.*

The Commentary thus conceived was bound to appeal to a large cross-section of people from the early-teenage day school student to the Hebrew teacher; from the college student seeking a traditional interpretation of a book of the Bible to the housewife; from the 'uninitiated' adult reader with limited Hebrew background to the young kollel scholar who has neither access to all the sources in their original, nor the time to investigate them individually. This, of course, encompasses a very wide range of background and ability; the completed book is, I hope, one that bridges the gap and fills the unique individual needs of each reader.

SCOPE OF THE COMMENTARY

The primary goal was to provide a free-flowing 'running commentary' to the text, removing first the 'surface difficulties.' It became immediately obvious that the standard JPS translation — which very often is at odds with the Talmudic translation of the Hebrew — simply would not do. A free-flowing, lucid, and literate translation in consonance with the interpretation of our Sages was absolutely essential to ensure the readability of the book and its faithfulness to the outlook of our Torah sages. The new translation eliminated many of the 'surface difficulties' dealt with by Rashi and Ibn Ezra because their interpretations were incorporated within the translation.

The Gemara and Midrashim were then consulted, and virtually every Chazal directly concerned with פְּשַׁט — the literal and intended meaning of the text, which could be meaningfully incorporated into the framework of an English-language commentary was included.

The classic commentaries — Rashi, Ibn Ezra, and Alschich — were then culled for essential comments not suggested in the translation or quoted in the Talmudic sources.

Next, the major commentaries were consulted: primarily the M'nos Halevi, by Rav Shlomo Alkabetz, Yosef Lekach by Rav Eliezer haRofe, the recently reprinted commentary of Rav Elisha Galico, the Vilna Gaon, the all-encompassing Yalkut Me'am Lo'ez, and the commentary of the Malbim. [An extensive bibliography — with brief biographical descriptions of the authorities consulted — has been added to the back of the volume.]

The problem was not finding material on the Megillah: it was limiting the vast material to that which would provide the best 'running commentary' within the scope of the work. I hope that the resulting volume does justice both to the Gaonim who have been cited and to the reader.

It must be made clear that this is not a so-called 'scientific' or 'apologetic' commentary on the Megillah. That area has, unfortunately, been too well-covered, resulting in violence to the Jewish faith as well as to correct interpretation. It is in no way the intention of this book to demonstrate the legitimacy or historicity of Esther or Mordechai to non-believers or doubters. Belief in the authenticity of every book of the Torah is basic to Jewish faith, and we proceed from there. It comes as no surprise to me — nor should it to any Orthodox Jew — that the palace in Shushan, as unearthed by archealogists, bears out the description of the palace in the Megillah in every detail; nor do we deem it necessary to prove, by means of the 'Persian borrow-words,' nor by whatever means, that the Book was, indeed, written in that contemporary period.

Rather, the aim was a specifically traditional commentary reflecting the Megillah as understood by Chazal. No non-Jewish sources have even been consulted, much less quoted. I consider it offensive that the Torah should need authentication from the secular or so-called 'scientific' sources. The sources of every excerpt has been documented. Whenever the author has inserted a comment of his own, it is inserted in brackets.

To add to the appeal of this book among Yeshivah students, much use has been made of Hebrew within the commentary. All such Hebrew references are vocalized and translated for the benefit of those less fluent in the language.

The transliteration of the Hebrew words posed a problem: Sephardi or Ashkenazi? It was decided that the pronunciation most acceptable to most readers was a cross between the Ashkenazi and Sefardi — Ashkenazi consonents, so to speak, with Sephardi vowels. Words that have become generally accepted, such as 'Ahasuerus' were not changed to conform to the above method of transliteration. Although there are several inconsistencies, in general the style has been held throughout the work.

The moment of bidding farewell to this book is indeed nostalgic and solemn. It marks the conclusion of a delightful quest, of many hours spent in intimate contact with חז״ל, our Sages, and their profound insight into every facet of Torah study.

I am deeply grateful for the frequent and inspiring sessions spent with my good friend, RABBI NOSSON SCHERMAN, throughout the compilation of this work. Reb Nosson has given of himself beyond every reasonable expectation; he was kind enough to further cramp his busy schedule to read, amend, research, expand and edit my manuscript. He put his scholarly mark on the book, and lent it the benefit of his erudition and flowing style. His very association with this work has raised its level beyond description. Appreciating the need for such a work, he also consented to write the most beautiful Introduction. I take this opportunity to express to him my warm and sincere thanks. Our association has taught me more than I can put into words.

Similarly, I owe a tremendous debt of gratitude to my colleague at ArtScroll and חָבֵר נֶאֱמָן, REB SHEAH BRANDER for providing the initial impetus in this project. His tireless efforts in seeing the graphics through every stage of production — with editing and constant changes — and his constant availability as a sounding-board for much of the material, provided a continuous source of inspiration. My wishes — often unreasonable, I fear — have had his sympathetic consideration and unyielding response.

Reb Nosson and Reb Sheah could have produced this work without me, but I could not have produced it without them.

To a considerable extent, this work was inspired by REBBETZIN MEYER FELDBRAND. She, with the assistance of her husband, a distinguished talmid chacham, prepared a manuscript in English that was an anthology of commentaries. The work in its original form was not publishable. It was mutually agreed that her project would be dropped and that I would attempt a new anthology with a different emphasis dedicated to the memory of Reb Mair Fogel ע״ה . Rebbetzin Feldbrand is to be commended, however, for her concept. It is hoped that this woman of considerable ability will find new vehicles to make her sensitivity and talent available to the Torah public.

ACKNOWLEDGEMENTS

And now, as I lay down my pen, it is my pleasant duty to express deep feelings of gratitude to the many friends who have given of themselves so nobly and offered such precious help:

First, my father HARAV ARON ZLOTOWITZ—"אֲשֶׁר מֵימָיו אֲנִי שׁוֹתֶה" for giving of his profound and phenomenal scholarship and for his constant advice and guidance. May he and my dear mother תחי׳, be rewarded with אֲרִיכוּת יָמִים וְשָׁנִים מִתּוֹךְ בַּרְיוּת גּוּפָא וּנְהוֹרָא מְעַלְיָא.

I owe a great debt of gratitude to my dear friend, MR. DAVID H. SCHWARTZ who responded to this project with great warmth and enthusiasm. He read the manuscript and made many practical suggestions which were incorporated into the work. I appreciate his constant concern and guidance.

RABBI JOSEPH ELIAS, who was kind enough to read and comment upon the manuscript of the first chapter in the initial stage of this work. His scholarly insights and friendly advice helped set the tone for the work as a whole, and his encouragement provided an important impetus. His encouragement and comments were of immeasurable benefit.

My very good friend, RABBI DAVID COHEN, from whom I learned in years gone by my first real lessons in research, and from whom I developed my great love for sefarim. He graciously took the time to read and comment on parts of the manuscript. He pointed out important concepts, made many stimulating suggestions, and provided insights from the spring of his original thought and phenomenal scholarship.

My long time friend, REB AVI SHULMAN, who shouldered the burden at ArtScroll during my involvement with this work and who, seeing the need for such a commentary, almost single-handedly ensured its dissemination on a broad scale.

RABBI NISSON WOLPIN, for making himself available during the formative stage of the work and for providing much encouragement and suggestions which helped shape the scope of the commentary and direction of the finished book.

Perhaps the single greatest 'יִישַׁר כֹּחַ' is due to HARAV DAVID FEINSTEIN, who I am privileged to call רַבִּי אֲלוּפִי וּמְיוּדָּעִי. He has read and commented upon nearly every selection. He graciously took time out from his busy schedule to read the manuscript on a daily basis and allowed me to benefit from the abundant storehouse of his learning. He removed stumbling blocks and guided me to interpretations I might otherwise have misunderstood. Most of all, he graciously gave me the gift of time, which cannot be repaid.

The responsibility, however, for what is included in, and what has been omitted from this book, is entirely mine. All the above were good enough to leave the final redaction of the book wholly to me. They are therefore absolved from any responsibility for errors or shortcomings in that which follows; such are completely my own.

I feel indebted to MRS. JUDY GROSSMAN for generously giving of her personal time to proof read the manuscript through its evolving stages of editing. She took it upon herself — within the short span of time allowed — to help ensure the accuracy of the final product. Many errors would have passed through uncorrected were it not for her keen eye.

MISS MIRIAM FLAM has been kind enough to assist in certain areas of research. In their capacities at ArtScroll, she, MISS MAZAL LANIADO and MISS PEARL EINHORN, have followed through the technical end of the publication in a most dedicated manner. They responded with great selflessness; their role is greatly appreciated.

My deepest gratitude is due my wife מנב״ת, RACHEL, who created the domestic atmosphere and inspiration conducive for Torah-study and for the compilation of such a work, and who graciously assisted in translating and proofreading. May השי״ת grant us both that in the z'chus of Harbatzas Torah we may merit to see בָּנִים וּבְנֵי־בָנִים עוֹסְקִים בַּתּוֹרָה וּבְמִצְוֹת.

E very author has hopes for the work that represents a slice of his life, a part of his being. Especially for a work like this — one that is intended as a monument to a dear friend — one presents his book to the public with a tefillah that it fulfill its purpose. Its purpose is this:

> To make accessible to the Torah public a *Chazal's* eye view of one of the twenty-four sacred books of *Tanach*; provide a glimpse of the treasure hidden in the depths of every verse of Torah; by so doing, to inspire others to open other parts of *Tanach* and find the treasures hidden there; what is more, to be a catalyst that will drive others to compile more and finer commentaries in our rich heritage of סִפְרֵי קֹדֶשׁ — holy books; most of all, to help Torah hurdle the language barrier that has condemned so many thousands of English-speaking Jews to varying degrees of spiritual pauperdom.

An ambitious purpose, this. If but part of it is realized than the thousands of cumulative man-hours invested in this volume will have been justly rewarded.

Meir Zlotowitz
Brooklyn, New York, Tu b'Shevat, 5736

An Overview—
The Period and the Miracle

אֶסְתֵּר מִן הַתּוֹרָה מִנַּיָן?
"וְאָנֹכִי הַסְתֵּר אַסְתִּיר פָּנַי"

Where is there an allusion to Esther
in the Torah?
"And I will hide My face" *(Deut. 31:18).*

—*Chullin 139b*

פירש"י . . בִּימֵי אֶסְתֵּר יִהְיֶה הֶסְתֵּר פָּנִים

". . . in the days of Esther
there will be a concealment
of the divine countenance" —*Rashi.*

אָמַר רַב שְׁמוּאֵל בַּר יְהוּדָה,
שָׁלְחָה לָהֶם אֶסְתֵּר לַחֲכָמִים, "קָבְעוּנִי לְדוֹרוֹת."
שָׁלְחוּ לָהּ, "קִנְאָה אַתְּ מְעוֹרֶרֶת עָלֵינוּ לְבֵין הָאוּמוֹת?
שָׁלְחָה לָהֶם, כְּבָר כְּתוּבָה אֲנִי עַל
דִּבְרֵי הַיָּמִים לְמַלְכֵי מָדַי וּפָרַס

Rav Shmuel bar Yehudah said,
Esther sent to the Sages, "establish me [the
festival marking my miracle] for all time." They
sent back, "Do you seek to arouse the jealousy
of the nations against us?" She sent them, "I am
already inscribed in the royal chronicle of Media
and Persia" —*Megillah 7a*

The
Historical
Background

It is hard to imagine how the Divine countenance
could be concealed during a prophetic period; surely the prophets would see it and reveal its grandeur!
In our confused times, many wonder how we will

It is hard to imagine
how the Divine
countenance could
be concealed during
a prophetic period:
surely the prophets
would see it and
reveal its grandeur!

know when מָשִׁיחַ—the Messiah arrives — who will tell us? "If only we had a prophet — then we would know; then we would follow."

There were still prophets during גָלוּת בָּבֶל — the Babylonian exile. Even in its closing years, Daniel, Mordechai, Baruch ben Neria, Ezra, Chaggai, Zechariah, Malachi, and more were still on the scene. Fifty-two years after the destruction of the Temple a prophecy was fulfilled. Cyrus, King of Persia, gave the order that the House of G-d be rebuilt in Jerusalem. The prophet Isaiah had foretold it about two hundred years before: אָמַר ה' לִמְשִׁיחוֹ לְכוֹרֶשׁ— So said G-d to His anointed, to Cyrus ... לְמַעַן עַבְדִּי יַעֲקֹב וְיִשְׂרָאֵל בְּחִירִי — For the sake of Jacob my servant and Israel my chosen ... הוּא יִבְנֶה עִירִי וְגָלוּתִי יְשַׁלֵּחַ — he shall build My city and he shall free My captives [Isaiah 45].

It was two years before Ahasuerus became King and over four years before the opening scene of Megillas Esther. To the Jewish people, intensely familiar with the prophecies of Isaiah, the gesture of Cyrus should have been a signal to converge upon Jerusalem to rebuild the Temple that had been razed by Nebuchadnezzar. Indeed, they should have considered it a rare opportunity that they, not Cyrus, were given this privilege of rebuilding the House of G-d — according to Isaiah's prophecy, it was the Divine will that Cyrus, not the Jews, build the House of G-d and bring its children back to its holy environs. But Cyrus gave the privilege to the Jewish people. [Megillah 12a]

Prophecy Unheeded

Cyrus, who wept
and groaned over
the Temple's
destruction, became
G-d's chosen
instrument to fulfill
the ancient
prophecy

Cyrus, who wept and groaned over the Temple's destruction [Seder Eliyahu Rabba, 19], became G-d's chosen instrument to fulfill the ancient prophecy and bring the glory of the Divine Presence back to the holy mountain where Abraham bound Isaac to the altar, where Jacob beheld the heavenly ladder, where David set his hopes, and where Solomon built the Temple of G-d. The righteous Persian monarch gave the order that the Jews might go home again — and only forty-two thousand heeded his call! Forty-two thousand heard the call of prophecy but millions stayed behind.

When G-d hides His face, such are the effects. Confusion, hesitation, fear. What does G-d want of us? Where and how are we to do His bidding? And what *is* His bidding?

This was the tapestry before which the actors in the Purim story entered the stage of history. The Jewish people were splintered and confused. Torah study was experiencing a renaissance in Babylon — but some of its outstanding sons were asking whether they, as a nation driven by its G-d from His land, still owed Him any more allegiance than a divorced woman driven from the home of her husband, or a freed slave sent away from the home of his master [*Sanhedrin 105a*]. A shocking question, one that can only be understood as one more saddening indication of the many veils behind which the Divine countenance was hidden.

Cyrus moved his royal capital to Shushan in the Land of Elam. With him went Mordechai and Daniel, but they were not able to teach Torah in Elam as they had, and their peers were still doing in the flowering academies of Babylon. Elam, the seat of royal power, the source of Jewish hope, was barren of Torah. More concealment of the Divine countenance.

Hope Extinguished

The work on the Temple in Jerusalem proceeded under Cyrus despite the harassment of hostile nations surrounding Jerusalem. In the last months of his reign, Cyrus had a change of heart. He forbade additional Jews to cross the river to the Land of Israel. This setback caused the Jewish pioneers in Jerusalem to despair and halt the work they had begun so hopefully. But the rebuilding had not been outlawed, only hindered [*Shir Hashirim Rabba 5:4*].

The reign of Cyrus did not long endure. Only two years after he ordered the rebuilding of the Temple, Ahasuerus was king of the vast Persian Empire. The new king was no friend of the Jews. Despite the impression common among us that he was an amiable drunkard who was manipulated by Haman, the Sages make it very clear that he was thoroughly evil [*Megillah 11a*] and that he hated the Jews even more than did Haman [*Esther Rabba 4:12*]. His queen, Vashti, a granddaughter of Nebuchadnezzar,

Torah study was experiencing a renaissance in Babylon — but some of its outstanding sons were asking whether they, as a nation driven by its G-d from His land, still owed Him any more allegiance than a divorced woman driven from the home of her husband, or a freed slave sold away from the home of his master

Despite the impression common among us that Ahasuerus was an amiable drunkard who was manipulated by Haman, the Sages make it very clear that he was thoroughly evil and that he hated the Jews even more than did Haman

fulminated furiously against the feeble attempts to rebuild the Temple and she insisted that Ahasuerus put an end to the holy task begun by Cyrus [*Esther Rabba 5:2*]. Finally, a vicious letter arrived from Jerusalem. It was written by enemies of the Jews — the sons of Haman prominent among them — and accused them of building the Temple as a prelude to rebellion. Ahasuerus was only too happy to accept the advice of his queen and the reports of his observers. He ordered an end to the work in Jerusalem [*Ezra 4*].

So another veil descended over the Divine countenance as it seemed plain that Isaiah's prophecy was not to be fulfilled. And if not, then perhaps, indeed, the Jewish people were no less adrift and alone than the wife and the slave driven from their former husband and master.

The Crucial Prophecy

There was another prophecy, more explicit and more imminent than Isaiah's, that was a source of confusion at best; and despair at worst:

כִּי כֹה אָמַר ה׳, כִּי לְפִי מְלֹאת לְבָבֶל שִׁבְעִים שָׁנָה אֶפְקֹד
אֶתְכֶם וַהֲקִימֹתִי עֲלֵיכֶם אֶת דְּבָרִי הַטּוֹב לְהָשִׁיב אֶתְכֶם
אֶל הַמָּקוֹם הַזֶּה

For thus says the L-rd, that after seventy years of Babylon are completed, I will remember you and perform my good word concerning you to make you return to this place

[Jeremiah 29:10].

אֲנִי דָנִיֵּאל בִּינֹתִי בַּסְּפָרִים מִסְפַּר הַשָּׁנִים אֲשֶׁר הָיָה דְבַר
ה׳ אֶל יִרְמְיָה הַנָּבִיא לְמַלֹּאות לְחָרְבוֹת יְרוּשָׁלַיִם
שִׁבְעִים שָׁנָה

I, Daniel, considered in the books the number of years whereof the word of the L-rd came to Jeremiah the prophet that he would complete seventy years of the ruins of Jerusalem

[Daniel 9:2]).

Perplexities of Concealment

Was Cyrus' order the fulfillment of the prophecy? And if it was, how could it have been so easily nullified by Ahasuerus? Was the gracious gesture of Cyrus a Divine invitation to the Jews to demonstrate their love of Jerusalem and, found wanting, were they denied even the fragile beginning of a redemption?

Another veil of concealment over the Divine countenance.

What happens when G-d's face is hidden? We no longer see His hand guiding history. The successes and failures of the Jewish people were historically dependent upon their allegiance to G-d and His Torah. Torah and Prophets are a series of pledges and warnings. When Jews were loyal to the dictates of their Creator, they were rewarded in this world as well as the next. And when they failed to heed His word, retribution was not long in coming. That was when G-d showed His face and His concern. When His countenance was concealed, Israel became subject to the whims of rulers, the mutations of nature and the vicissitudes of history. The smile of Cyrus seemed to matter more than the prophecy of Jeremiah, and the frown of Ahasuerus was more disastrous than the chastisements of Moses.

The smile of Cyrus seemed to matter more than the prophecy of Jeremiah, and the frown of Ahasuerus was more disastrous than the chastisements of Moses.

Who is Concealed?

אֶסְתֵּר מִן הַתּוֹרָה מְנַיִן
Where is there an allusion to Esther in the Torah?

On the surface, it seemed clear that it was G-d who had made Himself distant, but in reality, even the concealment was ordained by the Torah. It was the Jewish people that had created the distance between itself and its G-d. By neglecting its total dependence on G-d and its total belief in the supreme אָנֹכִי—I— the אָנֹכִי — I of the first commandment אָנֹכִי ה' אֱלֹקֶיךָ —*I am the L-rd your G-d*—the Jews created the conditions that beclouded the Divine Image and allowed a barrier to conceal His countenance from them. But He was still there. It was the challenge of that confused, baffled, frightened generation to strip away the veils — or, better said, to recognize that it was He who gave existence to *all* the veils, that nature itself was but an illusory veil that could conceal Him only from those who were blind. That was the challenge. It was the greatness of Mordechai and Esther that they found Him for themselves and revealed Him to others, and, in so doing, illuminated every darkness down through the centuries [*Maharsha, Chullin 139b*].

By neglecting its total dependence on G-d the Jews created the conditions that beclouded the Divine Image and allowed a barrier to conceal His countenance from them. But He was still there.

The Second Temple — A Dreaded Prophecy

Most of us have become indoctrinated with a non-Jewish, anti-Torah version of history. The existence or destruction of the Temple has been portrayed as a cultural sidelight to the existence of a Jewish nation-state. The Jerusalem awarded by Cyrus to his Jewish subjects consisted of only the city and its immediate environs, barely more than a dot on the world scene and surely of no greater significance than any casual amnesty of a kind-hearted ruler. Saturated as many of us have become with this version of history, we are thoroughly convinced that whatever importance the Holy Land possessed was primarily because it was the crossroads of three continents.

The authentic history of the period as seen through Torah eyes is far different. Jeremiah's prophecy hung like a sword over the heads of absolute monarchs. To them, the Temple was more than a building. It represented a philosophy of life that was dramatically opposed to theirs.

The authentic history of the period as seen through Torah eyes is far different. Jeremiah's prophecy hung like a sword over the heads of absolute monarchs. To them, the Temple was more than a building. It represented a philosophy of life that was dramatically opposed to theirs. The G-d of Israel was a power who had destroyed kings from Pharaoh to Sancherev. If His people were to be redeemed, then He could well lay low the masters, kings, and rulers of all lands as he had done whenever they menaced His people in past generations. When Haman sought to persuade Ahasuerus that the Jews could be exterminated with impunity, the Jew-hating king was reluctant.

"I am afraid that their G-d will do to me what He did to my predecessors," he argued.

Haman answered, "The Jews are sleeping. Because they no longer perform *mitzvos* as they once did, they do not merit heavenly intercession" [*Megillah* 13b.]

Haman and Ahasuerus saw more clearly than did the Jews. They, too, saw the veils of concealment, but the two plotters knew that the darkness was not imposed from on high; it was a reflection of Jewish attitudes below.

Monarchies Haunted

For more than a generation, Jeremiah's prophecy haunted monarchs and their advisors. The L-rd of Hosts said that Babylon would be ascendant for seventy years and that the ruins of Jerusalem would rot for seventy years. If the prophecy were to come true, crowns would topple and empires crumble. As long as the prophecy was pending, kings avoided gross acts of disrespect toward G-d lest they provoke His anger. They lived in fear, but they also lived with hope—the hope that the destruction of the Temple marked the end of G-d's ascendancy ו״ח or that the Jewish lethargy had allowed the bonds between them and G-d to slip apart. And the magic number was seventy. If seventy years went by without fulfillment of Jeremeiah's prophecy, then Jerusalem would forever remain a plowed field and a haven only to foxes.

Belshazzar, grandson of and successor to the throne of Nebuchadnezzar, watched the days go by with trepidation as the end of year number seventy grew closer. Jeremiah's prophecy was well known and well respected: *after seventy years of Babylon are completed.* The then current Babylonian Empire was founded by Nebuchadnezzar in the year 3318 (442 BCE). He reigned for forty-five years and was succeeded by his son, Evil Merodach, who reigned for another twenty-three. Balshazzar saw the months go by until he entered the third year of his reign. The seventy years were over! He rejoiced, but he was not content to be merely joyous; he had to show his contempt of the G-d whose power he no longer feared.

Belshazzar prepared the wild, orgiastic feast that has become legendary in the literature of excess. To celebrate, he did something that not even his brazen grandfather had dared do; he took out the sacred vessels of the Temple and used them in his wild, drunken revelry. And why not? Jeremiah was wrong. Babylon had survived his deadline and Jerusalem was not being rebuilt. But Belshazzar was wrong. By morning he was dead [*Megillah 11b*].

The arithmetic of the seventy years will be discussed later. For the moment, however, let us take note that no Babylonian king, even after the razing of Jerusalem, dared use its holy vessels. They knew full well that, though Judea was but a minor province in the world of *realpolitik*, it was a major spiritual force.

The prophecy was real, and if it came true, punishments too terrible to be contemplated would be visited upon the monarch who dared profane the holy vessels.

The Seat of Power Moves

Belshazzar's audacity was brutally punished that very night as he was murdered by Darius, the Mede, and his son-in-law, Cyrus, the Persian. Darius offered the throne to Cyrus, but the younger man demurred because Daniel had prophesied that the kingdom of Babylon would pass first to Media and then to Persia [*Yalkut Shimoni, Esther, 1049*]. So it was that a prophecy decided the highest of all affairs of state — the identity of the monarch and the seat of world dominion. Both reigns were brief — Darius' lasted a year and Cyrus' for less than three. In 3392, (368 BCE) Ahasuerus assumed the throne of the Persian Empire in the capital city of Shushan.

Belshazzar blundered miserably — and bloodily — in his computation; Ahasuerus was determined to do better.

He, too, kept one eye on the calendar. Seventy years — when would they end? Belshazzar blundered miserably — and bloodily — in his computation; Ahasuerus was determined to do better. According to his calculation, the seventy years ended with the third year of his reign. He celebrated with the fabulous 180-day feast with which *Megillas Esther* begins. And he, too, as an arrogant symbol of his new-found security from the Jeremiah prophecy, did something he had never dared do up to then — he profaned the sacred vessels of the Temple [*Megillah 11b*]. His calculation, too, was wrong, but he was spared from immediate retribution because G-d's plan called for Ahasuerus to become sire of the man who would finally bring fulfillment to the words of the prophets.

Anything — Except . . .

Nine years later, Esther came to plead for her people and Ahasuerus made his famous magnanimous gesture that she might make any request up to half the kingdom and it would be fulfilled. The Talmud (*Ibid*) says he that told her she might request anything וְלֹא דָבָר שֶׁחוֹצֵץ לַמַּלְכוּת — except for something that will interfere with the stability of the kingdom, וּמַאי נִיהוּ, בִּנְיַן בֵּית הַמִּקְדָּשׁ — and what is this thing? The building of the Holy Temple. Let us not forget that at that time, Ahasuerus had no idea that his queen was a Jewess, nor had she ever given him any reason to think that the half-finished, long-neglected Temple was of any interest to her. Nevertheless, when he made an offer as generous as any husband has ever made to a distraught wife, he felt it necessary to caution her that in all the world there was one request that he could not grant because it would irreparably disrupt the stability of his kingdom — the Temple must not be rebuilt.

There was one equest that he could not grant because it would irreparably disrupt the stability of his kingdom — the Temple must not be rebuilt.

Thus, it should be absolutely clear that, despite the fact that only forty-two thousand Jews had returned "home," the Holy City and Holy Land were very much on the minds of all rulers. In a broader sense, this should point up another vital realization. Because the study of history has always been of negligible importance in the world of Torah scholarship, the field has been forfeited to the "historians" who have all too often become its distorters. The three examples cited above throw a new light on one aspect of the period that is not found in the history books. We may justly say that the current world-view is a massive veil of concealment that obscures our vision of all too much.

Because the study of history has always been of negligible importance in the world of Torah scholarship, the field has been forfeited tol the "historians" who have all too often become its distorters.

The Mysterious Seventy Years

As mentioned above, Jeremiah spoke of seventy years of Babylon before the Jews would be remembered by G-d, and Daniel spoke of seventy years from the destruction of Jerusalem. As we have seen, the kings of the period dreaded the climax of the seventy years and each in turn attempted to determine when they would end. The following table gives some of the main dates and events of the period and shows which were crucial to the "seventy" and

The kings of the period dreaded the climax of the seventy years and each in turn attempted to determine when they would end

which were extraneous. [*The material is taken from Rabbi Joseph D. Epstein's excellent work,* Otzar Ha'iggeres, *a masterful compilation of halacha, aggada, history, and ethical thought on Purim and the Megillah. See* Otzar Ha'Iggeres *p. 149 for a far more extensive table of relevant dates and events.*]

THE YEAR	THE EVENT
3318	Nebuchadnezzar assumes the throne of Babylon
3319	Nebuchadnezzar conquers King Yeho-yakim of Judea. The Jewish land becomes a vassal state of Babylon.
3327	Nebuchadnezzar exiles King Yechaniah of Judea together with the leading scholars.
3338	Nebuchadnezzar destroys the Temple and exiles the Jewish nation.
3389	Belshazzar, dating the "seventy" from the accession to the throne of Nebuchadnezzar, celebrates and dies. He interprets "seventy years of Babylon" as a reference to the reigning dynasty.
3390	Cyrus orders the construction of the Temple. It is, indeed, seventy years since the first stage of the exile, the conquest of Judea. G-d has "remembered" Jerusalem as promised to Jeremiah, but not yet redeemed it.
3392	Ahasuerus becomes king and orders the cessation of construction of the Temple.
3394	Ahasuerus, in the third year of his reign, concludes that seventy years, dating from Yechaniah's exile, have ended. Although only 67 calendar years have elapsed, Ahasuerus follows the ancient custom of counting a fraction of a royal year as a full year. [*For a detailed explanation, see* Megillah 11b *and* Otzar Ha'iggeres].
3406	Ahasuerus dies and is succeeded by Darius, son of Esther.
3408	Darius orders that construction of the Temple begin again. It is seventy years since the destruction of Jerusalem.

Interpretation of Prophecy

At first glance, the varying interpretations of the mysterious seventy years may seem strange. Didn't the prophet convey the exact meaning of his words? Didn't the Torah sages understand?

The prophet understands what G-d wants him to understand and conveys what G-d wants him to convey. The present exile will end one day — that it will is one of Maimonides' Thirteen Principles that are the very basis of Jewish belief. When that day comes, the redeemed Jewish nation will understand the true meaning of the many prophecies dealing with exile and redemption. We will then understand how the prophets foretold the conditions of the exile and the deliverance from it, but their words will remain murky and obscure until then. It was never G-d's purpose to give us a history book in reverse, clearly outlining the exact course of all future events. Often, the prophet himself may not understand the full import of the Heavenly words conveyed through his lips.

It was never G-d's purpose to give us a history book in reverse... Often, the prophet himself may not understand the full implication of the Heavenly words conveyed through his lips.

The classic example is the prophet Jonah. His prophecy was וְנִינְוֵה נֶהְפָּכֶת — *and Nineveh will be overturned*. To him it was clear that he was foretelling the destruction of the great city. Nineveh would be overturned just as Sodom and Gomorrah were overturned. When the population repented and was spared, Jonah thought that he would be branded a false prophet. But Jonah did not know the true meaning of his own prophecy [*Sanhedrin 89b*]. Nineveh was *indeed* overturned, but in the moral, ethical, and religious sense. The prophetic words *"Nineveh will be overturned"* contained both potential meanings: without repentence, it would be literally overturned and destroyed; with repentence it would be spiritually overturned and saved [*Derech Hashem, III 4:7*].

The Ambiguous 400 Years

One of the pivotal prophecies of Jewish history was the declaration to Abraham כִּי גֵר יִהְיֶה זַרְעֲךָ

בְּאֶרֶץ לֹא לָהֶם וַעֲבָדוּם וְעִנּוּ אֹתָם אַרְבַּע מֵאוֹת שָׁנָה — *Your seed shall be a stranger in a land that is not theirs, and shall serve them; and they shall afflict them four hundred years.* [Gen. 15:13]

When would the four hundred years begin? Would there be a full four hundred years of slavery? Would the entire period be spent in one land?

Not until the Exodus ... was it clear that G-d in His mercy, dated the 400 years from the birth of Isaac rather than some later date

It was not until the Exodus that these questions were answered. Not until the Jews were freed exactly four hundred years after the birth of Isaac was it clear that G-d, in His mercy, dated the four hundred years from the birth of Isaac rather than from some later date [*Vilna Gaon on Haggadah of Pesach*]. Until then, no one could say that the first seventy-five years of Isaac's life — years that he spent together with his father, Abraham — would be considered part of the exile despite the incongruity of the fact that, although it may have been considered "exile" for Isaac, the exalted status of Abraham was such that even among the idolators of Canaan, he was not considered a "stranger" in an alien land [*Maharal, Gevuros Hashem, 10*].

...and the Future Redemption

That Rabbi Akiva was mistaken about Bar Kochba in no way diminishes either his own greatness or the unimpeachable truths that still await fulfillment.

When G-d wants His people to understand His words clearly, He makes them known clearly. But countless prophecies, including those foretelling the coming of the Messiah, the ultimate redemption, and the end of days, were not meant to be explicitly clear. Therefore, a giant like Rabbi Akiva could be convinced that Bar Kochba was the Messiah and represented the fulfillment of G-d's ultimate plan of creation and the realization of all the prophetic pledges. That Rabbi Akiva was mistaken about Bar Kochba in no way diminishes either his own greatness or the unimpeachable truths that still await fulfillment [*Mishneh Torah, Hilchos Melachim 11:3*]. Every Torah school child "knows" that G-d told Abraham of a four-hundred year exile that would begin with the birth of Isaac. But this knowledge did not become absolute and public until the Exodus actually took place. In the same way, future events will illuminate the apparent obscurities of the Torah like a flash of lightning.

An Overview/The Period and the Miracle [xxvi]

Misplaced Mercy

Only a few weeks after the Exodus, the Jews were attacked by Amalek. The prayers of Moses, the leadership of Joshua, and the faith of the Jews resulted in a great victory, a victory that was followed soon after by the giving of the Torah at Mount Sinai. The miracle of Purim was climaxed by another great victory over Amalek and it was followed by קִיְמוּ וְקִבְּלוּ, *they undertook and confirmed* [9:27] — which, as our Sages tell us, was a new acceptance of the Torah, one that was even more sweeping than that at Sinai. One of the three commandments required of Israel upon settling the land was the obliteration of Amalek [*Sanhedrin 20b*]. The commandment מָחֹה תִּמְחֶה אֶת זֵכֶר עֲמָלֵק — *you must blot out the memory of Amalek* — is still read annually in all Jewish congregations the Sabbath before Purim and it is a commandment that must be fulfilled before the final redemption can be accomplished.

The miracle of Purim was climaxed by another great victory over Amalek, and it was followed by a new acceptance of the Torah...

Superficially it would appear that the commandment is an act of revenge for a vicious sneak attack that happened in the year 2448. The many comments of the Sages and later commentators make it abundantly clear, however, that Amalek is the very embodiment of evil on earth, and that the attack in the desert was but a symptom, and indication of an incurable spiritual malaise. It is for this reason that G-d says that neither His Name nor His throne can be complete until the seed of Amalek is wiped from the face of the earth [*Midrash Shocher Tov 9:10.*]

Amalek is the embodiment of evil on earth and the attack in the desert was but a symptom, and indication of an incurable spiritual malaise.

Mercy is a Jewish trait, so much so that our Sages question the Jewish ancestry of a cruel person. Nevertheless, there are times when softheaded mercy is nothing more than a euphemism for cruelty. The "kind" mother who indulges her child's insatiable sweet tooth hardly deserves anyone's sympathy while she cringes at the sound of the drill and her beloved's screams as he sits in the hated dentist's chair — she put him there. On the other hand, the

There are times when soft-headed mercy is nothing more than a euphemism for cruelty.

"cruel" mother who supervises her beloved's eating habits earns temporary resentment when she snatches away gob upon gob of carbohydrates, but she will get a lifetime of gratitude for having raised a healthy child.

If someone had assassinated Hitler in 1933 (before assassination became 'respectable'), we may be sure that statesmen and editorialists would have fulminated against bringing the barrel of a gun into the political process. With our 20-20 hindsight, we now know that such an assassination would have been an act of mercy unparalleled in human history.

Human concepts of right and wrong, mercy and cruelty, are of necessity limited by the overriding fact of our very humanity. The sensitive human being might well feel revulsion at the commandment to murder an Amalekite in cold blood — it flies in the face of everything he has been taught about the sanctity of life and the virtues of compassion. But compassion and weakness are not always synonymous. The source of goodness and mercy is G-d. When He, in His supreme wisdom, decrees that the war against Amalek is the road to human perfection, then that is the only true course of mercy. To let Hitler live, to let Stalin live, to let Torquemada live, to let Titus live . . . to let Amalek live is not mercy at all.

To let Hitler live, to let Stalin live, to let Titus live ... to let Amalek live is not mercy at all

Saul and Agag

David was twenty-eight years old when Saul became king — not a mere stripling tending herds as distorted history would have us believe ...

As soon as Saul was anointed King of Israel, he was commanded to wage war against Amalek. He was no simple farmer's son, the new king. He was head and shoulders above the rest of his people spiritually as well as physically. In his entire lifetime he committed but one sin [*Yoma 22b*]. David was twenty-eight years old when Saul became king — not a mere stripling tending herds as distorted history would have us believe — and still Saul was chosen over him as Israel's finest son. In his great test, he was given the assignment of completing the task begun by Moses and Joshua 438 years earlier — to eradicate Amalek completely, even its livestock.

Saul said to himself, "If it is a calamity when even a single wayfarer dies, how tragic it would be to slaughter an entire nation! If the people have sinned, how have the livestock sinned? If the adults have sinned, how have the children sinned?" Logical questions; we might well ask them today. A heavenly voice said to him, "אַל תְּהִי צַדִּיק הַרְבֵּה — *Do not be too righteous!*" [*Koheles 7:16 ibid*].

Saul, righteous Saul, fell into the trap that was to cost him his throne; He substituted his own concept of mercy for G-d's. He thought he would be more merciful than the merciful G-d!

He attacked Amalek and a victory took place, but not a total victory — the people and Saul both found the commandment more than they could fulfill. One man, above all, was spared. He was King Agag, malevolent and obsequious ruler of the evil nation. Because he was spared, he lived with his wife and she conceived. She survived and gave birth. Many generations later, a descendant of Agag, born because of Saul's misplaced mercy, entered the stage of Jewish history. His name was Haman. And, because of an act of human "mercy" in opposing G-d's absolute and ultimate mercy, the Jewish people was threatened with the same extinction that it should have visited upon Amalek [*Megillah 13a*].

Many generations later, a descendant of Agag, born because of Saul's misplaced mercy, entered the stage of Jewish history. His name was Haman.

Samuel the prophet was told by G-d that the monarchy would be stripped from Saul. The prophet sadly and angrily delivered the message to his anointed, and asked that Agag be brought to him. Unctuously, Agag came with gifts and thanks. Samuel himself slayed the Amalekite king. Samuel — not a man of battle, not a man who ever had blood on his hands—a man of peace and kindness and *genuine* mercy. He did not ask for a warrior or a professional executioner to deliver the *coup de grace*, because one does not entrust acts of mercy to others. And carrying out the *mitzvah* of eradicating Amalek, because it contributes to the perfection of G-d's Name, throne, and the redemption, is the ultimate act of mercy. [See *I Samuel 16*].

Samuel did not ask for a professional executioner to deliver the coup de grace, because one does not entrust acts of mercy to others.

David and Shim'i

The popular impression of David is that of a bloody conqueror king, unable to build the Holy Temple because he was a man of war, not of peace. The impression is typical of the shallow readings of Prophets of which most of us are guilty. David was truly a man of peace and mercy. The fallen of his

David was truly a
man of peace and
mercy. The fallen of
his wars were like
offerings on the
Divine altar.

wars were like offerings on the Divine altar and he
was not permitted to build the Temple because his
people could not measure up to this level of purity
and righteousness [*Yalkut Shimoni II Samuel 145.
See Michtav Me'eliyahu II p. 275*].

When his son Absalom rebelled and drove David
from Jerusalem, the exiled king was pelted with
stones and bitter curses by Shim'i ben Gera, a
prophet, teacher of Solomon, and unreconciled
member of Saul's family. Shim'i, as a rebel against
the person of the king, was liable to the death penalty
[*Mishneh Torah, Hilchos Melachim 3:8*], and
David's loyal followers led by Avishai ben Zruyah
begged for permission to kill Shim'i:

לָמָה יְקַלֵּל הַכֶּלֶב הַמֵּת הַזֶּה אֶת אֲדֹנִי הַמֶּלֶךְ אֶעְבְּרָה נָא
וְאָסִירָה אֶת רֹאשׁוֹ.

*"Why should this dead dog curse my lord the
king? Let me go over and take off his head!"*
David refused. Even in his hour of deepest
anguish and hurt, his compassion did not desert him:

הַנִּחוּ לוֹ וִיקַלֵּל כִּי־אָמַר לוֹ ה', אוּלַי יִרְאֶה ה' בְּעֵינִי
וְהֵשִׁיב ה' לִי טוֹבָה תַּחַת קִלְלָתוֹ הַיּוֹם הַזֶּה.

*". . . let him alone and let him curse; for G-d
has bidden him. Perhaps G-d will look at my af-
fliction and requite me good for his cursing this
day."*[*II Samuel 16*]

So Shim'i lived and
had children thanks
to David's mercy.
One of his
descendants was
Mordechai!

So Shim'i lived and had children and descendants
thanks to David's mercy. One of his descendants
entered the center stage of Jewish history many
generations later — his name was Mordechai!

Not for naught did the Jews of Esther's time say,
"See what a Yehudi (of the tribe of Judah) did for me
and what a Benjaminite caused me." What did a
Yehudi do for me? — David did not kill Shim'i, and
Mordechai was born of him. What did a Benjaminite
cause me? — Saul did not kill Agag and Haman was
born of him to oppress the Jews [*Megillah 13a*].

There are two kinds of mercy — the true kind that
produced Mordechai and the false kind that
produced Haman.

Saul Vindicated

But Saul was still a great and righteous man
despite his lapse. The ways of G-d are mysterious;
how mysterious, exacting and righteous they are we

can only sometimes begin to fathom and even then it often takes centuries and a perspective bordering on the superhuman.

G-d in His providence utilized David's mercy to Shim'i to produce Mordechai and Esther, two descendants of Saul's royal family. When the product of Saul's grievous sin terrorized the Jews of Persia and Media and gloated over their assured extermination, it was Mordechai and Esther carrying on where their ancestor had failed, arising to bring the Jews to repentance, arousing G-d's compassion for His children, and foiling Haman's plot.

When the product of Saul's grievous sin terrorized the Jews of Persia and Media ... it was Mordechai and Esther carrying on where their ancestor had failed.

We begin to peek behind the veils of concealment and see G-d's hand at work. We are not done; we will see more.

Esther—A forlorn Wife

The poignancy of Esther's plight is almost certainly the most gripping part of the *Megillah* in purely personal terms. A Jewish girl hoping against hope not to become first lady of the world finds herself spending twelve months in an alien harem dedicated to the sole purpose of preparing for the king's pleasure. Then she is chosen queen and lives at the center of oriental intrigue and passion while guarding the secret of her origin and secretly holding fast to her religion.

According to our Sages, however, the personal suffering of Esther was even more acute. לְקָחָה מָרְדֳּכַי לוֹ לְבַת, אַל תִּקְרִי לְבַת אֶלָּא לְבַיִת — *Mordechai took her to himself like a daughter [Megillas Esther 2:7]*, do not read *like a daughter*, but like a "home" [meaning as a wife] [*Megillah 13a*]. Thus we have a married Jewess — who remained married to Mordechai all through her ordeal in the palace — simultaneously living with a gentile husband.

As a matter of fact, it was the very circumstance of her ordeal that convinced Mordechai that some higher Divine motive lay behind Esther's forced entry into Ahasuerus' grotesque, international beauty contest. Esther was a prophetess [*Megillah 14a*], a supremely righteous woman who, since she was married, should not even have been eligible for queenship according to the rules laid down by Ahasuerus' chamberlains. They violated their own rules by taking married women [see Commentary 2:17]. But Esther should have merited at least so minor a miracle that she should not stand out among the many hundreds of contestants. Instead, whoever saw her was captivated by her. Mordechai, a prophet possessed of the holy spirit in his own right, surely knew that a G-d-given חוּט שֶׁל חֶסֶד — thread of grace rested upon her enabling her to win the king's heart [ibid].

These were unmistakeable indications to him that G-d wanted her in the palace for some higher purpose than merely being Ahasuerus' consort

These were unmistakable indications to him that G-d wanted her in the palace for some higher purpose than merely being Ahasuerus' consort. So Esther remained brave and Mordechai bided his time.

We can feel the depth of her ordeal through her prayer and plaint to G-d as she prepared to break the law by appearing unbidden to beg Ahasuerus for the survival of her brethren:

"My G-d, my G-d, why have you forsaken me. Why have you changed the order of the world and the order of the Jewish mothers against me. Sarah was taken captive by Pharaoh for one night and he and his household were punished. I have been placed in the bosom of this evil man for so many years and no miracles have helped me. Jewish women have three special commandments and I keep them even here. Why have you forsaken me?"[Midrash Shocher Tov 22:26.]

Esther in Halachah

According to those who hold that Esther was married to Mordechai, her plight presents enormously complex halachic problems. She was involved in two sins — even though she was coerced — which every Jew must sacrifice his very life to avoid:

1) She was a married woman engaged in adultery, and

2) By living with Ahasuerus she caused a public חִילוּל הַשֵּׁם — desecration of the Name of G-d, also a sin that a Jew must give up life itself to avoid.

There is a third area of difficulty: a married woman who commits adultery is forbidden to her husband unless she was coerced. When Esther went to plead for her people, she went willingly, thus becoming forbidden to her husband.

The main Talmudic sources on these questions are *Kesubos 3b* and *Sanhedrin 74b* where *Tosafos* and other commentators deal with these matters at length. We will offer no more than a few of their main trends of thought. Anyone seeking a full understanding of the matter should, of course, consult the primary sources. It goes without saying that nothing that follows should be used as a basis for halachic decision.

Esther was never an active participant in either the sin of adultery or the sin of desecration at any time during her marriage to Ahasuerus [*Sanhedrin 74b*]. Her righteousness was of such magnitude that her initial revulsion at being forced to submit herself to the King was never in doubt, nor was there the slightest suspicion that it became eroded with the passage of time or the allures of palace life [*Tosefos, Kesubos 57b*]. An important element in any consideration of potential desecration of the Name חִילוּל הַשֵׁם is whether the non-Jew requiring the given act intends that the Jewish victim violate his religion [*Sanhedrin 74b*]. Ahasuerus was driven solely by passion; not knowing Esther was Jewish, he could have had no intention that she profane her religion. Even after she revealed her identity, Ahasuerus' desire to retain her as queen was purely a product of his love for her rather than as an intention to desecrate her religious beliefs. Until the fateful days when Esther voluntarily presented herself to Ahasuerus to pursue the salvation of her people, Mordechai had no doubts about her status as his wife. Then, she feared [*see Commentary 4:16*] that Mordechai might suspect her of acting the temptress and no longer wish to remain her husband despite the compelling circumstances under which she acted [*see Shitah Mekubetzes, Kesubos 3b*].

Esther's righteousness was of such magnitude that her initial revulsion at being forced to submit herself to the King was never in doubt.

The Veils Part

The history of the Jewish people up to the Babylonian Exile is replete with miracles. In virtually every generation, a Jew could reinforce his belief through miracles which he had seen himself or tales of such miracles from first person witnesses. A visit to the Holy Temple was, in itself, an opportunity to see the active hand of G-d [*Avos 5:8*]. True, Jewish belief is not based on miracles; belief must feed on deeper roots. Miracles can be rationalized, explained away or misinterpreted [*Mishneh Torah, Yesode Hatorah 8*]. But there is more. Reliance on miracles, even undue emphasis on miracles, can actually dilute belief because it can make one forget that the hand of G-d is as present in what, for lack of a better name, we refer to as "nature" as it was at the Splitting of the *Yam Suf* when the Jews left Egypt. It is not simply a pretty turn of phrase when we thank G-d in *Shmone Esrai* for נִסֶּיךָ שֶׁבְּכָל יוֹם עִמָּנוּ — the miracles that are done with us every day. Life exists because G-d makes it exist constantly; without His life-giving activity, the universe would cease to exist.

Reliance on miracles, even undue emphasis on miracles, can actually dilute belief because it can make one forget that the hand of G-d is as present in what, for lack of a better name, we refer to as "nature."

To the extent that that early history of the Jews is a chain of miracles and Divine intervention, it is itself a veiled picture of G-d. The very emphasis on G-d's miraculous activity can make one forget that His guidance is everywhere. The Hebrew word for the world, עוֹלָם, comes from a root that means "hidden," for, in this world, the existence of G-d *is* hidden. People may pray three times a day and observe *mitzvos* scrupulously, yet they are convinced that their business, professional, or military success is based on hard work, education, capital investment, superior strength, better planning, etc., etc., etc. Isn't G-d at least an equal partner in their success? Of course, but He is a silent and unseen partner, so silent and unseen that His very participation can be questioned.

The Hebrew word for the world, עוֹלָם, comes from a root that means "hidden," for, in this world, the existence of G-d is hidden. He places us in an עוֹלָם — world of hiddenness and expects us to find our way to the truth.

This is the purpose of עוֹלָם — world-hiddenness — to test man to find truth in the murkiness. The non-believer will always find bases for doubt and blasphemy. The מַבּוּל (Deluge) took place in the year 1656 after creation, so the builders of the tower of Babel had a theory: every 1656 years, the foundations of the universe tremble causing a flood; we are safe until then. Pharaoh explained away the plagues in a similar way. Belshazzar arrived at a computation on which to base his blasphemy. And so down through the ages. G-d does not drill faith into our minds and hearts; He places us in an עוֹלָם — world of hiddenness and expects us to find our way to the truth because He has given us enough tools — just enough, barely enough — to find the truth *if we really want to find it.*

The period of openly revealed miracles ended with Esther and Mordechai. A new emphasis was added to Jewish history. We had to find G-d's hand not in the splitting sea or heavenly fire, but in everyday events [See *R'sisei Loylo,* chapter 56].

G-d's Jigsaw Puzzle

Haman was enraged and sought vengeance against the entire Jewish people. Why? The reason was obvious: Mordechai refused to bow down to Haman. Quixotic Mordechai refused to acknowledge the King's Viceroy with the obeisance that was common protocol in the Orient, the same obeisance that Jacob paid Esau without a royal edict ordering him to do so. The *real* reason for the sword over Jewish heads was that the Jews allowed themselves to enjoy the feast of Ahasuerus despite Mordechai's insistence that they refrain from going. But the feast was in the *third* year of Ahasuerus' reign and the decree of extermination was in the *twelfth* year. How could there be a connection? Simple logic cried out that Mordechai was wrong!

Then the pieces of G-d's jigsaw puzzle began coming together. Suddenly widely separate links began to move together to form a chain and widely separated chains joined to become the anchor upon which Jewish survival was secured. And simple logic turned out to be wrong; quixotic Mordechai was right.

Then the pieces of G-d's jigsaw puzzle began coming together. Suddenly widely separate links began to move together to form a chain and widely separated chains joined to become the anchor upon which Jewish survival was secured. And simple logic turned out to be wrong; quixotic Mordechai was right.

One set of links: Ahasuerus' feast would become the undoing of the Jews later on, but first it resulted in the execution of Vashti which led to the coronation of Esther. Because Esther was Queen, she was in a position to approach the King to save her people and lull Haman into complacency by inviting him to her private banquet.

Another set of links: Bigsan and Teresh plotted to kill Ahasuerus. Because Esther secured a royal promotion for Mordechai he was positioned to overhear them and report the scheme to Esther. She told the King of Mordechai's loyalty. It was inscribed in the royal chronicle there to lay forgotten until the fateful night when G-d disturbed the sleep of the King.

Another set of links: The King promoted Haman and everyone was required to bow to the newly risen Agagite. Mordechai refused to bow. Haman, assured of his power and influence — even with the Queen! — built a gallows and came to seek royal permission to hang Mordechai just when Ahasuerus learned that it was Mordechai who had once saved his life.

When the appropriate climactic time arrived, G-d's pieces came together and formed the destruction of Haman and most of Amalek, and salvation for the Jews.

G-d's Absent Name

G-d's Name does not appear in the *Megillah* — the only one of the twenty-four sacred books where such a phenomenon occurs. True, commentators show how the word הַמֶּלֶךְ — the King, is always a reference to G-d, King of the Universe and His name appears occasionally in acrostic form [*see Commentary 5:4*]. Nevertheless, these hidden appearances of His name are still in marked contrast to the rest of *Tanach*.

Precisely. The miracle of Purim happened at the end of the Babylonian Exile, a time when G-d was behind myriad veils of concealment, a time when Jews were asking with poignant, tragic sincerity whether they owed Him more allegiance than a wife spurned or a slave set free. And the miracle happened in Elam, a spiritually forlorn province, almost devoid of Torah.

Yet it was at that time and in that place that "random" links began coming together and forming chains of salvation, chains eternally binding the Jews to the earlier days when G-d was everywhere. The miracle of Purim showed them that G-d was *still* everywhere, would always be everywhere, even when His presence could be divined only in the actions of this king or that, in acrostics of random events, in bafflements of history that, to the believing eye, spell out אֲנִי רִאשׁוֹן וַאֲנִי אַחֲרוֹן וּמִבַּלְעָדַי אֵין אֱלֹקִים — *I am the first and I am the last; and beside me there is no G-d* [Isaiah 44:6].

"Establish Me"

Esther asked the Sages to establish Purim as a festival for all generations [*see Talmudic quote at beginning of Introduction*]. The Sages refused on the grounds that, to do so, would inspire the jealousy and enmity of non-Jews. To which she responded that the story was *already* inscribed in the royal annals of Persia and Media.

To proclaim a festival and inscribe the tale in a sacred book would indicate that the chain of coincidental events leading up to the salvation was an open, obvious miracle. This, the Sages said, could not be done. The Jews were still under the dominion of the Persian Empire and its rulers would not respond kindly to a Jewish claim that G-dly intervention had been employed to best the highest officials of the empire.

Esther replied that such fears were groundless. The story is already inscribed in the royal annals, she countered. It is universally recognized that a miracle took place. There are simply too many coincidences and they fit together too well. Even the Persians and Medes recognized that G-d had taken a hand — albeit a gloved, concealed hand — in the events. The links came together too well for it to be anything else [*Resisei Laylah Chapter 56*].

Even the Persians and Medes recognized that G-d had taken a hand — albeit a gloved, concealed hand — in the events. The links came together too well for it to be anything else.

The Heavenly Reign

Of the ten סְפִירוֹת — emanations of Kabbalah, the last is מַלְכוּת — kingship. The king, as ruler of the nation, represents the public manifestation of authority and government. He may have ministers and advisers whose counsel and machinations help determine the course of events, but it is the king who is the only, ultimate symbol of government. Nowadays, for example, a chief of state is higher in the order of protocol than a head of government. A prime minister may wield effective power, but he does so in the name of the state; and the state is represented by the person of the king or president. The state is embodied in him.

In the Heavenly order, מַלְכוּת — kingship represents the final stage of G-d's will, His revelation on earth. It is the culmination of a lengthy chain of events resulting in His revelation.

Nowhere more than in *Megillas Esther* is this revealed. In the *Megillah*, G-d's name does not appear, but when all was done, His presence was recognized everywhere. Every piece fit, His jigsaw puzzle was perfect. And Esther could truthfully tell the Sages that everyone knew it. Everyone realized that G-d rules the affairs of man — directly as He had in Egypt, the desert, or the Land of Israel; or from the concealment of nature and coincidence as He had in Shushan. Because He does not appear in the *Megillah*, He is there more meaningfully than in any other sacred book. It is in the *Megillah* that we see מַלְכוּת — kingship, the final emanation of G-d's infinite wisdom and power as it is manifested in the apparently mundane affairs of this planet. [*ibid*]

This may be the deeper reason why G-d is alluded to in the Megillah by the word הַמֶּלֶךְ — *The King*. It is in the guise of temporal, natural rule of earth that His essence is represented most truly.

No, He is not concealed. He only seems to be. It is for us to find Him in every event in our lives. *Megillas Esther* shows us how if we but read its directions.

Rabbi Nosson Scherman

In the Megillah G-d's Name does not appear, but when all was done, His presence was recognized everywhere. Every piece fit, His jigsaw puzzle was perfect

מְגִלַּת אֶסְתֵּר

א וַיְהִי בִּימֵי אֲחַשְׁוֵרוֹשׁ הוּא אֲחַשְׁוֵרוֹשׁ
הַמֹּלֵךְ מֵהֹדּוּ וְעַד־כּוּשׁ שֶׁבַע וְעֶשְׂרִים
ב וּמֵאָה מְדִינָה: בַּיָּמִים הָהֵם כְּשֶׁבֶת|הַמֶּלֶךְ
אֲחַשְׁוֵרוֹשׁ עַל כִּסֵּא מַלְכוּתוֹ אֲשֶׁר
ג בְּשׁוּשַׁן הַבִּירָה: בִּשְׁנַת שָׁלוֹשׁ לְמָלְכוֹ
עָשָׂה מִשְׁתֶּה לְכָל־שָׂרָיו וַעֲבָדָיו חֵיל
פָּרַס וּמָדַי הַפַּרְתְּמִים וְשָׂרֵי הַמְּדִינוֹת
ד לְפָנָיו: בְּהַרְאֹתוֹ אֶת־עֹשֶׁר כְּבוֹד מַלְכוּתוֹ

יג"א ר' בקמץ

1. בִּימֵי אֲחַשְׁוֵרוֹשׁ — *In the days of Ahasuerus,* successor to Cyrus, toward the end of the 70 years of the Babylonian exile. [4th Century B.C.E.] *(Rashi).*

הַמֹּלֵךְ — *Who reigned.* Rav said: He elevated himself to the throne. Some interpret this to his credit, holding that no one else was equally qualified for the throne. Others say that he was not deserving of the throne, but that he owed his status to his vast wealth and lavish distribution of money with which he purchased his royal position, thus giving him dominion over the whole world *(Meg. 11b).*

מֵהֹדּוּ וְעַד־כּוּשׁ — *From Hodu to Cush.* i.e. the whole world. [The Sages differ as to the actual location of these two countries] *Meg. 11a).*

Hodu to Cush. [usually translated 'India to Ethiopia.']

שֶׁבַע וְעֶשְׂרִים וּמֵאָה מְדִינָה — *One hundred and twenty-seven provinces.* Rabbi Akiva was once giving a lecture when he noticed that his students were drowsing. In order to rouse them he asked, "Why was it seen fit that Esther should rule over one hundred and twenty-seven provinces? Because thus said

G-d: Let the daughter of Sarah who lived one hundred and twenty-seven years come and reign over one hundred twenty-seven provinces" *(Midrash).*

Why would these words alert the drowsing students more than the topic of the day? Rabbi Akiva wanted to impress upon his students the importance of time and the duty to use every second to best advantage. It was because Sarah's one hundred and twenty-seven years were perfect and completely sin-free that her granddaughter could hold sway over one hundred and twenty-seven provinces. Each second meant a family; each minute, a farm; each day, a village. Had Sarah idled away her time, Esther's kingdom would have been diminished. Time is too precious to waste. Sarah's time well-spent was rewarded during Esther's reign. Each of us, too, is presented with the fleeting gift of time—and the mission of utilizing it fully and well. Who can say what the rewards will be for each minute well-spent; or the penalty for each minute wasted?

This admonition brought Rabbi Akiva's students to attention *(Chidushei HaRim).*

[Please note: *The source of every excerpt has been documented. Whenever the author has inserted a comment of his own, it is framed in square brackets.*]

¹ **A**nd it came to pass in the days of Ahasuerus—the Ahasuerus who reigned from Hodu to Cush over a hundred and twenty-seven provinces— ² that in those days, when King Ahasuerus sat on his royal throne which was in Shushan the capitol, ³ in the third year of his reign, he made a feast for all his officials and his servants; the army of Persia and Media, the nobles and officials of the provinces being present; ⁴ when he displayed the riches of his glorious

The feasts of Ahasuerus

2. כְּשֶׁבֶת הַמֶּלֶךְ — *When the king sat.* i.e. 'sat securely.' He was a usurper to the throne and he wasn't securely established until after three years of political insecurity (Rashi).

בְּשׁוּשַׁן הַבִּירָה — *Shushan the Capitol* This was the palace compound which was surrounded by the less fortified עִיר שׁוּשָׁן, the residential part of Shushan where the Jews lived. [The capitol was separated from the city by a river.] Many citizens—including Mordechai [2:5]—as well as the King and his officers lived in the capitol. (See Ibn Ezra on 8:15, 9:12; M'nos Halevi on 8:14,15; Rav Yonasan Eybeschuetz on 4:17; Malbim on 9:13; Torah T'mimah on 4:17).

3. בִּשְׁנַת שָׁלוֹשׁ — *In the third year.* 3395 from Creation (Seder Hadoros).

It was the third anniversary of his ascension to the throne. He celebrated this anniversary with an annual feast, but in this third year, he had multiple cause for celebration:

According to his (erroneous) calculation, the seventieth year of the Jews' exile had passed thus belying the prophets who had foretold the exile's end after seventy

years [see Meg. 11b], and Ahasuerus rejoiced in this frustration of Jewish hope; he had completed the building of his magnificent throne; he was finally secure in his reign; he took Vashti as his queen. Thus the causes for such a lavish feast (Midrash; Ibn Ezra).

פָּרַס וּמָדַי — *Persia and Media.* The Persians and Medes were two peoples of the same racial stock who jointly established a vast empire. They made a stipulation with one another saying: 'If we supply the kings, you will supply the governors, and if you supply the kings we will supply the governors' (Meg. 12a).

Ahasuerus was a Persian, therefore Persia is mentioned first. However, at the end of the Megillah (10,2), Media is mentioned first because the Chronicles, referred to there, were begun when Darius, the Mede, was king (Me'am Loez).

הַפַּרְתְּמִים — *The nobles.* Royal descendants. It is uncertain whether this word is Hebrew or Persian, because it appears nowhere else except for the Books of Daniel and Esther (Ibn Ezra).

4. אֶת-עֹשֶׁר כְּבוֹד מַלְכוּתוֹ — *The*

וְאֶת־יְקָר תִּפְאֶרֶת גְּדוּלָתוֹ יָמִים רַבִּים
שְׁמוֹנִים וּמְאַת יוֹם: וּבִמְלוֹאת | הַיָּמִים
הָאֵלֶּה עָשָׂה הַמֶּלֶךְ לְכָל־הָעָם הַנִּמְצְאִים
בְּשׁוּשַׁן הַבִּירָה לְמִגָּדוֹל וְעַד־קָטָן מִשְׁתֶּה
שִׁבְעַת יָמִים בַּחֲצַר גִּנַּת בִּיתַן הַמֶּלֶךְ:
חוּר | כַּרְפַּס וּתְכֵלֶת אָחוּז בְּחַבְלֵי־בוּץ
וְאַרְגָּמָן עַל־גְּלִילֵי כֶסֶף וְעַמּוּדֵי שֵׁשׁ
מִטּוֹת | זָהָב וָכֶסֶף עַל רִצְפַת בַּהַט־וָשֵׁשׁ
וְדַר וְסֹחָרֶת: וְהַשְׁקוֹת בִּכְלֵי זָהָב וְכֵלִים

ה

ו

ז

וּבִמְלוֹאת ק׳

יח׳ רבתי

riches of his glorious kingdom. His
intention was to dazzle his subjects
with his great wealth so that they
would loyally support his reign;
subjects delight in an independently
wealthy monarch. Also, he did not
display the riches he confiscated
from the people—those they would
recognize. Rather, he displayed his
own *personal* wealth (*Me'am Loez*).

וְאֶת יְקָר תִּפְאֶרֶת גְּדוּלָתוֹ — *The splendor of his excellent majesty.* He
adorned himself with בִּגְדֵי כְהוּנָה —
the Jewish priestly robes. The word
תִּפְאֶרֶת splendor, used here is the
same word used in connection with
the priestly garments: לְכָבוֹד
וּלְתִפְאָרֶת, *for glory and splendor*
(*Exodus* 28:2), thus indicating that
he wore the robes looted from the
Jews during the conquest by Nebuchadnezzar (*Meg. 12a*).

שְׁמוֹנִים וּמְאַת יוֹם — *A hundred and
eighty days.* The last day was as
lavish as the first (*Midrash*).

Our sages have told us that
Nebuchadnezzar had one thousand
and eighty different treasures which
were buried in the bed of the river
Euphrates. G-d revealed this hiding
place to Cyrus, predecessor of

Ahasuerus, as a reward for having
given orders to rebuild the Temple.
Ahasuerus inherited this fortune
from him and he displayed the in-
heritance to the guests at this party.
The Midrash tells us that he showed
them six treasures a day as is symbolized by the six superlatives mentioned in the previous verse: עֹשֶׁר,
riches; כָּבוֹד, glory; מַלְכוּתוֹ, kingdom;
יְקָר splendor; תִּפְאֶרֶת excellence;
גְּדוּלָתוֹ majesty. At this pace, it took
him exactly one hundred and eighty
days to go through all his wealth,
for 180 x 6 equals 1,080 (*Vilna
Gaon*).

5. וּבִמְלוֹאת הַיָּמִים הָאֵלֶּה — *And
when these days were fulfilled.* Rav
and Shmuel differed in their interpretation. One said it was clever of
him to invite his distant subjects
first, because he could win the
loyalty of the Shushanites whenever he wished. The other held that
he was foolish; he should have
entertained the inhabitants of his
own city first so that, in case of a
rebellion by outsiders, they would
support him (*Meg. 12a*).

The Talmud asks: "Why did the
Jews of that generation deserve ex-

kingdom and the splendor of his excellent majesty for many days—a hundred and eighty days. ⁵ And when these days were fulfilled, the King made a week-long feast for all the people who were present in Shushan the capitol, great and small alike, in the court of the garden of the King's palace. ⁶ There were hangings of white, fine cotton, and blue, held with cords of fine linen and purple, upon silver rods and marble pillars; the couches of gold and silver were on a pavement of green and white, and shell and onyx marble. ⁷ The drinks were served in gold goblets—no two goblets

termination? Because they derived pleasure [נֶהֱנוּ] from the feast of that wicked one (Ahasuerus)''. The Talmud doesn't say ''because they *ate*'' — this the Jews could possibly justify by claiming they were subject to royal intimidation and were afraid not to eat. Rather the sin was that they *enjoyed* themselves and partook of the festivities *(Pirchei L'vanon).*

הַנִּמְצָאִים — *Who were present.* The Jewish notables, גְדוֹלֵי יִשְׂרָאֵל, had been there but they fled following the decree of Mordechai against participating in the festivities.

The Jews who remained in Shushan participated in the festivities and, although they did not partake of forbidden foods, their mere *presence* at such a gathering was sinful *(Me'am Loez; Rav Galico; Midr. Abba Gorion).*

לְמִגָּדוֹל וְעַד־קָטָן — *Great and small alike.* The small were served as lavishly as the great *(Kol Rinah).*

6. [This banquet took place outdoors in the courtyard that the King ordered decorated, in the

Oriental manor, with hanging curtains, etc., as enumerated in this verse].

חוּר *White [garments].* The letter ח [Ches] has the numerical value of 8. In the Megillah the Ches is enlarged to imply that on that climactic day Ahasuerus adorned himself with the eight garments of the High Priest. In punishment for this, he suffered the multiple evils of the resulting episode with Vashti, her death, his embarrasment, and his subsequent depression *(M'nos Halevi).*

7. The verse continues to describe the extravagance of the feast. The wine was drunk only from golden goblets, yet no drinking cup was used more than a single time, and no two goblets were alike. As magnificent as his utensils were, when the holy vessels of the Temple were brought in, the golden splendor of the others were dimmed — they turned dull as lead *(Yalkut Shimoni).*

The Jews who saw the Temple's holy vessels being used were greatly saddened at their profanation, and

פרק א

ח־י ח מִכֵּלִים שׁוֹנִים וְיֵין מַלְכוּת רָב כְּיַד הַמֶּלֶךְ: וְהַשְּׁתִיָּה כַדָּת אֵין אֹנֵס כִּי־כֵן יִסַּד הַמֶּלֶךְ עַל כָּל־רַב בֵּיתוֹ לַעֲשׂוֹת ט כִּרְצוֹן אִישׁ־וָאִישׁ: גַּם וַשְׁתִּי הַמַּלְכָּה עָשְׂתָה מִשְׁתֵּה נָשִׁים בֵּית י הַמַּלְכוּת אֲשֶׁר לַמֶּלֶךְ אֲחַשְׁוֵרוֹשׁ: בַּיּוֹם הַשְּׁבִיעִי כְּטוֹב לֵב־הַמֶּלֶךְ בַּיָּיִן אָמַר

they resolved to leave the feast. The King, not wanting them to be saddened, prepared a banquet for them outside. For his grievous sin of profaning the Temple's vessels Ahasuerus deserved to be punished immediately. It was only in the merit of Ahasuerus' future wife, Esther, and their son, Darius, who would one day allow the Jews to rebuild the Temple and return the vessels, that Ahasuerus was not punished with loss of his throne. Instead, his festivity was saddened by the death of Vashti for which he bore the onus (Me'am Loez).

וְיֵין מַלְכוּת רָב — And royal wine in abundance. Every one was served wine older, רָב, than himself (Megillah 12a).

The reason that all this splendor detailed here was not also enumerated when the first banquet for the nobility and officers was described, is, as our sages tell us: (Chag, 13b). A townsman who sees the king is not as a villager who sees the king. To the townsman the sight of the king is not such a novelty and he is less prone to indulge in lengthy descriptions; the villager, to whom the sight of the king is a rare thrill, is inclined to give his impressions at length. Here too, at the banquet for the nobility there was little need for lengthy description. But at the Shushan banquet held for all the people — not normally exposed to such lavishness — more description was called for (Imrei Moshe).

8. וְהַשְּׁתִיָּה כַדָּת אֵין אֹנֵס — And the drinking was according to the law; without coercion. Rabbi Levi said that the tradition among the inhabitants of Persia was that each individual was forced to drink from a large cup containing twenty-two reviis wine (over two quarts)! It made no difference to them whether an individual died or lost his sanity consuming this large amount of liquor. Ahasuerus decided to have this huge goblet on his table so that his guests would not think that he was stingy, but no one was forced to drink from it. He made the cup available realizing that perhaps someone would want to drink from this cup in particular.

This clarifies the meaning of the phrase, וְהַשְּׁתִיָּה כַדָּת and the drinking was according to the law, according to the regular proceedings. However, אֵין אֹנֵס without coercion; those who wished to drink from the traditional cup drank from it while those who wished to partake only a small amount were free to do so (Or Hachaim).

Also, there was no shortage of

alike—and royal wine in abundance, according to the
bounty of the King. ⁸ *And the drinking was according*
to the law; without coercion; for so the King had
ordered all the officers of his house that they should
do according to every man's pleasure.

⁹ *Queen Vashti also made a feast for the women in*
the royal house of King Ahasuerus. ¹⁰ *On the seventh*
day, when the heart of the King was merry with wine,

drinking utensils, so that אֵין אֹנֵס, *no one was coerced* into finishing his drink quickly in order to make his cup available to someone else *(Kad Hakemach).*

כִּרְצוֹן אִישׁ־וָאִישׁ — *According to every man's pleasure* [lit. *according to the pleasure of 'man and man'.]* According to the pleasure of even Mordechai and Haman [Mordechai and Haman both being referred to as אִישׁ, 'man' (2:5 and 7:6)]—Mordechai the Jew and Haman enemy of the Jews. They both wished that there be no compulsion to drink. Mordechai hoped that the Jews would not be forced to eat any part of the feast; while Haman hoped that the Jews would drink of their own free will, thus meriting punishment from G-d for having drunk willingly *(Me'am Loez).*

Another interpretation is that both Mordechai and Haman did not wish the Jews to participate in the festivities — Mordechai, so that they would not drink defiled wine; and Haman to deny them the honor of being invited to the feast *(Me'am Loez).*

9. גַּם וַשְׁתִּי הַמַּלְכָּה — *Queen Vashti also.* The word גַּם, *also,* always signifies something in addition to the plain meaning. Just as Ahasuerus opened six treasuries, so she opened six treasuries . . . just as

he wore the high-priestly garments, so she wore the high priestly garments" *(Midrash).*

"Another explanation of גַּם, also,: the time has come for Vashti also to be razed (לְגַמֵּם) to her foundation; the time has come for Vashti to be plucked; the time has come for Vashti to be trodden. Rav Huna said: The time of Vashti has come to die" *(Midrash).*

וַשְׁתִּי הַמַּלְכָּה — *Queen Vashti.* The daughter of Belshazzar, and granddaughter of Nebuchadnezzar *(Seder Hadoros).*

מִשְׁתֵּה נָשִׁים — *Feast for the women.* As explained above, one of the reasons for Ahasuerus' lavish banquet was his marriage to Vashti. Therefore she followed her husband's example and celebrated their marriage with her own banquet *(Me'am Loez).*

All this is written about her to show how great was the affluence into which Esther stepped *(Midrash).*

בֵּית הַמַּלְכוּת — *The royal house.* She set them in decorated rooms since 'a woman would rather have well-decorated rooms and beautiful clothes than eat fatted calves' *(Midrash).*

10. בַּיּוֹם הַשְּׁבִיעִי — *On the seventh day.* It was the Sabbath *(Rashi).*

The wicked Vashti used to take

לְמְהוּמָן בִּזְּתָא חַרְבוֹנָא בִּגְתָא וַאֲבַגְתָא זֵתַר וְכַרְכַּס שִׁבְעַת הַסָּרִיסִים הַמְשָׁרְתִים אֶת־פְּנֵי הַמֶּלֶךְ אֲחַשְׁוֵרוֹשׁ: לְהָבִיא אֶת־ יא

וַשְׁתִּי הַמַּלְכָּה לִפְנֵי הַמֶּלֶךְ בְּכֶתֶר מַלְכוּת לְהַרְאוֹת הָעַמִּים וְהַשָּׂרִים אֶת־יָפְיָהּ כִּי־ טוֹבַת מַרְאֶה הִיא: וַתְּמָאֵן הַמַּלְכָּה וַשְׁתִּי יב

לָבוֹא בִּדְבַר הַמֶּלֶךְ אֲשֶׁר בְּיַד הַסָּרִיסִים וַיִּקְצֹף הַמֶּלֶךְ מְאֹד וַחֲמָתוֹ בָּעֲרָה בוֹ: וַיֹּאמֶר הַמֶּלֶךְ לַחֲכָמִים יֹדְעֵי הָעִתִּים כִּי־ יג

כֵן דְּבַר הַמֶּלֶךְ לִפְנֵי כָּל־יֹדְעֵי דָּת וָדִין: וְהַקָּרֹב אֵלָיו כַּרְשְׁנָא שֵׁתָר אַדְמָתָא יד

תַרְשִׁישׁ מֶרֶס מַרְסְנָא מְמוּכָן שִׁבְעַת שָׂרֵי

the daughters of Israel, strip them of their clothing and make them work on the Sabbath. It was on the Sabbath, therefore, that her punishment overtook her, and, for the same reason, it was put into the King's heart to have her appear in public, stripped of all clothing (Meg. 12b).

Beginning with the first day of the King's banquet, Mordechai and the Sanhedrin fasted and prayed for six days that G-d should not destroy the Jews. On the seventh day, the Sabbath, G-d responded to their prayers by causing Vashti's rebellion (Me'am Loez).

11. בְּכֶתֶר מַלְכוּת — Wearing the royal crown. i.e. 'only with the royal crown,' i.e., unclothed, so her true beauty could be appreciated (Midrash).

12. וַתְּמָאֵן הַמַּלְכָּה וַשְׁתִּי — But Queen Vashti refused. Not because of modesty. The reason for her refusal was that G-d caused leprosy to break out on her, and paved the

way for her downfall (Meg. 12b).

Leprosy was punishment for her conceited manner (M'nos Halevi).

When Ahasuerus sent for her, he called her וַשְׁתִּי הַמַּלְכָּה, 'Vashti the Queen,' implying that her title was of secondary importance. He was suggesting that she was simply 'a Vashti', a commoner, who had been elevated to the throne because it pleased him to do so.

She, on the other hand, referred to herself as הַמַּלְכָּה וַשְׁתִּי, 'Queen Vashti,' to make it plain that she was of royal blood even before her marriage, and that her dignity was not to be trifled with.

Further on, when he wished to spare her, Ahasuerus referred to her as Queen Vashti, reminding his advisors that she was a queen — the daughter of a great ruler, a royal personage in her own right (Vilna Gaon).

וַיִּקְצֹף הַמֶּלֶךְ מְאֹד — And the King therefore became very incensed. Vashti responded to the King's re-

I
11-14

he ordered Mehuman, Bizzetha, Charbonah, Bigtha and Abagtha, Zethar, and Carcas, the seven chamberlains who attended King Ahasuerus, ¹¹ to bring queen Vashti before the King wearing the royal crown, to show off to the people and the officials her beauty; for she was beautiful to look upon. ¹² But Queen Vashti refused to come at the King's commandment conveyed by the chamberlains; the King therefore became very incensed and his anger burned in him.

The King seeks advice ¹³ *Then the King conferred with the experts who knew the times (for such was the King's procedure [to turn] to all who knew law and judgment.* ¹⁴ *Those closest to him were Carshena, Shesar, Admasa, Tarshish, Meres, Marsena and Memuchan, the seven*

---

quest by sending back scoffing and degrading messages via the chamberlains. This enraged him (*Meg. 12b*).

13. לַחֲכָמִים — *With the experts.* Literally the 'wise men.' The Talmud (*Meg. 12b*) understands this to be the Rabbis.

יֹדְעֵי הָעִתִּים — *Who knew the times.* That is, who knew how to calculate the timing of leap years and fix new moons (*Meg. 12b*).

Ibn Ezra, however, interprets this as referring to astrologers or those familiar with the historical precedents of earlier monarchs.

Ahasuerus, seeking impartial and trusted counsel, turned first to the Jewish sages and asked them to pass sentence on his Queen. The sages thought to themselves: 'If we condemn the Queen to death we shall suffer for it as soon as Ahasuerus becomes sober and hears that it was upon our advice that she was executed. If we advise clemency and advise him to pardon her, he will accuse us of not paying due reverence to the majesty of the King.' They, therefore, resolved to take a position of neutrality. They said to him, "From the day the Temple was destroyed and we were exiled from our land, we lost the power to give judgment in capital cases. Better seek counsel with the wise men of Ammon and Moab who have dwelt at ease in their land." Thereupon, he sought advice from his seven officials, as we read וְהַקָּרֹב אֵלָיו כַּרְשְׁנָא וכו׳, *those closest to him were Carshena, etc.* (*Meg. 12b*).

כִּי־כֵן דְּבַר הַמֶּלֶךְ -- *For such was the King's procedure.* [The King did not pass judgment upon her himself because, legally, a King may not have sole jurisdiction over a serious offense. Rather he is to seek counsel from יֹדְעֵי דָּת וָדִין, those *'who knew law and judgment.'* (See comm. to verse 19 s.v. יָצָא).]

פָּרַס וּמָדַי רֹאֵי פְּנֵי הַמֶּלֶךְ הַיֹּשְׁבִים
רִאשֹׁנָה בַּמַּלְכוּת: כְּדָת מַה־לַעֲשׂוֹת
בַּמַּלְכָּה וַשְׁתִּי עַל|אֲשֶׁר לֹא־עָשְׂתָה אֶת־
מַאֲמַר הַמֶּלֶךְ אֲחַשְׁוֵרוֹשׁ בְּיַד הַסָּרִיסִים:
וַיֹּאמֶר מְמוּכָן לִפְנֵי הַמֶּלֶךְ וְהַשָּׂרִים לֹא
עַל־הַמֶּלֶךְ לְבַדּוֹ עָוְתָה וַשְׁתִּי הַמַּלְכָּה כִּי
עַל־כָּל־הַשָּׂרִים וְעַל־כָּל־הָעַמִּים אֲשֶׁר
בְּכָל־מְדִינוֹת הַמֶּלֶךְ אֲחַשְׁוֵרוֹשׁ: כִּי־יֵצֵא
דְבַר־הַמַּלְכָּה עַל־כָּל־הַנָּשִׁים לְהַבְזוֹת
בַּעְלֵיהֶן בְּעֵינֵיהֶן בְּאָמְרָם הַמֶּלֶךְ
אֲחַשְׁוֵרוֹשׁ אָמַר לְהָבִיא אֶת־וַשְׁתִּי
הַמַּלְכָּה לְפָנָיו וְלֹא־בָאָה: וְהַיּוֹם הַזֶּה
תֹּאמַרְנָה|שָׂרוֹת פָּרַס־וּמָדַי אֲשֶׁר שָׁמְעוּ
אֶת־דְּבַר הַמַּלְכָּה לְכֹל שָׂרֵי הַמֶּלֶךְ וּכְדַי
בִּזָּיוֹן וָקָצֶף: אִם־עַל־הַמֶּלֶךְ טוֹב יֵצֵא
דְבַר־מַלְכוּת מִלְּפָנָיו וְיִכָּתֵב בְּדָתֵי פָרַס־

---

14. רֹאֵי פְּנֵי הַמֶּלֶךְ — *Who had access to the King.* Ordinarily, the Persian King was accessible to the public, but these seven advisers had constant accessibility (literally 'saw the face') to the King.

הַיֹּשְׁבִים רִאשֹׁנָה בַּמַּלְכוּת — *Sat first in the kingdom.* [They were the highest ranking officials of the kingdom.]

15. This verse is a continuation after the parenthetical break of verse 13: 'Then the King conferred with the experts' (Rashi).

כְּדָת — *Legally.* i.e. from a legal standpoint. Ahasuerus was concerned about treating the wicked Vashti only according to law. Yet this same wicked Ahasuerus barbarously condemned the whole of the Jewish people to destruction without ever consulting the law (Midrash Panim Acherim).

16. וַיֹּאמֶר מוּמְכָן—*Memuchan declared.* A Tanna taught: 'Memuchan is Haman. Why was he called Memuchan? Because he was destined [מוּכָן] for destruction. Rav Kahana said: 'From here we see that an ignoramus always thrusts himself to the forefront.' [Memuchan is mentioned last in verse 14, yet he speaks first.] (Meg. 12b; Midrash).

Everywhere else he is referred to as מְמוּכָן but here he is called מוּמְכָן a combination of the two words מוּם כֵּן, meaning "a blemish is here."

officers of Persia and Media, who had access to the King, and who sat first in the kingdom—) [15] as to what should be done, legally, to Queen Vashti for not obeying the bidding of the King Ahasuerus conveyed by the chamberlains.

Memuchan's
suggestion

[16] Memuchan declared before the King and the officials: 'It is not only the King whom Vashti has wronged, but also all the officials and all the people in all the provinces of King Ahasuerus. [17] For this deed of the Queen will come to the attention of all women, making their husbands contemptible in their eyes, by saying: King Ahasuerus commanded Queen Vashti to be brought before him but she did not come! [18] And this day the princesses of Persia and Media who have heard of the Queen's deed will cite it to all the King's officials, and there will be much contempt and wrath.

Vashti is
deposed

[19] If it please the King, let there go forth a royal edict from him, and let it be written into the laws of the

The blemish is his discourtesy in speaking out of turn. The Torah is not tolerant of boorishness (Mesoras Habris).

17. When the word gets out that the queen acted contemptibly to the king, every woman will consider this as license to act likewise to her own husband (Rashi).

Memuchan therefore warned the King of two dire results of her action:

1. Her refusal would undoubtedly have a bad influence on her peers. When it becomes known that King Ahasuerus commanded that Queen Vashti be brought before him, but she refused to obey, other wives will feel free to be disrespectful of their husbands as well; 2. Women were

there when she belittled the King and will inform their husbands of the manner in which she deprecated her husband resulting in them poking fun at the King (Nachal Eshkol).

18. וּכְדֵי בִּזָּיוֹן וָקָצֶף — And there will be much contempt and wrath, i.e. this affair, if allowed to get out of hand, is fraught with the danger of excessive contempt and wrath (Rashi, Ibn Ezra).

19. אִם־עַל־הַמֶּלֶךְ טוֹב — If it please the King. [A deferential, almost obsequious phrase].

יֵצֵא דְבַר־מַלְכוּת מִלְּפָנָיו — Let there go forth a royal edict from him. Memuchan suggested that Ahasuerus abolish the requirement that a King consult learned men for advice

וּמָדַי וְלֹא יַעֲבוֹר אֲשֶׁר לֹא־תָבֹא וַשְׁתִּי
לִפְנֵי הַמֶּלֶךְ אֲחַשְׁוֵרוֹשׁ וּמַלְכוּתָהּ יִתֵּן
כ הַמֶּלֶךְ לִרְעוּתָהּ הַטּוֹבָה מִמֶּנָּה: וְנִשְׁמַע
פִּתְגָם הַמֶּלֶךְ אֲשֶׁר־יַעֲשֶׂה בְּכָל־מַלְכוּתוֹ
כִּי רַבָּה הִיא וְכָל־הַנָּשִׁים יִתְּנוּ יְקָר
כא לְבַעְלֵיהֶן לְמִגָּדוֹל וְעַד־קָטָן: וַיִּיטַב הַדָּבָר
בְּעֵינֵי הַמֶּלֶךְ וְהַשָּׂרִים וַיַּעַשׂ הַמֶּלֶךְ כִּדְבַר
כב מְמוּכָן: וַיִּשְׁלַח סְפָרִים אֶל־כָּל־מְדִינוֹת
הַמֶּלֶךְ אֶל־מְדִינָה וּמְדִינָה כִּכְתָבָהּ וְאֶל־

prior to making an important decision. We have been informed of this tradition previously [verse 13]: *'Then the King conferred with the experts who knew the times, for such was the King's procedure to turn to all who knew laws and judgment'* (Yosef Lekach).

Memuchan felt that it was not necessary for the King to discuss his judgment with others.

It was ordained by G-d that this new law giving sweeping powers to the King be inscribed in their judicial canons so that it could later be the instrument of Haman's death, as it says: [chapter 7, v9]: *Then Charbonah, one of the chamberlains said, "Behold the gallows ... " Then the King said, "hang him on it!"* The King then passed independent judgment upon Haman, no questions asked. Thus, Haman inadvertantly brought about his own downfall (Me'am Loez).

וְלֹא יַעֲבוֹר — *that it be not revoked.* The law should be permanent for all women who ever show contempt for their husbands (Rashi).

אֲשֶׁר לֹא־תָבֹא וַשְׁתִּי — *That Vashti*

never again appear. Haman was still worried that Ahasuerus might reconsider and pardon Vashti — thereby reversing the tables — for Memuchan would hardly want to face the consequences of a re-instated Vashti. He therefore requested that the decree be irrevocable, and that Vashti never again be permitted to appear before the King (Meam Loez).

Rashi understands this in the past tense, i.e., that Vashti *did not appear* before the King (at his command) and therefore she deserved the death penalty.

[Note the probably deliberate omission here of the title מַלְכָּה — 'Queen.']

לִרְעוּתָהּ הַטּוֹבָה מִמֶּנָּה — *Upon another who is better than she.* Memuchan had told Ahasuerus that his second wife would most certainly be more obedient than her predecessor having made note of the manner in which Vashti was killed, and having read the stern decree proclaimed throughout the land. His second wife would realize that if the King could not find it in his heart to forgive his first love, his beloved

Persians and the Medes, that it be not revoked, that Vashti never again appear before King Ahasuerus; and let the King confer her royal estate upon another who is better than she. ²⁰ Then, when the King's decree which he shall proclaim shall be resounded throughout all his kingdom—great though it be—all the wives will show respect to their husbands, great and small alike.' ²¹ This proposal pleased the King and the officials, and the King did according to the word of Memuchan; ²² and he sent letters into all the King's provinces, to each province in its own script, and to

wife, for having disobeyed him, she, as his second choice, would have to tread very carefully *(Me'am Loez).*

20. וְנִשְׁמַע פִּתְגָם הַמֶּלֶךְ — *The King's decree shall be resounded.* [Literally: 'shall be heard.']

וְכָל-הַנָּשִׁים יִתְּנוּ יְקָר לְבַעֲלֵיהֶן — *All the wives will show respect to their husbands.* [Once they see the revenge taken against Vashti, they will show respect to their own husbands. Ahasuerus accepted the advice and had her killed].

All this was written in such detail to teach us how the Almighty weaves a web of intrigue and paradox to accomplish miracles for Israel! Ahasuerus issued a decree designed to accomodate the wishes of even his lowliest subject; yet he did not hesitate to make the outrageous and humiliating demand upon his own wife — his Queen, daughter of royalty — to appear unclothed in public against her will. His caprice resulted in her death, and paved the way for Esther and the ultimate miracle *(Vilna Gaon).*

לְמִגָּדוֹל וְעַד-קָטָן — *Great and small alike.* [I.e. both the upper and lower classes.]

21. וַיִּיטַב הַדָּבָר בְּעֵינֵי הַמֶּלֶךְ — *This proposal pleased the King.* "He gave the order and they brought in her head on a platter" *(Midrash).*

22. אֶל-מְדִינָה וּמְדִינָה כִּכְתָבָהּ — *To each province in its own script.* Ahasuerus wrote the proclamation in the various local scripts and languages. A King usually commands his subjects to learn one "official" language. Ahasuerus, however, went out of his way not to burden each province to give up its native tongue; a device to win the gratitude of his subjects and further consolidate his throne *(Yosef Lekach).*

לִהְיוֹת כָּל-אִישׁ שֹׂרֵר בְּבֵיתוֹ — *That every man should rule in his own home.* The relevance of this part of the decree is difficult to understand. Raba said that had it not been for this decree, even a shred would not have remained of the Jews. People said: 'What does he mean by

עַם וָעָם כִּלְשׁוֹנוֹ לִהְיוֹת כָּל־אִישׁ שֹׂרֵר
בְּבֵיתוֹ וּמְדַבֵּר כִּלְשׁוֹן עַמּוֹ:

פֶּרֶק ב
א־ד

א אַחַר הַדְּבָרִים הָאֵלֶּה כְּשֹׁךְ חֲמַת הַמֶּלֶךְ
אֲחַשְׁוֵרוֹשׁ זָכַר אֶת־וַשְׁתִּי וְאֵת אֲשֶׁר־
עָשָׂתָה וְאֵת אֲשֶׁר־נִגְזַר עָלֶיהָ: ב וַיֹּאמְרוּ
נַעֲרֵי הַמֶּלֶךְ מְשָׁרְתָיו יְבַקְשׁוּ לַמֶּלֶךְ
ג נְעָרוֹת בְּתוּלוֹת טוֹבוֹת מַרְאֶה: וְיַפְקֵד
הַמֶּלֶךְ פְּקִידִים בְּכָל־מְדִינוֹת מַלְכוּתוֹ
וְיִקְבְּצוּ אֶת־כָּל־נַעֲרָה־בְתוּלָה טוֹבַת
מַרְאֶה אֶל־שׁוּשַׁן הַבִּירָה אֶל־בֵּית
הַנָּשִׁים אֶל־יַד הֵגֶא סְרִיס הַמֶּלֶךְ שֹׁמֵר
ד הַנָּשִׁים וְנָתוֹן תַּמְרֻקֵיהֶן: וְהַנַּעֲרָה אֲשֶׁר
תִּיטַב בְּעֵינֵי הַמֶּלֶךְ תִּמְלֹךְ תַּחַת וַשְׁתִּי

sending us word that every man should rule in his own home? Of course he should! Even a weaver in his own home must be boss!' (Meg. 12b)

The commentaries explained that upon reading this first decree, everyone saw how foolish the King was. Later, therefore, when they read his second decree about exterminating the Jews on the 13th of Adar, they were afraid that the King issued this decree while intoxicated and that he would change his mind and reverse the order the next morning. Were it not for this mockery, they would have responded immediately to the second decree by "jumping the gun," and would not have waited for the appointed date to exterminate the Jews (Me'am Loez).

II

1. זָכַר אֶת־וַשְׁתִּי — He remembered Vashti. i.e. with affection and remorse.

He remembered the order he had given her to appear unclothed before him and how she refused, and how he had been wroth with her and put her to death (Midrash).

each people in its own language, to the effect that every man should rule in his own home, and speak the language of his own people.

II
1-4

¹**A**fter *these things, when the wrath of King Ahasuerus subsided, he remembered Vashti, and what she had done, and what had been decreed against her.* ²*Then the King's pages said: "Let there be sought for the King beautiful young maidens;* ³*and let the King appoint commissioners in all the provinces of his kingdom, that they may gather together every beautiful young maiden to Shushan the capitol to the harem, under the charge of Hege the King's chamberlain, custodian of the women; and let their cosmetics be given them.* ⁴*Then, let the girl who pleases the King be queen instead of Vashti."* This

Ahasuerus seeks a new Queen

The King obviously *mentioned* his recriminations or how else would his pages know to respond? *(Yosef Lekach).*

וְאֵת אֲשֶׁר־נִגְזַר עָלֶיהָ — *And what had been decreed against her.* A decree that was patently unjust. The *Midrash* explains that Vashti deserved to suffer this miserable fate because she prevailed upon Ahasuerus to halt the construction of the Temple which had begun with the permission of Ahasuerus' predecessor, Cyrus. She used to say to him, 'Do you seek to build what my ancestors destroyed?'

3. פְּקִידִים — *Commissioners.* Local commissioners were chosen from each of the 127 provinces, rather than from Shushan, because a local commissioner would more readily be able to find the most beautiful girls in his province *(M'nos Halevi; see Rashi).*

וְיִקְבְּצוּ — *That they may gather together.* They gathered girls even by snatching them against their will *(Me'am Loez).*

Why did G-d subject the Persian women to the humiliation of being taken to the King and then rejected in favor of Esther [the Jewess]? Because the Persian women used to pour contempt on the daughters of Israel, calling them ugly and saying none would look at them *(Midrash).*

פֶּרֶק ב
ה-ז

וַיִּיטַב הַדָּבָר בְּעֵינֵי הַמֶּלֶךְ וַיַּעַשׂ כֵּן:
ה אִישׁ יְהוּדִי הָיָה בְּשׁוּשַׁן הַבִּירָה וּשְׁמוֹ
מָרְדֳּכַי בֶּן יָאִיר בֶּן־שִׁמְעִי בֶּן־קִישׁ אִישׁ
ו יְמִינִי: אֲשֶׁר הָגְלָה מִירוּשָׁלַיִם עִם־הַגֹּלָה
אֲשֶׁר הָגְלְתָה עִם יְכָנְיָה מֶלֶךְ־יְהוּדָה
ז אֲשֶׁר הֶגְלָה נְבוּכַדְנֶצַּר מֶלֶךְ בָּבֶל: וַיְהִי

4. וַיַּעַשׂ כֵּן — *And he followed it,* by sending out the commissioners. Ahasuerus was afraid that, if they knew they were to be drafted for the harem, the beautiful girls would hide or flee the kingdom. He told his commissioners, therefore, not to make their real mission known, but to go about their normal routine while secretly compiling a list of the whereabouts of the beautiful girls. Then the King dispatched other officers to round them up without warning (*Me'am Loez*).

5. אִישׁ יְהוּדִי — *A Jewish man.* All those who were exiled along with the Kings of Judah were called 'Yehudi' by the gentiles — regardless of their original tribe (*Rashi*).

The term 'Yehudi' (derived from Yehudah, or Judah, fourth son of Jacob) has become a synonym for Jew. Yehudah's mother gave him that name because, as she said, 'I will praise (אוֹדֶה) G-d.' Yehudah is thus a declaration that Jews always praise G-d, hence the common name Yehudi regardless of tribal origin (*Sfas Emes*).

He was the only one who remained in Shushan, but did not partake of the food during the King's banquet (*Rav Galico*).

The title אִישׁ — *man* indicates

that Mordechai in his generation was equal to Moses in his, for of Moses, too, it is written: וְהָאִישׁ מֹשֶׁה עָנָו מְאֹד, *And the 'man' Moses was very humble* [Numbers 12:3] (*Midrash*).

He was a member of the Sanhedrin (*Midrash*).

This verse, as well as the verses: לַיְּהוּדִים הָיְתָה [8:15], וּמָרְדֳּכַי יָצָא [8:16] and כִּי מָרְדֳּכַי הַיְּהוּדִי אוֹרָה [10:3] are read aloud by the Congregation during the reading of the Megillah in the Synagogue. Among the reasons offered for this wide-spread custom are: to popularize the miracle [פִּרְסוּמֵי נִיסָא]; these verses express the essence of the miracle through Mordechai; and to keep the children alert and prevent them from dozing off. The congregation recites the verses loudly as an expression of the joy of the day. The reader then repeats the verses because each verse must be read from the Megillah (*RaMA, Orach Chayim 690:17; Mishneh Brurah ad. loc. Mishne Brurah 689:16. See Abudarham; Kol Bo; Levush*).

בְּשׁוּשַׁן הַבִּירָה — *In Shushan the capitol.* He acted as a Jew not only in the privacy of his home, nor only in his study-house, but even in Shushan — in the street, among people... (*R. Yonasan Eybescheutz*).

advice pleased the King, and he followed it.

⁵There was a Jewish man in Shushan the capitol whose name was Mordechai, son of Yair, son of Shim'i, son of Kish, a Benjaminite, ⁶who had been exiled from Jerusalem along with the exiles who had been exiled with Jechoniah, King of Judah, whom Nebuchadnezzar, King of Babylon had exiled. ⁷And

וּשְׁמוֹ מָרְדֳּכַי — *Whose name was Mordechai.* In Scripture, the names of the wicked are given before the word שֵׁם (name); as it says: נָבָל שְׁמוֹ — *Nabal was his name;* גָּלְיָת שְׁמוֹ — *Goliath was his name;* שֶׁבַע בֶּן בִּכְרִי שְׁמוֹ —*Sheva son of Bichri was his name.* But the names of the righteous are preceeded by the word שֵׁם—'*name*'— as it says: וּשְׁמוֹ מָנוֹחַ *And his name was Manoach;* וּשְׁמוֹ קִישׁ — *And his name was Kish;* וּשְׁמוֹ אֶלְקָנָה — *And his name was Elkanah;* וּשְׁמוֹ שָׁאוּל — *And his name was Saul;* וּשְׁמוֹ בֹּעַז — *And his name was Boaz;* וּשְׁמוֹ יִשַׁי — *And his name was Jesse;* וּשְׁמוֹ מָרְדֳּכַי — *And his name was Mordechai.* They thus resemble their Creator of whom it is written וּשְׁמִי ה' — '*But by My Name* HASHEM *I made me not known to them'* [Ex. 6:2] (*Midrash Rabba; Midrash Abba Gorion*).

מָרְדֳּכַי — *Mordechai.* Where is Mordechai alluded to in the Torah? — In the verse מָר־דְּרוֹר — *flowing myrrh* [*Exod.* 30:22] which the *Targum* renders as מֵירָא דַכְיָא '*Mira Dachia*' [which both in spelling and sound resemble מָרְדֳּכַי — *Mordechai* — (*Chulin* 139b).

Just as myrrh is the foremost of spices, so Mordechai was the foremost of the righteous of his generation (*Midrash*).

בֶּן יָאִיר בֶּן־שִׁמְעִי בֶּן־קִישׁ — *Son of*

Yair, son of Shim'i, son of Kish. He wasn't literally: '*son of*' but rather '*descendant of*' (*Megilas Sesarim*).

אִישׁ יְמִינִי — *A Benjaminite.* Mordechai, as a descendant of Benjamin, deserved to be instrumental in saving the Jewish people because Benjamin was the only brother who did not participate in מְכִירַת־יוֹסֵף selling Joseph into bondage. The descendants of the other brothers are perpetually punished for this crime (*Me'am Loez*).

[Mordechai was a descendant of King Saul and thus was instrumental in correcting Saul's iniquity of allowing Agag to escape and beget a son who was the forefather of Haman].

The Hebrew for 'Benjaminite' is אִישׁ יְמִינִי, *man from the right —*i.e. Mordechai never swerved to the left (*Tiferes Shlomo*).

6. אֲשֶׁר הָגְלָה — *Who had been exiled.* They had all been exiled but Mordechai particularly is so described because he continually anguished over the Exile (*Tiferes Shlomo*).

Another interpretation offered by the Sages: Mordechai went into self-exile before the rest of his people to establish a holy atmosphere in Persia so the Jews could survive the exile there. He followed the example of Jacob, who went down to Egypt

אֹמֵן אֶת־הֲדַסָּה הִיא אֶסְתֵּר בַּת־דֹּדוֹ כִּי אֵין לָהּ אָב וָאֵם וְהַנַּעֲרָה יְפַת־תֹּאַר וְטוֹבַת מַרְאֶה וּבְמוֹת אָבִיהָ וְאִמָּהּ לְקָחָהּ מָרְדֳּכַי לוֹ לְבַת: וַיְהִי בְּהִשָּׁמַע דְּבַר־ הַמֶּלֶךְ וְדָתוֹ וּבְהִקָּבֵץ נְעָרוֹת רַבּוֹת אֶל־ שׁוּשַׁן הַבִּירָה אֶל־יַד הֵגָי וַתִּלָּקַח אֶסְתֵּר אֶל־בֵּית הַמֶּלֶךְ אֶל־יַד הֵגַי שֹׁמֵר הַנָּשִׁים:

ט וַתִּיטַב הַנַּעֲרָה בְעֵינָיו וַתִּשָּׂא חֶסֶד לְפָנָיו וַיְבַהֵל אֶת־תַּמְרוּקֶיהָ וְאֶת־מָנוֹתֶהָ לָתֵת לָהּ וְאֵת שֶׁבַע הַנְּעָרוֹת הָרְאֻיוֹת לָתֶת־ לָהּ מִבֵּית הַמֶּלֶךְ וַיְשַׁנֶּהָ וְאֶת־נַעֲרוֹתֶיהָ לְטוֹב בֵּית הַנָּשִׁים: י לֹא־הִגִּידָה אֶסְתֵּר

before the enslavement of his children, to sow the seeds of holiness which sustained them in their exile (Tiferes Shlomo).

7. אֹמֵן — *Reared.* This word connotes the constant supervision and ministering demanded of a mother by her child. Mordechai, despite being a renowned member of the Sanhedrin, did not hesitate to perform these services for the child Esther (Me'am Loez).

הֲדַסָּה — *Hadassah.* There is a difference of opinion among the Sages (Meg. 13a) whether Hadassah was her proper name and Esther was added later, or *vice-versa.* Both names are descriptive of her virtues. Hadassah is derived from the Hebrew word הֲדַס—'myrtle'; Esther from אִסְתַּהַר — *Istahar* ['as beautiful as the moon' — (Rashi).]

'Just as the myrtle [הֲדַס] has a sweet smell but a bitter taste, so Esther was sweet to Mordechai but bitter to Haman' (Midrash).

'Where is Esther alluded to in the Torah? — In the verse וְאָנֹכִי הַסְתֵּר אַסְתִּיר פָּנַי בַּיּוֹם הַהוּא, 'And I will surely hide (אַסְתִּיר) My face on that day [Deut. 31:18] (Chulin 139b).

[The verse in *Devarim* speaks of the many evils which will ח"ו befall Israel if they forsake G-d's ways, evils symbolized by G-d's 'hiding' His benevolent Face].

In Esther's lifetime G-d seemingly diverted (הַסְתִּיר) His attention from Israel because of their evil ways (The Chortkover Rebbe).

וּבְמוֹת אָבִיהָ וְאִמָּהּ — *And when her father and mother had died.* Her father died before her birth, and her mother at her birth (Megilla 13a).

לְקָחָהּ לוֹ לְבַת — *Adopted her as his daughter.* 'A Tanna taught in the name of Rav Meir: Read not "as a daughter" [לְבַת] but "for a home" [לְבַיִת] i.e. "a wife" ' (Meg. 13a). [See *Overview.*]

8. בְּהִשָּׁמַע — *Were published.* [Lit.

he had reared Hadassah, that is, Esther, his uncle's daughter; since she had neither father nor mother. *The girl was finely featured and beautiful, and when her father and mother had died, Mordechai adopted her as his daughter. ⁸So it came to pass, when the King's bidding and decree were published, and when many young girls were being brought together to Shushan the capitol, under the charge of Hegai, that Esther was taken into the palace, under the charge of Hegai, guardian of the women. ⁹The girl pleased him, and she obtained his kindness; he hurriedly prepared her cosmetics and her allowance of delicacies to present her; along with the seven special maids from the palace; and he transferred her and her maidens to the best quarters in the harem. ¹⁰Esther had not told of*

Esther is
brought to
the harem

'were heard'].

וַתִּלָּקַח אֶסְתֵּר — *Esther was taken.* It is obvious from the phrase *'was taken'* that when the edict was promulgated Mordechai had tried to hide Esther and that she was ultimately taken to the harem by force (*Targum Sheni, Yosef Lekach*).

9. וַתִּיטַב הַנַּעֲרָה בְעֵינָיו — *The girl pleased him,* not only with superficial beauty. Unlike some who only appear good from afar, Esther was pleasing even after one got to know her well (*Maamar Mordechai*).

וְאֵת שֶׁבַע הַנְּעָרוֹת הָרְאֻיוֹת — *With the seven special maids.* The Talmud explains that there were seven so that she could count the days of the week through rotating their schedule so that the same one always served her on a given day. The commentators wonder. why

Esther — a prophetess — would need such a system to keep track of the Sabbath. Esther was keeping her identity as a Jewess hidden. Forever mindful that בַּטָּלָה מְבִיאָה לִידֵי שִׁיעְמוּם *laziness leads to indolence* — she kept herself busy throughout the week. Afraid that her maids would notice that on the Sabbath she performed no work and guess she was Jewish, she appointed a different maid for each day of the week. Those who ministered her during the week didn't see her rest on the Sabbath; the Sabbath maid, meanwhile, assumed that just as she did no work on the Sabbath, she did no work on *any* days of the week (*Yaaros Devash*).

10. לֹא הִגִּידָה אֶסְתֵּר — *Esther had not told.* She guarded the secret for nine years until Haman's downfall in the twelfth year of Ahasuerus' reign (*Me'am Loez*).

אֶת־עַמָּהּ וְאֶת־מְוֹלַדְתָּהּ כִּי מָרְדֳּכַי צִוָּה
יא עָלֶיהָ אֲשֶׁר לֹא־תַגִּיד: וּבְכָל־יוֹם וָיוֹם
מָרְדֳּכַי מִתְהַלֵּךְ לִפְנֵי חֲצַר בֵּית־הַנָּשִׁים
לָדַעַת אֶת־שְׁלוֹם אֶסְתֵּר וּמַה־יֵּעָשֶׂה בָּהּ:
יב וּבְהַגִּיעַ תֹּר נַעֲרָה וְנַעֲרָה לָבוֹא | אֶל־
הַמֶּלֶךְ אֲחַשְׁוֵרוֹשׁ מִקֵּץ הֱיוֹת לָהּ כְּדָת
הַנָּשִׁים שְׁנֵים עָשָׂר חֹדֶשׁ כִּי כֵּן יִמְלְאוּ
יְמֵי מְרוּקֵיהֶן שִׁשָּׁה חֳדָשִׁים בְּשֶׁמֶן הַמֹּר
וְשִׁשָּׁה חֳדָשִׁים בַּבְּשָׂמִים וּבְתַמְרוּקֵי
יג הַנָּשִׁים: וּבָזֶה הַנַּעֲרָה בָּאָה אֶל־הַמֶּלֶךְ
אֵת כָּל־אֲשֶׁר תֹּאמַר יִנָּתֵן לָהּ לָבוֹא עִמָּהּ
יד מִבֵּית הַנָּשִׁים עַד־בֵּית הַמֶּלֶךְ: בָּעֶרֶב|הִיא
בָאָה וּבַבֹּקֶר הִיא שָׁבָה אֶל־בֵּית הַנָּשִׁים
שֵׁנִי אֶל־יַד שַׁעֲשְׁגַז סְרִיס הַמֶּלֶךְ שֹׁמֵר

Many reasons are given for keeping Esther's Jewishness secret: Mordechai must have realized that if Esther was chosen to be Queen it could only be that she was to be instrumental in saving Israel from some impending calamity. He reasoned that if her origins as a Jew were known, Ahasuerus would never choose her and she would lose her opportunity (R. Eleazar of Worms).

Mordechai had Esther keep her relationship to him secret so others would not be secretive in his presence (Yosef Lekach).

Rashi comments that she did not declare her royal lineage (as a descendant of the family of King Saul) so that the king might think that she was of humble origin and send her away.

Ibn Ezra explains that the purpose of her secrecy was so that she might secretly observe her religion. Had she declared her faith, she would have been forced to transgress.

According to the Vilna Gaon, Mordechai was afraid that his family and nation would be killed for having kept Esther hidden for so long, and for not surrendering her voluntarily when she was finally discovered. Now that she was made Queen, however, and no one even rebuked her for having hidden, the reason for withholding her identity no longer applied. Nevertheless לֹא הִגִּידָה אֶסְתֵּר, Esther had not told, in deference to Mordechai כִּי מָרְדֳּכַי צִוָּה עָלֶיהָ — for Mordechai instructed her.

11. מִתְהַלֵּךְ — Used to walk about. Mordechai did not make it obvious

her people or her kindred, for Mordechai had instructed her not to tell. ¹¹Every day Mordechai used
to walk about in front of the court of the harem to
find out about Esther's well-being and what would
become of her.

¹²Now when each girl's turn arrived to come to
King Ahasuerus, after having been treated according
to the manner prescribed for women for twelve
months (for so was the prescribed length of their
annointing accomplished: six months with oil of
myrrh, and six months with perfumes, and feminine
cosmetics) — ¹³when then the girl thus came to the
king, she was given whatever she desired to accompany her from the harem to the palace. ¹⁴ In the evening she would come, and the next morning she would
return to the second harem in the custody of

that he was interested in Esther; to
do that would have revealed her
Jewishness. The verb used in this
verse is not הוֹלֵךְ — 'walk' but
מִתְהַלֵּךְ 'walked about', i.e. 'strolled'
around the court of the harem so
that his true intention of inquiring
after Esther's welfare would not be
realized by the guards (Me'am
Loez).

שְׁלוֹם אֶסְתֵּר — Esther's well-being.
To answer ritual questions (Midrash).

וּמַה־יֵּעָשֶׂה בָּה — And what would
become of her. i.e. 'And what would
be accomplished בָּה — through her'
[As mentioned earlier (Commentary
v. 10), Mordechai realized that
Esther's torment must have been so
that she could become the Divine
instrument for saving her people.]
(Rashi, Yosef Lekach).

12. שְׁנֵים עָשָׂר חֹדֶשׁ — Twelve
months. Ahasuerus wanted to make
sure that none of the girls were dis-
eased. He therefore ordained that
twelve months should elapse so that
any symptoms of illness would surface during that time (M'nos
Halevi).

כִּי כֵּן יִמְלְאוּ — For so was the prescribed length [This parenthetical
phrase indicates to us that twelve
months was not an arbitrarily long
waiting period, but that it took that
long for the cosmetics and
annointing to have the desired ef-
fect].

13. כָּל־אֲשֶׁר תֹּאמַר — Whatever she
desired. To enhance her beauty, she
was given whatever she desired in
the way of jewelry or dress (Rav
Galico).

הַפִּילַגְשִׁים לְא־תָבְוֹא עוֹד אֶל־הַמֶּלֶךְ כִּי
אִם־חָפֵץ בָּהּ הַמֶּלֶךְ וְנִקְרְאָה בְשֵׁם:
טו וּבְהַגִּיעַ תֹּר־אֶסְתֵּר בַּת־אֲבִיחַיִל | דֹּד
מָרְדֳּכַי אֲשֶׁר לָקַח־לוֹ לְבַת לָבוֹא אֶל־
הַמֶּלֶךְ לֹא בִקְשָׁה דָּבָר כִּי אִם אֶת־אֲשֶׁר
יֹאמַר הֵגַי סְרִיס־הַמֶּלֶךְ שֹׁמֵר הַנָּשִׁים
וַתְּהִי אֶסְתֵּר נֹשֵׂאת חֵן בְּעֵינֵי כָּל־רֹאֶיהָ:
טז וַתִּלָּקַח אֶסְתֵּר אֶל־הַמֶּלֶךְ אֲחַשְׁוֵרוֹשׁ
אֶל־בֵּית מַלְכוּתוֹ בַּחֹדֶשׁ הָעֲשִׂירִי הוּא־
חֹדֶשׁ טֵבֵת בִּשְׁנַת־שֶׁבַע לְמַלְכוּתוֹ:
יז וַיֶּאֱהַב הַמֶּלֶךְ אֶת־אֶסְתֵּר מִכָּל־הַנָּשִׁים
וַתִּשָּׂא־חֵן וָחֶסֶד לְפָנָיו מִכָּל־הַבְּתוּלוֹת
וַיָּשֶׂם כֶּתֶר־מַלְכוּת בְּרֹאשָׁהּ וַיַּמְלִיכֶהָ
יח תַּחַת וַשְׁתִּי: וַיַּעַשׂ הַמֶּלֶךְ מִשְׁתֶּה גָּדוֹל

14. בֵּית הַנָּשִׁים שֵׁנִי — *The second harem.* Having consorted with the King, it would not be proper for them to marry other men. They were required to return to the harem and remain there for the rest of their lives as concubines, to await the possibility of being crowned Queen if the King found no one better (*Ibn Ezra; Alshich*).

15. וּבְהַגִּיעַ תֹּר־אֶסְתֵּר בַּת־אֲבִיחַיִל — *Now when the turn came for Esther, daughter of Avichail.* Why is her family background and her father's name given for the first time only here? One also wonders why the fact that Mordechai adopted Esther is repeated at this point.

The reason is to let us know that precisely *because* she was acutely aware of her background, she asked for nothing. She kept in mind that her father was Avichail, and that her relative and savior and adoptive father was Mordechai. With these images before her, she did not request any artificial beauty aids, in the hope of lessening her chances of finding favor in the eyes of Ahasuerus so that she would be rejected and possibly even be sent home to her family (*M'nos Halevi*).

וַתְּהִי אֶסְתֵּר נֹשֵׂאת חֵן — *Esther would captivate.* i.e. even though she requested nothing, her true beauty and grace found favor. 'R. Judah said: She was like a statue upon which a thousand persons look and admire equally. R. Nehemiah said: They placed Median women and Persian women on either side of her, and she was more beautiful than all of them' (*Midrash*).

II
15-18

Shaashgaz, the King's chamberlain, guardian of the concubines. She would never again go to the King unless the King desired her, and she were summoned by name.

Esther is chosen Queen

¹⁵Now when the turn came for Esther, daughter of Avichail the uncle of Mordechai (who had adopted her as his own daughter) to come to the King, she requested nothing beyond what Hegai the King's chamberlain, guardian of the women, had advised. Esther would captivate all who saw her; ¹⁶Esther was taken to King Ahasuerus into his palace in the tenth month, which is the month of Teves, in the seventh year of his reign. ¹⁷The King loved Esther more than all the women, and she won more of his grace and favour than all the other girls; so that he set the royal crown upon her head, and made her queen in place of Vashti. ¹⁸Then the King made a great banquet for all

'Rav Eleazar said: Everyone claimed her as a member of his own people' (Megilla 13a).

16. וַתִּלָּקַח אֶסְתֵּר — *Esther was taken.* By force, against her will (Midrash).

17. מִכָּל־הַנָּשִׁים *More than all the women.* i.e., 'more than the wives he already had' (Alshich).

According to the Midrash, married women were also brought before him. [This explains why, according to the Rabbis who hold that Esther was legally married to Mordechai, Esther's claim that she was a married woman would not have saved her from being taken by force to the King's harem. Had the King been assembling maidens only, Esther could have exempted

herself by claiming she was married.]

מִכָּל־הַבְּתוּלוֹת — *Than all the other girls.* Although other maidens were awaiting their turn in the harem, once Ahasuerus saw Esther he instantly crowned her as his Queen without bothering to see the other beautiful candidates (Alshich).

According to the Talmud, Esther had the qualities both of a maiden and of a married woman (Megilla 13b) [See Overview.]

תַּחַת וַשְׁתִּי — *In place of Vashti.* Even though Vashti was of royal descent and Esther's origins were unknown, Ahasuerus loved Esther as much as he had loved Vashti (Alshich).

18. וַיַּעַשׂ הַמֶּלֶךְ מִשְׁתֶּה גָדוֹל — *Then the King made a great banquet.* In

לְכָל־שָׂרָיו וַעֲבָדָיו ׀ אֵת מִשְׁתֵּה אֶסְתֵּר וַהֲנָחָה לַמְּדִינוֹת עָשָׂה וַיִּתֵּן מַשְׂאֵת כְּיַד הַמֶּלֶךְ: יט וּבְהִקָּבֵץ בְּתוּלוֹת שֵׁנִית וּמָרְדֳּכַי יֹשֵׁב בְּשַׁעַר־הַמֶּלֶךְ: כ אֵין אֶסְתֵּר מַגֶּדֶת מוֹלַדְתָּהּ וְאֶת־עַמָּהּ כַּאֲשֶׁר צִוָּה עָלֶיהָ מָרְדֳּכָי וְאֶת־מַאֲמַר מָרְדֳּכַי אֶסְתֵּר עֹשָׂה כַּאֲשֶׁר הָיְתָה בְאָמְנָה אִתּוֹ: כא בַּיָּמִים הָהֵם וּמָרְדֳּכַי יוֹשֵׁב בְּשַׁעַר־הַמֶּלֶךְ קָצַף בִּגְתָן וָתֶרֶשׁ שְׁנֵי־סָרִיסֵי הַמֶּלֶךְ מִשֹּׁמְרֵי הַסַּף וַיְבַקְשׁוּ לִשְׁלֹחַ יָד בַּמֶּלֶךְ אֲחַשְׁוֵרֹשׁ: כב וַיִּוָּדַע הַדָּבָר לְמָרְדֳּכַי וַיַּגֵּד לְאֶסְתֵּר הַמַּלְכָּה וַתֹּאמֶר אֶסְתֵּר לַמֶּלֶךְ בְּשֵׁם

an effort to draw the secret of Esther's descent from her, Ahasuerus arranged for great festivities. He made a feast for her and she did not tell him; he remitted taxes in her name and she did not tell him; he sent gifts in her name and she still did not tell him (Megillah 13a).

19. וּבְהִקָּבֵץ בְּתוּלוֹת שֵׁנִית — *And when the maidens were gathered together the second time.* He [Ahasuerus] went and took counsel of Mordechai who said: The way to rouse a woman is to make her jealous; nevertheless, she did not tell' (Megilla 13a).

Ahasuerus had mentioned to Esther that he wished he had a Jewish advisor like Daniel, the trusted servant of Nebuchadnezzar. Esther told him of a wise man who was a descendant of King Saul who would make a good mentor. The King appointed Mordechai to sit at the gate and judge the people.

Ahasuerus then took counsel of Mordechai as to how he could extract from Esther the secret of her origin. Mordechai suggested that the King once again organize a gathering of beautiful young maidens from throughout the kingdom. Esther, fearing that she would be replaced as Queen, would certainly divulge her secret.

Mordechai made this suggestion because he wanted to ascertain whether Esther's coronation was truly the will of Heaven. If the King could find no superior to Esther, Mordechai would be assured that her reign was part of G-d's plan (Me'am Loez).

Why did no Israelite or self-seeking opportunist divulge Esther's secret to the King? First, they would not have been believed, because every nation claimed her as its own; second, the feared Mordechai who was then the King's advisor (M'nos Halevi).

II
19-22

his officers and his servants — it was Esther's Banquet — and he proclaimed an anmesty for the
provinces, and gave gifts worthy of the King.

¹⁹And when the maidens were gathered together
the second time, and Mordechai sat at the King's
gate, ²⁰(Esther still told nothing of her kindred or her
people as Mordechai had instructed her; for Esther
continued to obey Mordechai, just as when she was
raised by him.)

Mordechai
foils a plot
against the
King

²¹In those days, while Mordechai was sitting at the
King's gate, Bigsan and Seresh, two of the King's
chamberlains of the guardians of the threshold,
became angry and planned to assassinate King
Ahasuerus. ²²The plot became known to Mordechai,
who told it to Queen Esther, and Esther informed the

---

20. וְאֶת־מַאֲמַר מָרְדְּכַי אֶסְתֵּר עֹשָׂה —
For Esther continued to obey
Mordechai. [Even though she was
now the Queen, she still maintained
her filial piety and obedience].

21. בְּשַׁעַר הַמֶּלֶךְ — At the King's
gate. The commentators stress that
Mordechai, sensing perilous times,
left his position at the Sanhedrin
and stationed himself at the King's
gate where he would be the first to
overhear any threats against the
Jews and thereby thwart them
(Me'am Loez).

The King's gate was not a gathering place for idlers, but the assembly of the dignitaries of the land
(as we find all throughout the
Scriptures that the elders, judges,
and even kings sat at the gate of the
city); for Mordechai was the most
notable Jew in Shushan, and
according to the Persian practice

was highly respected by the government (Torah Nation).

קָצַף — Became angry, at Mordechai's elevation in their stead
(Midrash).

לִשְׁלֹחַ יָד — To assassinate i.e. to
poison the King (Rashi).

22. וַיִּוָּדַע הַדָּבָר לְמָרְדְּכַי — The plot
became known to Mordechai. Being
a member of the Sanhedrin Mordechai knew seventy languages. They
spoke in their native Tarsian tongue
in Mordechai's presence, not ex-
pecting him to understand them
(Megilla 13b).

בְּשֵׁם מָרְדְּכַי — In Mordechai's name.
'Whoever repeats a thing in the
name of him that said it brings
redemption to the world' (Pirke
Avos 6:6).

פֶּרֶק ב כג מָרְדְּכָי: וַיְבֻקַּשׁ הַדָּבָר וַיִּמָּצֵא וַיִּתָּלוּ
כג שְׁנֵיהֶם עַל־עֵץ וַיִּכָּתֵב בְּסֵפֶר דִּבְרֵי
הַיָּמִים לִפְנֵי הַמֶּלֶךְ:

פֶּרֶק ג א אַחַר | הַדְּבָרִים הָאֵלֶּה גִּדַּל הַמֶּלֶךְ
א־ב אֲחַשְׁוֵרוֹשׁ אֶת־הָמָן בֶּן־הַמְּדָתָא הָאֲגָגִי
וַיְנַשְּׂאֵהוּ וַיָּשֶׂם אֶת־כִּסְאוֹ מֵעַל כָּל־
ב הַשָּׂרִים אֲשֶׁר אִתּוֹ: וְכָל־עַבְדֵי הַמֶּלֶךְ
אֲשֶׁר־בְּשַׁעַר הַמֶּלֶךְ כֹּרְעִים וּמִשְׁתַּחֲוִים

---

23. וַיִּכָּתֵב — *It was recorded.* i.e. the goodness which Mordechai did in behalf of the King (*Rashi*).

Some commentators explain that *'it was recorded'* miraculously, by itself. That is why later [Chapter 6:2], when the insomniac King asked that the book of chronicles be read to him, the verse says *'it was found written'* because Ahasuerus did not remember it being written (*Me'am Loez*).

III

1. אַחַר הַדְּבָרִים הָאֵלֶּה — *After these things.* 'It was only *after* G-d had prepared for the future by establishing Mordechai's reputation that the monarch elevated Haman . . .' (*Torah Nation*).

גִּדַּל הַמֶּלֶךְ — *The King promoted.* G-d caused Haman to be raised to power in order to make his eventual fall greater. The Holy One, Blessed be He, said: 'Should Haman be slain when he goes down to stop the building of the Temple, no one will know who he was. Let him, therefore, become great and famous and *afterwards* be hanged.' (*Midrash*)

הָמָן — *Haman,* a descendant of Agag, King of Amalek [I *Samuel* 15,9].

With the exception of Korach he was the richest man who ever lived, for he stole the treasures of the Judean kings and of the Temple (*Midrash*).

2. כֹּרְעִים וּמִשְׁתַּחֲוִים—*Would bow down and prostrate....* Haman claimed divine powers for himself, therefore Mordechai would not bow down or prostrate himself (*Rashi*).

To make it manifest that the homage due him was of an idolatrous character, Haman had the image of an idol fastened to his

אסתר [64]

King in Mordechai's name. ²³*The matter was in-*
vestigated and corroborated, and they were both
hanged on a gallows. It was recorded in the book of
chronicles in the King's presence.

¹**A**fter these things King Ahasuerus promoted
Haman, the son of Hammedasa the Agagite, and
advanced him; he set his seat above all the officers
*who were with him.*² *All the King's servants at the*
King's gate, would bow down and prostrate
themselves before Haman, for this is what the King

clothes, so that whoever bowed down before him worshipped an idol at the same time (*Midrash*)

[It is interesting to note that wherever else both words כֹּרְעִים וּמִשְׁתַּחֲוִים, 'bowing and prostrating' appear together in the Bible they always refer to obeisance to G-d. Haman was not content with simple obeisance from his subjects; he insisted upon the kind of bowing and prostration reserved for G-d, hence the Midrash tells us he wore an image to enhance the idolatrous nature of the homage he desired. Mordechai לֹא יִכְרַע וְלֹא יִשְׁתַּחֲוֶה — would not bow down or prostrate himself — under any circumstances—before Haman. (Quite possibly, though, Mordechai would acknowledge Haman in some form, but this did not suffice Haman's vanity.) As pointed out later [verse 5], when Haman saw that Mordechai would not כֹּרֵעַ וּמִשְׁתַּחֲוֶה לוֹ — bow down and

prostrate himself before Haman, he grew angry. He knew that Mordechai's refusal was religiously motivated and there was no point in punishing Mordechai alone — the whole Jewish people deserved punishment in Haman's eyes.

But when Haman formulated the decree to annihilate the Jews and Mordechai found out about it, the next time the two met [5:9], וְלֹא־קָם וְלֹא־זָע מִמֶּנּוּ, Mordechai neither stood up nor stirred before him. This time, general חֵמָה, fury, against the Jews as a whole, was not enough. Haman directed his anger specifically עַל מָרְדְּכַי, at Mordechai, the individual].

כִּי־כֵן צִוָּה־לוֹ הַמֶּלֶךְ — For this is what the King commanded. [Prostration before top-ranking officials was universal in the Orient. It seems strange, therefore, that the King had to give a special command for the benefit of Haman. It would seem that there was some reluctance on

פרק ג

ג־ז

לְהָמָן כִּי־כֵן צִוָּה־לוֹ הַמֶּלֶךְ וּמָרְדֳּכַי לֹא
יִכְרַע וְלֹא יִשְׁתַּחֲוֶה: וַיֹּאמְרוּ עַבְדֵי הַמֶּלֶךְ
אֲשֶׁר־בְּשַׁעַר הַמֶּלֶךְ לְמָרְדֳּכָי מַדּוּעַ אַתָּה
עוֹבֵר אֵת מִצְוַת הַמֶּלֶךְ: וַיְהִי *בְּאָמְרָם
אֵלָיו יוֹם וָיוֹם וְלֹא שָׁמַע אֲלֵיהֶם וַיַּגִּידוּ
לְהָמָן לִרְאוֹת הֲיַעַמְדוּ דִּבְרֵי מָרְדֳּכַי כִּי־
הִגִּיד לָהֶם אֲשֶׁר־הוּא יְהוּדִי: וַיַּרְא הָמָן
כִּי־אֵין מָרְדֳּכַי כֹּרֵעַ וּמִשְׁתַּחֲוֶה לוֹ וַיִּמָּלֵא
הָמָן חֵמָה: וַיִּבֶז בְּעֵינָיו לִשְׁלֹחַ יָד
בְּמָרְדֳּכַי לְבַדּוֹ כִּי־הִגִּידוּ לוֹ אֶת־עַם
מָרְדֳּכָי וַיְבַקֵּשׁ הָמָן לְהַשְׁמִיד אֶת־כָּל־
הַיְּהוּדִים אֲשֶׁר בְּכָל־מַלְכוּת אֲחַשְׁוֵרוֹשׁ
עַם מָרְדֳּכָי: בַּחֹדֶשׁ הָרִאשׁוֹן הוּא־חֹדֶשׁ
נִיסָן בִּשְׁנַת שְׁתֵּים עֶשְׂרֵה לַמֶּלֶךְ

*כְּאָמְרָם ק׳

ג

ד

ה

ו

ז

the part of his subjects to do so necessitating a special order by the King.]

Haman was aware that Mordechai would not bow. He persuaded the King, therefore, to enact a law requiring everyone to bow down to him. Thus it would become obvious that Mordechai was disobeying a royal decree. The so-called felony would provide Haman with the provocation he desired to destroy the Jews (Sfas Emes).

וּמָרְדֳּכַי לֹא יִכְרַע — But Mordecai would not bow down. Why is this verse written in future — יִכְרַע [lit. 'will bow']—rather than past tense—כָּרַע — [bowed]? The future tense signifies a decision not to bow under any circumstances rather than a decision taken for a particular occasion (Shaar Bas Rabim). The Midrash Chazis states that,

at the request of Esther, Ahasuerus himself freed Mordechai from the obligation of prostrating himself before Haman. Rav Yonasan Eybeschuetz infers this explanation from the verse itself. The words כִּי־כֵן צִוָּה־לוֹ הַמֶּלֶךְ — 'for this is what the King had commanded' apply to the end of the verse rather than the beginning. Read thus: This is what the King had commanded concerning him: וּמָרְדֳּכַי לֹא יִכְרַע — 'That Mordechai should not bow, etc.' This also explains the use of the future tense יִכְרַע — 'should not bow.'

4. יוֹם וָיוֹם — Day after day. At first they thought he was a gentile. When they discovered he was a Jew, they despised him and reported him to Haman. Others say that they hated Haman's demeaning behavior toward his fellow subjects and they,

אסתר [66]

Haman
plans the
destruction
of all the
Jews

had commanded concerning him. But Mordechai
would not bow down or prostrate himself. ³ So the
King's servants at the King's gate said to Mordechai,
'Why do you disobey the King's command?' ⁴ Finally, when they said this to him day after day and he
did not heed them, they told Haman, to see whether
Mordechai's words would avail; for he had told them
that he was a Jew. ⁵ When Haman, himself, saw that
Mordechai did not bow down and prostrate himself
before him, then Haman was filled with rage.
⁶ However it seemed contemptible to him to lay
hands on Mordechai alone, for they had made known
to him the people of Mordechai. So Haman sought to
destroy all the Jews—the people of Mordechai—who
were throughout the entire kingdom of Ahasuerus.
⁷ In the first month, which is the month of Nissan, in

---

too, considered not bowing down to
him. They reported Mordechai as a
test case to see הַיַעַמְדוּ דִּבְרֵי מָרְדֳּכַי —
*Whether Mordechai's words would
avail.* If his actions were tolerated,
they would become a precedent for
the refusal of others to bow to
Haman (*Me'am Loez*).

דִּבְרֵי מָרְדֳּכַי — *Mordechai's words.*
i.e., that, as a Jew, he could never
prostrate himself idolatrously
(*Rashi*).

5. וַיַּרְא הָמָן — *Haman, himself, saw.*
'The use the wicked make of their
eyes draws them to Gehinnom'
(*Midrash*).

אֵין מָרְדֳּכַי כֹּרֵעַ — *Mordechai did not
bow down.* Even when Haman
removed the idol from his clothing
(*Alshich*).

6. [The reaction of Haman to a
personal affront is typical of the
most rabid anti-Semites throughout
the ages.]

בְּמָרְדֳּכַי לְבַדּוֹ — *On Mordechai
alone.* When Haman became aware
that Mordechai did not bow before
him on religious grounds, he not
only wanted to punish מָרְדֳּכַי לְבַדּוֹ —
Mordechai as an individual—for
having embarassed him, he also
wished to take revenge upon him as
a Jew, for Mordechai's refusal to
bow was caused by his religious
beliefs (*Akeidas Yitzchak*). [See
commentary to verse 2.]

First he aimed at 'Mordechai
alone,' then at 'the people of
Mordechai'. Who are these? — the
Rabbis; and finally at 'all the Jews'
(*Meg 13b*).

אֲחַשְׁוֵרוֹשׁ הִפִּיל פּוּר הוּא הַגּוֹרָל לִפְנֵי
הָמָן מִיּוֹם|לְיוֹם וּמֵחֹדֶשׁ לְחֹדֶשׁ שְׁנֵים־
עָשָׂר הוּא־חֹדֶשׁ אֲדָר: ח וַיֹּאמֶר הָמָן לַמֶּלֶךְ
אֲחַשְׁוֵרוֹשׁ יֶשְׁנוֹ עַם־אֶחָד מְפֻזָּר וּמְפֹרָד
בֵּין הָעַמִּים בְּכֹל מְדִינוֹת מַלְכוּתֶךָ
וְדָתֵיהֶם שֹׁנוֹת מִכָּל־עָם וְאֶת־דָּתֵי הַמֶּלֶךְ
אֵינָם עֹשִׂים וְלַמֶּלֶךְ אֵין־שֹׁוֶה לְהַנִּיחָם:
ט אִם־עַל־הַמֶּלֶךְ טוֹב יִכָּתֵב לְאַבְּדָם
וַעֲשֶׂרֶת אֲלָפִים כִּכַּר־כֶּסֶף אֶשְׁקוֹל עַל־

7. הִפִּיל פּוּר ... לִפְנֵי הָמָן — *The lot was cast in Haman's presence.* [Literally: 'he cast a pur...' the 'he' presumably referring to one of Haman's servants.]

Haman would always cast lots to determine his course of action. He wanted to take revenge against the Jews immediately and he cast lots for the very next day—14 Nissan—but that day proved inauspicious. So he cast lots for every successive day and month until the 13th of Adar. He should have realized from this that G-d's will was to allow the Jews time to be redeemed, and therefore it says—לִפְנֵי הָמָן [literally, *before Haman*] — i.e., that the lot was prepared *before Haman* rather than for the Jews — it would result in *his* destruction (*Malbim*).

Haman could not have drawn lots to determine Israel's 'unlucky' day — it is known that the fate of the Jews is not governed by מַזָּל—luck, or constellations. Rather, Haman cast the lots to determine when *his own* luck would be best, therefore — לִפְנֵי הָמָן — *before Haman* specifically (*Vilna Gaon*).

8. יֶשְׁנוֹ עַם־אֶחָד — *There is a certain people.* 'There was never a slanderer so skillful as Haman.'

Haman said to Ahasuerus: 'Come, let us destroy them.' 'I am afraid of their G-d,' the King answered, 'lest He do to me as He did to my predecessors.' . Haman said: יְשֵׁנִים, they are asleep [i.e., "negligent"; a play on the word יֶשְׁנוֹ] of the precepts.' 'There are Rabbis among them [who *do* keep the precepts],' Ahasuerus replied. עַם אֶחָד — *they are one people [and all hang together],*' said Haman (*Meg. 13b*).

מְפֻזָּר וּמְפֹרָד — *Scattered and dispersed.* And hence defenseless and disunified. Haman told this to the King to assure him that he need not fear reprisals (*Yaaros D'vash*).

וְדָתֵיהֶם שֹׁנוֹת — *Their laws are different.* 'They do not eat our food nor intermarry with us' (*Meg. 13b*).

וְלַמֶּלֶךְ אֵין־שֹׁוֶה לְהַנִּיחָם—*It is not befitting the King to tolerate them.* Haman said: 'They eat and drink and despise the throne. For if a fly falls into a Jew's cup, he throws out the fly and drinks the wine; but if his majesty were to touch his cup,

*the twelfth year of King Ahasuerus, pur (that is, the
lot) was cast in the presence of Haman from day to
day, and from month to month, to the twelfth month,
which is the month of Adar.*

Haman
slanders the
Jews to the
King

*⁸ Then Haman said to King Ahasuerus: 'There is a
certain people scattered abroad and dispersed among
the peoples in all the provinces of your realm. Their
laws are different from every other people's. They do
not observe even the King's laws; therefore it is not
befitting the King to tolerate them. ⁹ If it please the
King, let it be recorded that they be destroyed; and I
will pay ten thousand silver talents into the hands of*

he would throw it to the ground and
not drink from it' (Meg. 13b).

9. יִכָּתֵב — *Let it be recorded*, i.e.,
'with a simple stroke of the pen'
(Midrash).

Haman did not suggest that the
King himself direct the destruction
— but rather that it be *'recorded'*,
i.e., that blanket permission be
granted to destroy the Jews. The
populace — as enemies of the Jews
— will gladly carry out the extermination (Yosef Lekach).

וְעֲשֶׂרֶת אֲלָפִים כִּכַּר־כֶּסֶף — *Ten thousand silver talents.* [Haman felt that
by giving away a huge sum of
money equal to the value of the entire nation, he would be assured that
his prey would not escape his
clutches]:

'Resh Lakish said: It was revealed before He who said, "Let the
world come into existence" that
Haman would count off shekalim
for the right to destroy Israel.
Therefore, He anticipated his
shekalim with those of Israel [i.e.,
He ordained that the Jews should

give shekalim for a holy purpose
before Haman gave shekalim for a
fane purpose], as the Mishnah
says, "On the first of Adar the an-
nouncement is made that the
shekalim must be given" ' [G-d
thus negated Haman's plan.] (Megillah 13b).

According to the *Tosafos* [Megil-
lah 16a] the half-shekalim given by
the 600-thousand adult Jewish
males after the Exodus are equal to
10-thousand silver talents. This
calculation is most difficult, however, because one talent equals
3,000 shekalim. The 600-thousand
half-shekalim given by the 600-
thousand Jews equal 300-thousand
shekalim — only 100 talents!

To resolve this difficulty, we
must say that the copyist erred in
transcribing *Tosafos. Tosafos* wrote
the abbreviation ח״ש which the
copyist assumed to be חֲצִי שֶׁקֶל, half
a shekel. In reality, however,
Tosafos meant חֲמִשִּׁים שְׁקָלִים, fifty
shekalim, referring to the 50-shekel
valuation ascribed to an adult male
(Leviticus 27:3). If so, the 50-shekel

יְדֵי עֹשֵׂי הַמְּלָאכָה לְהָבִיא אֶל־גִּנְזֵי
הַמֶּלֶךְ: וַיָּסַר הַמֶּלֶךְ אֶת־טַבַּעְתּוֹ מֵעַל יָדוֹ
וַיִּתְּנָהּ לְהָמָן בֶּן־הַמְּדָתָא הָאֲגָגִי צֹרֵר
הַיְּהוּדִים: וַיֹּאמֶר הַמֶּלֶךְ לְהָמָן הַכֶּסֶף
נָתוּן לָךְ וְהָעָם לַעֲשׂוֹת בּוֹ כַּטּוֹב בְּעֵינֶיךָ:
וַיִּקָּרְאוּ סֹפְרֵי הַמֶּלֶךְ בַּחֹדֶשׁ הָרִאשׁוֹן
בִּשְׁלוֹשָׁה עָשָׂר יוֹם בּוֹ וַיִּכָּתֵב כְּכָל־אֲשֶׁר־
צִוָּה הָמָן אֶל אֲחַשְׁדַּרְפְּנֵי־הַמֶּלֶךְ וְאֶל־
הַפַּחוֹת אֲשֶׁר| עַל־מְדִינָה וּמְדִינָה וְאֶל
שָׂרֵי עַם וָעָם מְדִינָה וּמְדִינָה כִּכְתָבָהּ
וְעַם וָעָם כִּלְשׁוֹנוֹ בְּשֵׁם הַמֶּלֶךְ אֲחַשְׁוֵרֹשׁ
נִכְתָּב וְנֶחְתָּם בְּטַבַּעַת הַמֶּלֶךְ: וְנִשְׁלוֹחַ
סְפָרִים בְּיַד הָרָצִים אֶל־כָּל־מְדִינוֹת
הַמֶּלֶךְ לְהַשְׁמִיד לַהֲרֹג וּלְאַבֵּד אֶת־כָּל־

valuation per person of 600-thousand comes to 30-million shekalim which is exactly equal to the ten thousand silver talents given Ahasuerus by Haman [600,000 x 50 = 30,000,000 ÷ 3,000 = 10,000] (Torah T'minah) [Kad Hakemech].

The 10,000 silver talents corresponded to the 10,000 Jewish leaders exiled by Nebuchadnezzar. [See II Kings 24:14.] Haman thus reminded Ahasuerus that the fact that Nebuchadnezzar found it necessary to exile the Jews proves that they are an evil people worthy of destruction (Me'am Loez).

He also told the King not to be concerned with the loss of tax revenue that the Jews' destruction would bring. Haman more than compensated for that with his exhorbitantly large bribe (Vilna Gaon).

[One כִּכָּר — talent contains 3,000 shekalim (see Exodus 35:24). A shekel contains approximately .80 ounces of silver. Thus, a talent of silver is equal to about 2,400 ounces. The price Haman was ready to pay for the right to exterminate the Jews, 10,000 talents, was 24 million ounces, or 750 tons of silver! Even in today's inflationary times, that is a huge fortune. We can only begin to imagine the enormity of the treasure by ancient standards.]

עֹשֵׂי הַמְּלָאכָה — Those who perform the duties. Haman promised Ahasuerus that the campaign will cost the King nothing; he will finance the entire annihilation and the perpetrators will perform this task with relish (Malbim).

III
10-13

The King
consents to
the
destruction
of the Jews

those who perform the duties for deposit in the King's treasuries.' ¹⁰ So the King took his signet ring from his hand, and gave it to Haman, the son of Hammedasa the Agagite, the enemy of the Jews. ¹¹ Then the King said to Haman: 'The silver is given to you, the people also, to do with as you see fit.' ¹² The King's secretaries were summoned on the thirteenth day of the first month, and everything was written exactly as Haman had dictated, to the King's satraps, to the governors of every province, and to the officials of every people; each province in its own script, and to each people in its own language; in King Ahasuerus' name it was written, and it was sealed with the King's signet ring. ¹³ Letters were sent by courier to all the King's provinces, to destroy, to slay, and to exterminate all Jews, young and old,

---

10. טַבַּעְתּוֹ — *His signet ring.* Transference of the King's signet ring was symbolic that Haman now had full authority to act on the King's behalf (*Rashi*).

[The signet ring was used to seal official documents, and with it, in effect, Haman had autonomous control over the Jews].

'Our Rabbis said: Ahasuerus hated the Jews more than the wicked Haman. Usually the buyer gives a pledge to the seller, but here the seller gave the pledge' (*Midrash*).

11. 'When Haman offered a huge sum of money for the privilege of destroying the Jews throughout the Persian Empire, *it was exactly what*

Ahasuerus had hoped. "Like two men, one of whom had a mound in his field and the other had a hole in his field . . . Said the owner of the hole to the owner of the mound: Sell me your mound for money. Replied the other: Take it for nothing and welcome to it" (*Megillah* 14a; *Torah Nation*).

הַכֶּסֶף — *The silver.* The גִימַטְרִיָא [numercal value] of הַכֶּסֶף — 'silver' [165] *equals that of* הָעֵץ — 'the gallows' [a hint of Haman's ultimate end] (*Midrash*).

נָתוּן לָךְ — *Is given to you.* i.e., 'consider your money as having already been accepted by me and use it to execute your avowed purpose of annihilating the people in any way you wish' (*M'nos Halevi*).

הַיְּהוּדִים מִנַּעַר וְעַד־זָקֵן טַף וְנָשִׁים בְּיוֹם
אֶחָד בִּשְׁלוֹשָׁה עָשָׂר לְחֹדֶשׁ שְׁנֵים־עָשָׂר
הוּא־חֹדֶשׁ אֲדָר וּשְׁלָלָם לָבוֹז: פַּתְשֶׁגֶן
הַכְּתָב לְהִנָּתֵן דָּת בְּכָל־מְדִינָה וּמְדִינָה
גָּלוּי לְכָל־הָעַמִּים לִהְיוֹת עֲתִידִים לַיּוֹם
הַזֶּה: הָרָצִים יָצְאוּ דְחוּפִים בִּדְבַר הַמֶּלֶךְ
וְהַדָּת נִתְּנָה בְּשׁוּשַׁן הַבִּירָה וְהַמֶּלֶךְ וְהָמָן
יָשְׁבוּ לִשְׁתּוֹת וְהָעִיר שׁוּשָׁן נָבוֹכָה:

יד

טו

וּמָרְדֳּכַי יָדַע אֶת־כָּל־אֲשֶׁר נַעֲשָׂה וַיִּקְרַע
מָרְדֳּכַי אֶת־בְּגָדָיו וַיִּלְבַּשׁ שַׂק וָאֵפֶר וַיֵּצֵא

א

14. פַּתְשֶׁגֶן ... גָּלוּי לְכָל־הָעַמִּים — *The copies ... published to all [the] peoples.* Haman was afraid to openly and publicly decree the annihilation of the entire Jewish people. In the confidential decree to *'the satraps, governors, and high officials,'* [verses 12 and 13], he clearly spelled out that the purpose was to utterly destroy the Jews on the 13th of Adar. On the פַּתְשֶׁגֶן הַכְּתָב, *the copies of the documents,* — which were publicly displayed in every town square and גָּלוּי לְכָל־הָעַמִּים *published to all the peoples,* however, it was written only that on the thirteenth of Adar they must all be prepared for a military action whose nature will then be revealed. That is why the next verse follows with וְהָעִיר שׁוּשָׁן נָבוֹכָה — *but the city of Shushan was bewildered,* for no one knew who would be involved in this action (*Vilna Gaon*).

15. יָצְאוּ דְחוּפִים — *Went forth quickly.* There were several reasons for the strange haste in publishing a decree that would not be executed for eleven months. Haman was afraid that the fickle King would have a change of heart. He wanted to prolong the agony of the Jews throughout the kingdom by telling them of the impending massacre so far in advance (*Rav Galico*).

G-d desired a lapse of so many months to give the children of Israel a chance to repent (*Me'am Loez*).

וְהַמֶּלֶךְ וְהָמָן יָשְׁבוּ לִשְׁתּוֹת —*The King and Haman sat down to drink.* [To celebrate the decree of annihilation].

According to the *Midrash,* Haman deliberately intended to intoxicate the King out of fear that he might reconsider the edict before the couriers were securely on their way.

III
14-15

children and women, in a single day, the thirteenth day of the twelfth month, which is the month of Adar, and to plunder their possessions. ¹⁴ The copies of the document were to be promulgated in every province, and be published to all peoples, that they should be ready for that day. ¹⁵ The couriers went forth hurriedly by order of the King, and the edict was distributed in Shushan the capitol. The King and Haman sat down to drink; but the city of Shushan was bewildered.

IV
I

¹ Mordechai learned of all that had been done; and Mordechai tore his clothes and put on sackcloth with ashes. He went out into the midst of

וְהָעִיר שׁוּשָׁן נָבוֹכָה — *But the city of Shushan was bewildered.* The Jews cried and wailed loudly while, simultaneously, the Persians rejoiced at the new decree. Listeners were bewildered trying to differentiate between the cries of anguish and the shouts of joy *(Me'am Loez).*

'If a Jew went out to the market to shop, a Persian would taunt him and say: "Tomorrow I am going to kill you and plunder your property" '*(Midrash)*

Scarcely had the edict been promulgated against the Jews when all sorts of misfortunes began to happen to Persians in the city. Women hanging out their wash to dry on the roofs of houses fell to their death; men going to draw water fell into the wells and drowned. While Ahasuerus and Haman were making merry in the palace, the city was thrown into consternation and mourning *(Panim Acherim).*

IV

1. וּמָרְדֳּכַי יָדַע — *And Mordechai learned.* He was told in a dream *(Rashi).* He didn't learn it via רוּחַ הַקֹּדֶשׁ — the holy spirit, because Shushan was in turmoil and prophesy dwells only amidst joy

(Yismach Lev).

Others hold that Elijah the Prophet told him *(Midrash; Rav Eleazar of Worms;).*

וַיִּקְרַע...אֶת־בְּגָדָיו — *He tore his*

[73]   Esther

פרק ד
ב־ד

בְּתוֹךְ הָעִיר וַיִּזְעַק זְעָקָה גְדוֹלָה וּמָרָה:
וַיָּבוֹא עַד לִפְנֵי שַׁעַר־הַמֶּלֶךְ כִּי אֵין לָבוֹא
אֶל־שַׁעַר הַמֶּלֶךְ בִּלְבוּשׁ שָׂק: וּבְכָל־
מְדִינָה וּמְדִינָה מְקוֹם אֲשֶׁר דְּבַר־הַמֶּלֶךְ
וְדָתוֹ מַגִּיעַ אֵבֶל גָּדוֹל לַיְּהוּדִים וְצוֹם
וּבְכִי וּמִסְפֵּד שַׂק וָאֵפֶר יֻצַּע לָרַבִּים:
וַתָּבוֹאינָה נַעֲרוֹת אֶסְתֵּר וְסָרִיסֶיהָ וַיַּגִּידוּ
לָהּ וַתִּתְחַלְחַל הַמַּלְכָּה מְאֹד וַתִּשְׁלַח
בְּגָדִים לְהַלְבִּישׁ אֶת־מָרְדֳּכַי וּלְהָסִיר

ב
ג

יתיר י׳ ד

clothes, etc., as a manifestation of mourning and grief. When Mordechai learned of the plan, he no longer cared to sit in royal attire at the King's gate. He tore off his royal robes and put on sackcloth as if to say 'My place is now with the multitude' (P'dus Yaakov).

וַיִּזְעַק זְעָקָה גְדוֹלָה וּמָרָה — And cried loudly and bitterly. Why did Mordechai cry out — did he think that silent prayer is less effective? Chana whispered to herself as it says [I. Sam. 1:13] וְחַנָּה הִיא מְדַבֶּרֶת עַל לִבָּהּ Chana prayed silently, and yet G-d heard her, as the episode concludes: The G-d of Israel will grant your request. . .

— Mordechai cried out and said: אָבִי יִצְחָק — My ancestor Isaac! What have you done to me? Esau cried out before you and you heeded his cries and blessed him. Now we are to be sold and slaughtered [by Haman, a descendant of Esau]! Therefore he cried out (Yalkut Shimoni, Panim Acherim).

2. עַד לִפְנֵי שַׁעַר־הַמֶּלֶךְ — Until the front of the King's gate. Mordechai surely knew the rule that 'It was forbidden to enter the King's

gate clothed in sackcloth.' Had he wanted to enter the palace he surely would have appeared in his regular attire. Rather, his purpose was to publicize his cause to Esther and seek compassion — through fasting and prayer — from G-d. He might have been expected to first appear in his official attire to communicate the facts of the emergency to Esther so that she could attempt to intercede with the King. Only then should he have donned sackcloth to seek divine intervention. Mordechai, however, chose the opposite course. He placed his faith in G-d (Yosef Lekach).

3. וּבְכָל־מְדִינָה וּמְדִינָה — In every province. The further from Shushan, the greater was the mourning. The Jews in Shushan — living in close proximity to the King — felt assured they would not be slaughtered before the destined 13th of Adar. Not so those Jews who lived in the provinces. There, away from the King, the danger was very real that upon receipt of the edict, the populace would begin the slaughter (Yad Hamelech).

שַׂק וָאֵפֶר יֻצַּע לָרַבִּים — Most of them

*the city, and cried loudly and bitterly. ² He came until
the front of the King's gate, for it was forbidden to
enter the King's gate clothed with sackcloth. ³ (In
every province, wherever the King's command and
his decree extended, there was great mourning among
the Jews, with fasting, and weeping, and wailing;
most of them lying in sackcloth and ashes.)*

*⁴ And Esther's maids and chamberlains came and
told her about it, and the Queen was greatly distressed; she sent garments to clothe Mordechai so that he*

---

lying in sackcloth and ashes.
[Literally: 'sackcloth and ashes were
spread out under the many.']

'Many', רַבִּים, is open to several
interpretations:

According to R. Moshe Arama:
רַבִּים—'many', implies 'the most
prominent,' i.e. the rich, Persianized
Jews shared the danger of annihilation with their poorer, more pious
brethren. Also, "רַבִּים" were the
גְּדוֹלִים —*the religious leaders* who
were the first to mourn publicly;
The Midrash *Panim Acherim* states
that absolutely *everyone* slept on
sackcloth. A novel interpretation of
"רַבִּים" is offered by *Yosef Lekach*:
רַבִּים means "public"—in the sense
of רְשׁוּת הָרַבִּים, 'public domain;' i.e.
the mourning took place in public,
rather than in private.

4. וַיַּגִּידוּ לָהּ —*And they told her,* i.e.
about Mordechai and his sackcloth
(Alshich).

Esther had not yet revealed her
origins, but her interest in Mordechai—who had always inquired
about her welfare—was well-known
throughout the palace *(Yosef
Lekach).*

Esther was very modest and she

appreciated her privacy. That was
why she had not heard about the
decree *(Rav Galico).*

וַתִּתְחַלְחַל — *greatly distressed.*
[literally: 'became full of hollows.']
Rav said: she became a נִדָּה — ritual-
ly unclean; Rav Yirmiya said her
stomach was loosened' *(Meg. 15a).*

Some say she was pregnant, and
upon hearing the news she miscar-
ried, never to give birth again;
others say she conceived only once
after this miscarriage and gave birth
to Darius *(Midrash; Panim
Acherim).*

Esther instantly realized that
Mordechai's public mourning could
not have been the result of a personal bereavement, or he would not
have appeared in public. Realizing
that he was bewailing a public
calamity, she was greatly distressed
at the fact that Mordechai had not
informed her personally *(M'nos
Halevi; Alshich).*

וַתִּשְׁלַח בְּגָדִים — *And she sent garments,* so that, properly attired,
Mordechai could enter the palace to
speak with her personally
(Alshich).

ה שַׁקּוּ מֵעָלָיו וְלֹא קִבֵּל: וַתִּקְרָא אֶסְתֵּר
לַהֲתָךְ מִסָּרִיסֵי הַמֶּלֶךְ אֲשֶׁר הֶעֱמִיד
לְפָנֶיהָ וַתְּצַוֵּהוּ עַל־מָרְדֳּכָי לָדַעַת מַה־זֶּה
ו וְעַל־מַה־זֶּה: וַיֵּצֵא הֲתָךְ אֶל־מָרְדֳּכָי אֶל־
רְחוֹב הָעִיר אֲשֶׁר לִפְנֵי שַׁעַר־הַמֶּלֶךְ:
ז וַיַּגֶּד־לוֹ מָרְדֳּכַי אֵת כָּל־אֲשֶׁר קָרָהוּ וְאֵת |
פָּרָשַׁת הַכֶּסֶף אֲשֶׁר אָמַר הָמָן לִשְׁקוֹל
עַל־גִּנְזֵי הַמֶּלֶךְ בַּיְּהוּדִיִּים לְאַבְּדָם: וְאֶת־
פַּתְשֶׁגֶן כְּתָב־הַדָּת אֲשֶׁר־נִתַּן בְּשׁוּשָׁן
לְהַשְׁמִידָם נָתַן לוֹ לְהַרְאוֹת אֶת־אֶסְתֵּר
וּלְהַגִּיד לָהּ וּלְצַוּוֹת עָלֶיהָ לָבוֹא אֶל־
הַמֶּלֶךְ לְהִתְחַנֶּן־לוֹ וּלְבַקֵּשׁ מִלְּפָנָיו עַל־

וְלֹא קִבֵּל — *but he would not accept them*. He did not want to stop praying even for a moment lest he appear to substitute reliance on a human being for dependence on the mercy of G-d (*Malbim*).

5. הֲתָךְ — *Hasach*. He was a great man, Esther's confidant, one who could keep secrets, and whom no one would suspect or dare to question about his mission (*Alshich, Malbim*).

'Rav said: Hasach was Daniel. Why was he called Hasach? Because he was degraded [חֲתָכוּהוּ] from his position [which he held during the reigns of Belshazzar, Darius and Cyrus — (*Rashi*)] (*Meg. 15a*).

Another reason he was called Hasach was that he made decisions [חָתָךְ] on affairs of state (*Meg. 15a; Midrash*).

מַה־זֶּה וְעַל־מַה־זֶּה — *What this was about and why*. [lit. 'what this was and why it was.'] i.e. what the edict was and for what great sin were the

Jews being punished (*Alshich, Yosef Lekach*).

Esther told him: 'Go and say to Mordechai that never in their history have the Jews been in such a crisis as this ... Have the Jews perhaps denied the Tablets of which it is written, מִזֶּה וּמִזֶּה הֵם כְּתוּבִים, *on the one side and on the other side* [lit. 'on *this* and on *this*'] were they written [*Exodus 32:15*] (*Meg. 15a; Midrash*).

6. רְחוֹב הָעִיר — *City square*. i.e. Hasach walked roundabout through the city square in order to make it seem that he 'happened' to meet Mordechai by coincidence (*Alshich*).

They purposely spoke in the public square so that no one could spy on them and overhear their conversation. Furthermore, no one would suspect them of speaking about vital matters pertaining to the King in such a place (*Me'am Loez*).

7. וַיַּגֶּד־לוֹ מָרְדֳּכַי — *And Mordechai*

*might take off his sackcloth; but he would not accept
them.*

⁵ *Then Esther summoned Hasach, one of the
King's chamberlains whom he had appointed to attend her, and ordered him to go to Mordechai, to
learn what this was about and why.* ⁶ *So Hasach went
out to Mordechai unto the city square, which was in
front of the King's gate,* ⁷ *and Mordechai told him of
all that had happened to him, and all about the sum
of money that Haman had promised to pay to the
royal treasuries for the annihilation of the Jews.* ⁸ *He
also gave him a copy of the text of the decree which*

Mordechai
asks Esther
to intercede *was distributed in Shushan for their destruction — so
that he might show it to Esther and inform her, bidding her to go to the King, to appeal to him, and to*

---

told him, at great length *(Alshich).*

He told him everything — how
his refusal to prostrate himself
before Haman resulted in the edict,
but that its underlying cause was
the sin of the Jews in partaking of
Ahasuerus' feast *(M'nos Halevi,
Alshich, Meam Loez).*

אֲשֶׁר קָרָהוּ — *That had happened to
him.* Mordechai said to Hasach:
"Go tell her 'The descendant of
karahu, קָרָהוּ, [lit. 'met him'.
Amalek is meant] of whom it is said
אֲשֶׁר קָרְךָ בַּדֶּרֶךְ *"Who he met thee
[kar'cha] by the way* [Deut. 25:18].
(Midrash).

פָּרָשַׁת — *The sum of money.*
Mordechai conveyed the message
that far more than mere talk
between Haman and the King
resulted in the decree; a great sum
of money was involved *(R. Eleazar
of Worms).*

Mordechai also wanted to

impress Esther that the King could
not be 'bought off' with money,
because Haman offered Ahasuerus
10,000 silver talents and the King
was reluctant to accept this huge
sum *(Divrei Shaul).*

בַּיְּהוּדְיִים לְאַבְּדָם — *For the annihilation of the Jews.* Mordechai
revealed to Esther that, although the
public copies of the decree
published in the outer provinces
mentioned only 'readiness' and
made no mention of 'annihilation'
[see Commentary to 3:14]; the true
intent *was* annihilation *(Vilna
Gaon).*

8. לְהַשְׁמִידָם — *for their
destruction.* Apparently only the
Shushan copy of the edict mentioned 'destruction' — those copies
published in the other provinces
made no mention of 'destruction'
(see above on 3:14) *(Alshich).*

The word לְהַשְׁמִידָם — *'for their*

עַמָּהּ: וַיָּבוֹא הֲתָךְ וַיַּגֵּד לְאֶסְתֵּר אֵת דִּבְרֵי
מָרְדֳּכָי. וַתֹּאמֶר אֶסְתֵּר לַהֲתָךְ וַתְּצַוֵּהוּ
אֶל־מָרְדֳּכָי: כָּל־עַבְדֵי הַמֶּלֶךְ וְעַם
מְדִינוֹת הַמֶּלֶךְ יוֹדְעִים אֲשֶׁר כָּל־אִישׁ
וְאִשָּׁה אֲשֶׁר־יָבוֹא אֶל־הַמֶּלֶךְ אֶל־הֶחָצֵר
הַפְּנִימִית אֲשֶׁר לֹא־יִקָּרֵא אַחַת דָּתוֹ
לְהָמִית לְבַד מֵאֲשֶׁר יוֹשִׁיט־לוֹ הַמֶּלֶךְ
אֶת־שַׁרְבִיט הַזָּהָב וְחָיָה וַאֲנִי לֹא
נִקְרֵאתִי לָבוֹא אֶל־הַמֶּלֶךְ זֶה שְׁלוֹשִׁים
יוֹם: וַיַּגִּידוּ לְמָרְדֳּכָי אֵת דִּבְרֵי אֶסְתֵּר:
וַיֹּאמֶר מָרְדֳּכַי לְהָשִׁיב אֶל־אֶסְתֵּר אַל־
תְּדַמִּי בְנַפְשֵׁךְ לְהִמָּלֵט בֵּית־הַמֶּלֶךְ מִכָּל־
הַיְּהוּדִים: כִּי אִם־הַחֲרֵשׁ תַּחֲרִישִׁי בָּעֵת

ט פרק ד
י ט־יד
יא

יב
יג
יד

---

destruction', was not part of the
document. This word was
Mordechai's own addition as a
natural inference (Yosef Lekach).

עַל־עַמָּהּ — for her people. The time
was now ripe for Esther to divulge
the identity of her people and thus
win the King's mercy (Alshich).

9. וַיַּגֵּד לְאֶסְתֵּר — And told Esther.
He fully elaborated upon the grave
situation of the Jews as related by
Mordechai (M'nos Halevi).

10. וַתְּצַוֵּהוּ אֶל־מָרְדֳּכָי — To return
to Mordechai with this message. [lit.
'she commanded him to Mordechai'] knowing that her reply was
not favorable to Mordechai, Hasach
might not want to convey it. Esther,
therefore, commanded him to convey it (Alshich).

Esther also cautioned Hasach to
be very diplomatic in conveying her
response, seeing that Mordechai
was in great anguish (D'na Pashra).

[But, as explained in commentary
to verse 12, Hasach did not personally deliver this recalcitrant
response].

11. כָּל־עַבְדֵי הַמֶּלֶךְ — All the King's
servants.

Esther explained to Mordechai
why his request was impossible:
'Everyone knows the law against
approaching the King unsummoned, hence feigning ignorance of
the law would be no excuse for me.
Moreover, the prohibition was not
an expression of personal prefer-
ence on the part of King Ahasuerus;
it was a public law known by עַם
מְדִינוֹת הַמֶּלֶךְ, the people of the King's
provinces — so transgression would
be a public offense, like the sin of
Vashti.' Esther continued that there
was no exception to the law of אִישׁ
וְאִשָּׁה, man or woman. Even were the
King to forgive her by extending his
שַׁרְבִיט הַזָּהָב — gold scepter — it

IV
9-14

plead with him for her people.

⁹ *Hasach came and told Esther what Mordechai had said.* ¹⁰ *Then Esther told Hasach to return to Mordechai with this message:* ¹¹ *'All the King's servants and the people of the King's provinces are well aware that if anyone, man or woman, approaches the King in the inner court without being summoned, there is but one law for him: that he be put to death; except for the person to whom the King shall extend the gold scepter so that he may live. Now I have not been summoned to come to the King for the past thirty days.'*

¹² *They related Esther's words to Mordechai.* ¹³ *then Mordechai said to reply to Esther: 'Do not imagine that you will be able to escape in the King's palace any more than the rest of the Jews.* ¹⁴ *For if you persist in keeping silent at a time like this, relief*

would be a most inopportune time to plead also on behalf of her people because she would already owe her life solely to the King's mercy.

Her alternate suggestion was to take a more secure and less risky approach: 'It is already שְׁלוֹשִׁים יוֹם, *thirty days*, that I was not summoned by the King. I will definitely be summoned within the next few days; at that advantageous time I will plead for my people. It is best to wait' (Malbim).

12. וַיַּגִּידוּ לְמָרְדֳּכָי—*They related to Mordechai.* Hasach was not the one to deliver the recalcitrant message. Reluctant to deliver Esther's negative response, he sent another in his place. (Meg. 15a).

Others say that Haman grew suspicious of Hasach and had him murdered. (Me'am Loez).

13. [Mordechai warns Esther of the catastrophe of placing her personal safety first.]

אַל־תְּדַמִּי בְנַפְשֵׁךְ — *Do not imagine.* [Literally: *form an idea in your soul*] i.e. Mordechai said: 'You may, by some remote twist of fate, manage to save your body. But how will you save your soul?' (M'nos Halevi).

14. אִם־הַחֲרֵשׁ תַּחֲרִישִׁי — *If you persist in keeping silent.* 'If you keep silent now and refrain from pleading for your nation, in the end you will be silent in the time to come and you will not be able to justify yourself, because you had the opportunity of doing good in your lifetime and you did not do it. And do you imagine that the Holy One, Blessed be He, will abandon

פֶּרֶק ד
טו-טז

הַזֹּאת רֶוַח וְהַצָּלָה יַעֲמוֹד לַיְּהוּדִים מִמָּקוֹם אַחֵר וְאַתְּ וּבֵית־אָבִיךְ תֹּאבֵדוּ וּמִי יוֹדֵעַ אִם־לְעֵת כָּזֹאת הִגַּעַתְּ לַמַּלְכוּת. וַתֹּאמֶר אֶסְתֵּר לְהָשִׁיב אֶל־ מָרְדֳּכָי: לֵךְ כְּנוֹס אֶת־כָּל־הַיְּהוּדִים הַנִּמְצְאִים בְּשׁוּשָׁן וְצוּמוּ עָלַי וְאַל־ תֹּאכְלוּ וְאַל־תִּשְׁתּוּ שְׁלֹשֶׁת יָמִים לַיְלָה

טו

טז

Israel? — In any case, He will rise up and deliver them *(Midrash)*.

מִמָּקוֹם אַחֵר —*from some other place.* [Obviously a reference to divine help, but deliberately avoiding the use of G-d's Name. (See *Overview*).]

According to another interpretation:

Mordechai told Esther that G-d has many means at His disposal to save the Jews. G-d could send a foreign King to war with Ahasuerus and kill him. Thus, those living בְּבֵית הַמֶּלֶךְ in the palace, would be in the most imminent danger. He therefore warned her: רֶוַח וְהַצָּלָה יַעֲמוֹד לַיְּהוּדִים מִמָּקוֹם אַחֵר — *deliverance will come to the Jews from some other place,* i.e. G-d will send a foreign King, and thus will the Jews be saved, וְאַתְּ וּבֵית־אָבִיךְ תֹּאבֵדוּ — *while you and your father's house will perish,* because as a Queen you will be murdered along with the King, וּמִי יוֹדֵעַ אִם־לְעֵת כָּזֹאת הִגַּעַתְּ לַמַּלְכוּת i.e. *and who knows if you will still be reigning at this time next year?* *(Me'am Loez; Ma'amar Mordechai; see also Yosef Lekach; Rashi).*

Why did Mordechai insist that Esther endanger her life by going into the King's chambers immediately when there was nearly a full year left before the execution of the decree? Furthermore, by waiting just a little longer Esther would probably have been summoned by the King and could have pleaded her cause more effectively without endangering her life. — Mordechai knew the decree was sealed in Heaven, but אֵלִיָּהוּ הַנָּבִיא — *Elijah the Prophet* revealed to him that he could avert the decree by repentance and prayer. Mordechai, therefore, roused the Children of Israel to full repentance. He knew that G-d would never turn away prayers uttered in such fervent purity — especially during the month of Nissan when G-d was particularly compassionate toward the Jews. He was apprehensive that, as time passed, the Jews would lose hope and their spirits would flag. Thus, he told Esther: 'If you persist in maintaining your silence at such an opportune time, then help will come from elsewhere and another such opportunity may never arise again' *(Me'am Loez).*

וּמִי יוֹדֵעַ אִם־לְעֵת כָּזֹאת הִגַּעַתְּ לַמַּלְכוּת — *And who knows whether it was just for such a time as this that you attained the royal position!* [Our translation follows *Ibn Ezra*: 'Who knows? Maybe you attained the royal position solely for this oppor-

אסתר [80]

and deliverance will come to the Jews from some other place, while you and your father's house will perish. And who knows whether it was just for such a time as this that you attained the royal position!'

Esther agrees to go unsummoned to the King

15 The Esther sent this return answer to Mordechai: 16 'Go, assemble all the Jews to be found in Shushan, and fast for me. Do not eat or drink for three days, night or day; I , with my maids, will fast

---

tunity of being instrumental in saving the Jews.']

Esther had wanted to delay going to the King (see commentary on verse 11). Mordechai therefore said: "This opportunity cannot be delayed. Do not delude yourself into thinking you can achieve this salvation in a few days, for you have been elevated to the throne by G-d *just for this very moment.*" (*Malbim*).

Rashi, Alshich and *Yosef Lekach* undersand לְעֵת כָּזֹאת to mean: *a similar time next year*, i.e., the day of the slaughter. Hence: Who knows if you will still retain your royal position a year from now [i.e.,therefore 'hurry and be instrumental in saving the Jews now, for by next year you may yourself be deposed, for one reason or another, and powerless to save them'].

An interesting interpretation is given by *Rav Galico:* 'Who knows if your being Queen at that time will exempt you from Haman's decree?

15. לְהָשִׁיב — *This return answer.* Esther answered in a soothing manner, that she understands her special role and obligation. She is not concerned with self-preservation; the fate of all the Jews

is foremost in her mind. She only asks for a few days time to take advantage of this most auspicious occasion to present the facts of Haman's slander and expose him (*M'nos Halevi*).

16. כְּנוֹס — *Assemble.* Esther said, "Let us contradict Haman's slander [3:8] that the Jews are *'scattered and dispersed'*; let us assemble all the Jews in unity and determination" (*M'nos Halevi*).

בְּשׁוּשָׁן — *In Shushan.* Esther limited the assembly to the Jews in Shushan because it would have been impossible to assemble Jews living further away on such short notice (*Vilna Gaon*).

וְצוּמוּ עָלַי — *And fast for me.* Usually the most important part of a fast-day is prayer and charity. But here the fast was atonement for the sin of enjoying Ahasuerus' banquet.The essence of this fast, therefore, was abstinence from food and drink (*Me'am Loez*).

שְׁלֹשֶׁת יָמִים — *For three days.* 'This was an unprecedented effort of prayer, *never before or after equalled.* A tremendous wave of repentance swept over the Jews everywhere then they heard the stunning decree of the wicked ruler and

וָיוֹם גַּם־אֲנִי וְנַעֲרֹתַי אָצוּם כֵּן וּבְכֵן אָבוֹא
אֶל־הַמֶּלֶךְ אֲשֶׁר לֹא־כַדָּת וְכַאֲשֶׁר
אָבַדְתִּי אָבָדְתִּי: וַיַּעֲבֹר מָרְדֳּכָי וַיַּעַשׂ כְּכֹל
אֲשֶׁר־צִוְּתָה עָלָיו אֶסְתֵּר:

פֶּרֶק ד
יז

יז

וַיְהִי | בַּיּוֹם הַשְּׁלִישִׁי וַתִּלְבַּשׁ אֶסְתֵּר
מַלְכוּת וַתַּעֲמֹד בַּחֲצַר בֵּית־הַמֶּלֶךְ
הַפְּנִימִית נֹכַח בֵּית הַמֶּלֶךְ וְהַמֶּלֶךְ יוֹשֵׁב

פֶּרֶק ה
א

א

his Amaleki executioner. The spirit of Israel was so greatly renewed thereby that "they accepted the Torah anew in the days of Achashverosh" (Shabbos 88a); and G-d accepted their prayers (Torah Nation).

וְכַאֲשֶׁר אָבַדְתִּי אָבָדְתִּי — And if I perish, I perish [literally: 'What I have lost, I have lost'].

Esther said: 'Just as I have forfeited the sanctity of my soul by marrying a non-Jew, I now will sacrifice my body to save Israel' (Alshich).

The Talmud [Meg. 15a], holding that Esther was Mordechai's wife [see Commentary to 2:7] quotes Esther as saying to Mordechai: 'As I am lost to my father's house, so shall I be lost to thee' [i.e., by submitting voluntarily to Ahasuerus she would be forever forbidden to her legitimate husband, Mordechai. This is according to Torah law that forbids a wife to her husband if she voluntarily had relations with another man (see Overview).]

17. וַיַּעֲבֹר — then left. The Hebrew וַיַּעֲבֹר can mean either 'transgressed' or 'crossed over.' Rav, [in Talmud, Meg. 15a] holds that Mordechai transgressed the law by fasting on Yom Tov because the three fast days included the first day of Passover. Samuel held that the word means 'crossed.' i.e. he crossed the river which divided Shushan the capitol from the city of Shushan (Rav Yonasan Eybescheutz).

Mordechai protested to Esther, 'But these three days of fasting include the first day of Passover?' And she replied: 'If there is no Israel why should there be a Passover!' (Midrash).

Mordechai prayed to G-d: 'It is fully known before the throne of Thy glory, O Lord of all worlds, that I did not act from pride in not bowing down to Haman. Rather, through fear of Thee I do so — lest I assign Thy honor to flesh and blood; I was unwilling to bow down before anyone but Thee. For who am I that I should not bow down to

IV
17

*also. Then I will go in to the King though it's unlaw-
ful. And if I perish, I perish.'* [17] *Mordechai then left
and did exactly as Esther had commanded him.*

V
1

[1] **N**ow *it came to pass on the third day, Esther
donned royalty and stood in the inner court of
the King's palace facing the King's house while the*

Haman for the salvation of Thy
people Israel? For that, I would even
kiss his shoe latchet. Now therefore,
our G-d, deliver us, we pray Thee,
from his hand and let him fall into
the pit which he has dug and let him
be caught in the snare he has hidden
for the feet of Thy saints, and let
the swine know that Thou has not
forgotten the promise Thou has

made to us' (*Lev. 26:44*):

"בִּהְיוֹתָם בְּאֶרֶץ אֹיְבֵיהֶם לֹא־מְאַסְתִּים
וְלֹא־גְעַלְתִּים לְכַלֹּתָם לְהָפֵר בְּרִיתִי אִתָּם
כִּי אֲנִי ה' אֱלֹהֵיהֶם."

'When they are in the land of their
enemies, I will not reject them,
neither will I abhor them, to destroy
them utterly, and to break My cove-
nant with them; for I am the Lord
their (*Megillah 15a*).

V

1. בַּיּוֹם הַשְּׁלִישִׁי — *Third day* [of the
fast (*M'nos Halevi*)]. It was the first
day of Passover (*Rashi*).

מַלְכוּת — *Royalty.* i.e. 'royal apparel.' Until now, Esther detested
royal robes, but now that Mordechai impressed upon her the importance of the mission, and how
the salvation of Israel was dependent on her, she consented to make
the best possible impression and she
donned her most magnificent royal
garments (*M'nos Halevi*).

According to the *Talmud*: The
word 'royalty' refers not to clothing

but to spiritual royalty, i. e. the holy
[prophetic] spirit clothed her
(*Megillah 15a*).

וַתַּעֲמֹד— *And stood.* i. e. Esther
stopped and prayed. עֲמִידָה—
'standing' always indicates 'praying' (*M'nos Halevi*)

'Esther arrived at the inner court
facing the King and stood before
him. The King was sitting on his
royal throne ... and when he
noticed Esther standing in front of
him, he was furiously angry
because she had broken his law by
coming before him without being

עַל־כִּסֵּא מַלְכוּתוֹ בְּבֵית הַמַּלְכוּת נֹכַח
פֶּתַח הַבָּיִת: וַיְהִי כִרְאוֹת הַמֶּלֶךְ אֶת־
אֶסְתֵּר הַמַּלְכָּה עֹמֶדֶת בֶּחָצֵר נָשְׂאָה חֵן
בְּעֵינָיו וַיּוֹשֶׁט הַמֶּלֶךְ לְאֶסְתֵּר אֶת־
שַׁרְבִיט הַזָּהָב אֲשֶׁר בְּיָדוֹ וַתִּקְרַב אֶסְתֵּר
וַתִּגַּע בְּרֹאשׁ הַשַּׁרְבִיט: וַיֹּאמֶר לָהּ הַמֶּלֶךְ
מַה־לָּךְ אֶסְתֵּר הַמַּלְכָּה וּמַה־בַּקָּשָׁתֵךְ
עַד־חֲצִי הַמַּלְכוּת וְיִנָּתֵן לָךְ: וַתֹּאמֶר
אֶסְתֵּר אִם־עַל־הַמֶּלֶךְ טוֹב יָבוֹא הַמֶּלֶךְ
וְהָמָן הַיּוֹם אֶל־הַמִּשְׁתֶּה אֲשֶׁר־עָשִׂיתִי
לוֹ: וַיֹּאמֶר הַמֶּלֶךְ מַהֲרוּ אֶת־הָמָן לַעֲשׂוֹת

called ... Esther grew frightened ... but the Al-mighty gave her grace in the King's eyes and invested her with new beauty and new charm. The King then rose from his throne, ran to Esther and embraced her. "Esther, my queen," he said. "Why do you tremble? This law does not apply to you — you are my beloved and my companion."

He also said to her: "When I saw you, why did you not speak to me?"

"Your Majesty," replied Esther, "when I beheld you, I was overcome by your high dignity".' (Midrash)

2. שַׁרְבִיט הַזָּהָב — *Gold scepter.* The scepter is symbolic of the rulership. By extending the scepter, the King demonstrates that he is taking her under his protection (*Me'am Loez*).

According to the Talmud (*Meg.* 15b] an angel was sent to stretch out the gold scepter for Ahasuerus. Once Esther touched the scepter, the King was no longer doing her a favor because he had thereby symbolically welcomed her into his domain (*Eshkol Hakofer*).

3. מַה־לָּךְ אֶסְתֵּר הַמַּלְכָּה — *'What is your petition, Queen Esther?'* [Lit. 'What is to you....']. The King noticed that Esther's face was pale from fasting, and he realized that Esther's sudden, unsummoned appearance, potentially a capital offense, indicated that she had a most urgent request. Either she was being unbearably harassed by someone, or her petition was on behalf of others; whichever it was, it could only be of the most serious nature imaginable. He offered to fulfill her request whatever the case (*Vilna Gaon*).

חֲצִי הַמַּלְכוּת — *Half the kingdom.* Esther could have up to half the kingdom — but not the whole kingdom. Nor could she request something that would disturb the stability of the kingdom: The rebuilding of the Temple (*Meg.15b*).

V
2-5

Esther goes
before the
King

Esther lays a
trap for
Haman

King was sitting on his throne in the throne room
facing the chamber's entrance. ² When the King
noticed Queen Esther standing in the court, she won
his favor. The King extended to Esther the gold
scepter that was in his hand, and Esther approached
and touched the tip of the scepter.

³ The King said to her: 'What is your petition, Queen
Esther? Even if it be half the kingdom, it shall be granted
you.' ⁴ Esther said: 'If it please the King, let the King
and Haman come today to the banquet that I have
prepared for him.' ⁵ Then the King commanded: 'Tell
Haman to hurry and fulfill Esther's wish.' So the King

---

4. יָבוֹא הַמֶּלֶךְ וְהָמָן — *Let the King
and Haman come.*

Esther answered the King that,
indeed, she had something very important, to ask of him, but that this
was not the right time. It would be
more opportune if he were to visit
her. During a social visit at her banquet he would be more relaxed.
Then she would present her request. The King ordered his servants to 'hurry Haman' so the banquet could start early thus allowing
Esther to make her request and
relieve her of her sadness (*Vilna
Gaon*).

The Sages offered many reasons
for Esther's desire to have Haman
present when she petitioned the
King. Among them:

To set a trap for him and surprise
him; so that he would have no opportunity to form a conspiracy and
rebel; since Ahasuerus was fickle
and likely to change his mind she
wanted Haman present; so that
Ahasuerus would impetuously
commit himself; she was purposely
showing a great interest in Haman

to arouse the King's jealousy and to
disarm Haman; to arouse fears in
the hearts of Israel that Esther was
catering to Haman — thus they
would repent and pray rather than
be complacent in the knowledge
that they had a 'sister' in the palace
(*Meg. 15b*).

The first Hebrew letters of the
words יָבֹא הַמֶּלֶךְ וְהָמָן הַיּוֹם form the
Holy Name of G-d. This is one of
the several places throughout the
Megillah where G-d's Name is indirectly hinted. [For reasons that
G-d's Name is not explicitly mentioned in the Megillah; see *Overview*.] (*Rabbeinu Bachyai ben
Asher*).

5. מַהֲרוּ — *Hurry.* Since Esther had
already prepared the banquet,
Ahasuerus insisted that she not be
kept waiting (*Shaarei Binah*).

The King was also concerned that
Haman might leave — so he ordered
him taken even against his will, to
do Esther's bidding (*Megillas
Sesarim*).

אֶת־דְּבַר אֶסְתֵּר וַיָּבֹא הַמֶּלֶךְ וְהָמָן אֶל־
הַמִּשְׁתֶּה אֲשֶׁר־עָשְׂתָה אֶסְתֵּר: וַיֹּאמֶר
הַמֶּלֶךְ לְאֶסְתֵּר בְּמִשְׁתֵּה הַיַּיִן מַה־
שְׁאֵלָתֵךְ וְיִנָּתֵן לָךְ וּמַה־בַּקָּשָׁתֵךְ עַד־חֲצִי
הַמַּלְכוּת וְתֵעָשׂ: וַתַּעַן אֶסְתֵּר וַתֹּאמַר
שְׁאֵלָתִי וּבַקָּשָׁתִי: אִם־מָצָאתִי חֵן בְּעֵינֵי
הַמֶּלֶךְ וְאִם־עַל־הַמֶּלֶךְ טוֹב לָתֵת אֶת־
שְׁאֵלָתִי וְלַעֲשׂוֹת אֶת־בַּקָּשָׁתִי יָבוֹא
הַמֶּלֶךְ וְהָמָן אֶל־הַמִּשְׁתֶּה אֲשֶׁר אֶעֱשֶׂה
לָהֶם וּמָחָר אֶעֱשֶׂה כִּדְבַר הַמֶּלֶךְ: וַיֵּצֵא
הָמָן בַּיּוֹם הַהוּא שָׂמֵחַ וְטוֹב לֵב וְכִרְאוֹת
הָמָן אֶת־מָרְדֳּכַי בְּשַׁעַר הַמֶּלֶךְ וְלֹא־קָם
וְלֹא־זָע מִמֶּנּוּ וַיִּמָּלֵא הָמָן עַל־מָרְדֳּכַי

*חצי הספר בפסוקים

וַיָּבֹא הַמֶּלֶךְ וְהָמָן — *so the King and Haman came.* [i.e. they came immediately. This phrase does not begin a new verse, to indicate how quickly they arrived].

6. [Ahasuerus realized that Esther would not have risked her life merely to come and invite him to a banquet. Therefore, he repeated his inquiry into the real nature of Esther's petition.]

שְׁאֵלָתֵךְ...בַּקָּשָׁתֵךְ *Request ... petition.* שְׁאֵלָה ['request'] implies a personal request; בַּקָּשָׁה ['petition'] implies that which one petitions on behalf of others. Therefore, the verse says: 'What is your [personal] request? וְיִנָּתֵן לָךְ — 'It shall be granted you. And what is your petition [on behalf of another]? ... וְתֵעָשׂ — It shall be fulfilled (Vilna Gaon).

[According to the *Masorah*, with the end of verse 6, half of the verses in the Megillah have been completed.]

7. שְׁאֵלָתִי וּבַקָּשָׁתִי — *My petition and my request* — 'My request and petition are not for half the kingdom; nor are they for money; nor was rebuilding the Temple my aim ...'(Targum).

8. אֲשֶׁר אֶעֱשֶׂה לָהֶם — *That I shall prepare for them.* 'Them' i.e. Ahasuerus and Haman equally. Esther's aim was to arouse jealousy of Haman on the part of the King (M'nos Halevi).

כִּדְבַר הַמֶּלֶךְ — *The King's bidding.* 'Tomorrow I will ask the great favor of the King' (Alshich).

According to *Rashi,* Esther promised, 'Tomorrow I will do what the King has asked me many times: I will reveal my people and my ancestry.'

V
6-9

and Haman came to the banquet that Esther had prepared.

The first banquet

⁶ The King said to Esther during the wine feast: 'What is your request? It shall be granted you. And what is your petition? Even if it be half the kingdom, it shall be fulfilled.' ⁷ So Esther answered and said: 'My request and my petition: ⁸ If I have won the King's favor, and if it pleases the King to grant my petition and to perform my request — let the King and Haman come to the banquet that I shall prepare for them, and tomorrow I will do the King's bidding.'

Haman resolves to hang Mordechai

⁹ That day Haman went out joyful and exuberant. But when Haman noticed Mordechai in the King's gate and that he neither stood up nor stirred before him, Haman was infuriated with Mordechai.

---

9. שָׂמֵחַ וְטוֹב לֵב — *Joyful and exuberant.* 'Joyful' — at the special honor he received; and *'exuberant'* —at having dined so well (*M'nos Halevi*).

Esther's ruse worked. When Haman arrived at Esther's banquet, he was apprehensive of Esther's reason for inviting him. He suspected a connection between the new edict concerning the Jews and his invitation. Only now, having left the first party at which he was overwhelmed with flattery, was he joyous and confident. He was unprepared, therefore, for the consequences of Esther's next banquet (*M'nos Halevi*).

'When they had eaten and drunk, Haman said to himself: "The King promotes me and his wife honors me, and there is none greater than I in all the kingdom." And he rejoiced in his heart exceedingly.' (*Midrash*)

עַל־מָרְדֳּכַי חֵמָה — *Infuriated with Mordechai.* Until now, Haman rationalized that Mordechai's well known friendship with the Queen allowed him to refuse bowing down and prostrating before him. It was now obvious that Esther didn't care for Mordechai — after all, she invited only Haman, not Mordechai, to her banquet. Haman became more infuriated than ever at Mordechai's refusal to bow down to him. In fact, Mordechai didn't even 'stir' in Haman's presence! This was the first time since the decree was published that Haman saw Mordechai (*Yosef Lekach*).

Until this point, Haman considered it beneath his dignity [וַיִּבֶז בְּעֵינָיו (3:6)] to punish Mordechai alone. Now that the decree was promulgated — everyone knowing that it was the result of Mordechai's refusal to bow — Mordechai remained obstinate, and refused

חֵמָה: וַיִּתְאַפַּק הָמָן וַיָּבוֹא אֶל־בֵּיתוֹ
וַיִּשְׁלַח וַיָּבֵא אֶת־אֹהֲבָיו וְאֶת־זֶרֶשׁ
אִשְׁתּוֹ: וַיְסַפֵּר לָהֶם הָמָן אֶת־כְּבוֹד עָשְׁרוֹ
וְרֹב בָּנָיו וְאֵת כָּל־אֲשֶׁר גִּדְּלוֹ הַמֶּלֶךְ וְאֵת
אֲשֶׁר נִשְּׂאוֹ עַל־הַשָּׂרִים וְעַבְדֵי הַמֶּלֶךְ:
וַיֹּאמֶר הָמָן אַף לֹא־הֵבִיאָה אֶסְתֵּר
הַמַּלְכָּה עִם־הַמֶּלֶךְ אֶל־הַמִּשְׁתֶּה אֲשֶׁר־
עָשָׂתָה כִּי אִם־אוֹתִי וְגַם־לְמָחָר אֲנִי
קָרוּא־לָהּ עִם־הַמֶּלֶךְ: וְכָל־זֶה אֵינֶנּוּ שֹׁוֶה
לִי בְּכָל־עֵת אֲשֶׁר אֲנִי רֹאֶה אֶת־מָרְדֳּכַי
הַיְּהוּדִי יוֹשֵׁב בְּשַׁעַר הַמֶּלֶךְ: וַתֹּאמֶר לוֹ

יא

יב

יג

יד

---

even to 'stir' — וְלֹא־זָע מִמֶּנּוּ. This
could not be attributed to his Jewishness; his religion might forbid
him to bow, but surely he could
have no legitimate reason to ignore
Haman entirely. At the very least,
he should have showed some fear in
view of the impending extermination of the Jews. His obstinance
could only be an indication of the
man's arrogance. Then Haman
grew infuriated with Mordechai —
and wanted to kill him even before
the date of the decree (R. Galico,
Alshich, Malbim).[See bracketed
comment on 2:2.]

10. וַיִּתְאַפַּק הָמָן — Haman
restrained himself.

He was afraid to take revenge
without permission (Rashi).

וְאֶת־זֶרֶשׁ אִשְׁתּוֹ — And Zeresh his
wife. She was extremely cruel, and
the only one of his friends and
counselors capable of advising him.
She advised that since Mordechai
was of Jewish stock Haman would
not be able to overcome him unless
he contrived a punishment no Jew

had ever experienced. Hananiah
and his companions were delivered
from fire, Daniel from a lion's den,
Joseph from a dungeon.
Mordechai's ancestors, banished
into the wilderness, were fruitful
and multiplied there and withstood
many trials; and Samson killed the
Philistines even after his eyes were
gouged out. 'Therefore,' advised
Zeresh, 'hang Mordechai on a gallows for we have not found that any
of his people were ever delivered
from that.' *This suggestion pleased
Haman (Midrash).*

11. ...אֶת־כְּבוֹד עָשְׁרוֹ — *His wealth
etc.* By recounting his wealth and
good fortune he hoped to get out of
his despondent mood (*Yosef
Lekach; Vilna Gaon*).

Three things make a man happy:
wealth, children, and greatness
(*Alshich*).

Haman wished to prove that he
had all three and, as a result, could
easily dispose of his arch-enemy,
Mordechai: 1— כְּבוֹד עָשְׁרוֹ, *'the
glory of his riches'* — he had suf-

V
10-14

¹⁰ *Nevertheless Haman restrained himself and went home. He sent for his friends and his wife, Zeresh,* ¹¹ *and Haman recounted to them the glory of his wealth and his large number of sons, and every instance where the King had promoted him and advanced him above the officials and royal servants.* ¹² *Haman said: 'Moreover, Queen Esther invited no one but myself to accompany the King to the banquet that she had prepared, and tomorrow, too, I am invited by her along with the King.* ¹³ *Yet all this means nothing to me so long as I see that Jew Mordechai sitting at the King's gate.'* ¹⁴ *Then his wife, Zeresh, and*

---

ficient financial means to bring about Mordechai's downfall; 2—וְרֹב בָּנָיו, 'his large number of sons' all very capable; 3 — אֲשֶׁר נִשְׂאוֹ עַל־הַשָּׂרִים — 'and advanced him above the officials' — endowing him with the power to kill anyone he wishes. 'Lastly,' Haman said, 'even the Queen herself would not save Mordechai. It was I, alone, not Mordechai, whom she invited to the banquet.' Eventually, Haman was proved wrong in all these cases: *His wealth* was given to Mordechai; *his sons* were hung; *the King who had honored him* humbled him before Mordechai; and *Esther* exposed him as her enemy and intent on her people's death.

12. כִּי אִם־אוֹתִי — *No one but myself.* Foremost among Haman's causes for vanity was his conviction that Esther held Mordechai in contempt *(Alshich).*

In his arrogance, Haman was convinced that Esther held him in such high esteem that she arranged a special, intimate banquet solely for the purpose of having him present when she made a major personal request of the King. She was relying on Haman's influence to sway the King in her favor *(Malbim).*

13. Now Haman came to the main point of his discussion: He had not recounted the glories of his wealth, children, and power simply to make conversation. Obviously, his wife and friends were well aware of his family and status. Rather, he told them all this just to lead up to the point of how debilitatingly frustrated he was at Mordechai's refusal to acknowledge his superiority *(Yosef Lekach).*

יוֹשֵׁב בְּשַׁעַר הַמֶּלֶךְ — *Sitting at the King's gate.* Notice that Haman did not mention to his wife and children that he was angry because of Mordechai's refusal to bow down to him; he thought it beneath his dignity to admit that such a minor slight could ruffle him so. Rather he claimed that he was angry because

זֶ֫רֶשׁ אִשְׁתּוֹ וְכָל אֹהֲבָ֗יו יַעֲשׂוּ־עֵץ֮ גָּבֹ֒הַּ
חֲמִשִּׁים אַמָּה֒ וּבַבֹּ֡קֶר אֱמֹ֣ר לַמֶּ֣לֶךְ וְיִתְל֣וּ
אֶת־מָרְדֳּכַ֗י עָלָיו֮ וּבֹ֣א עִם־הַמֶּ֣לֶךְ אֶל־
הַמִּשְׁתֶּ֣ה שָׂמֵ֔חַ וַיִּיטַ֧ב הַדָּבָ֛ר לִפְנֵ֥י הָמָ֖ן
וַיַּ֥עַשׂ הָעֵֽץ׃

פרק ו א בַּלַּ֣יְלָה הַה֔וּא נָדְדָ֖ה שְׁנַ֣ת הַמֶּ֑לֶךְ וַיֹּ֕אמֶר
א לְהָבִ֗יא אֶת־סֵ֤פֶר הַזִּכְרֹנוֹת֙ דִּבְרֵ֣י הַיָּמִ֔ים

'the Jew Mordechai was sitting at the King's gate' and he was totally unworthy of such a high honor (Me'am Loez).

14. יַעֲשׂוּ־עֵץ — *Let a gallows be made.* Since no Jew had ever befòre been miraculously saved from hanging, this is the one punishment that, in the opinion of his advisors, Haman could hope to inflict on Mordechai (*Midrash; see Commentary on verse 10*).

גָּבֹהַּ חֲמִשִּׁים אַמָּה — *Fifty cubits high.* The gallows were built that high to enable Haman to see it and rejoice at its sight while feasting with the King (*Ma'amar Mordechai*).

'Haman searched for a 50-foot beam but could not find one. So his son, Parshandasa, who was the governor of the Mt. Ararat area, supplied him with a beam from the remains of Noah's Ark, which was 50-feet long' (*Midrash Abba Gorion*).

— וּבֹא עִם־הַמֶּלֶךְ אֶל־הַמִּשְׁתֶּה שָׂמֵחַ — *Then in good spirits accompany the King to the banquet.* 'In good spirits' — at the death of Mordechai (*Alshich*).

וַיַּעַשׂ־הָעֵץ—*And he had the gallows erected.* Haman didn't undress or go to sleep. He *immediately* called artisans to build the gallows. His sons banged with hammers and rejoiced; Zeresh his wife played musical instruments with Haman and boasted that she would pay for the construction, and she arranged a feast (*Targum*).

VI

1. נָדְדָה שְׁנַת הַמֶּלֶךְ — *Sleep eluded the King.* [literally: 'the sleep of the King was shaken'].

Allegorically understanding the word 'King' as G-d, 'The King of the Universe,' the *Midrash* com-

all his friends said to him: 'Let a gallows be made, fifty cubits high; and tomorrow morning speak to the King and have them hang Mordechai on it. Then, in good spirits, accompany the King to the banquet.' This suggestion pleased Haman; and he had the gallows erected.

VI
1

¹*That night sleep eluded the King so he ordered that the record book, the annals, be brought and*

ments that the cries of the Jews caused 'the heavens, the throne of the Supreme King of Kings, the Holy One, blessed be He, to be shaken when He saw Israel in such distress.' Taken this way, the verse is saying that G-d's sleep was disturbed. Obviously — even allegorically — 'sleep' cannot be attributed to G-d Almighty. There are times when G-d, in His wisdom, chooses to ignore human needs, almost as if He 'were asleep,' a sleep that can be shaken by the repentance of Israel *(Torah T'mimah).*

'King Ahasuerus' sleep was also disturbed by a dream in which he saw Haman seizing a sword to kill him. He awoke in terror and told his secretaries to bring the book of chronicles to see what events had occurred *(Midrash).*

In the Talmud, 'Rava said: It means literally *"the sleep of King Ahasuerus."* A thought occurred to Ahasuerus: What is the meaning of Esther having invited Haman to the feast? Perhaps they are conspiring to kill me? He thought again: If that

is so, don't I have any friends who would tell me? Then he thought again: Perhaps someone has done me a valuable service and gone unrewarded. If I am guilty of such ingratitude then I may have forfeited the friendship of loyal subjects; they will not inform me of conspiracies against me. He, therefore, *ordered the record book, the annals to be brought'* (Megillah 15b).

To account for his sleeplessness, Ahasuerus thought he might have been poisoned and he was about to order the execution of those charged with the preparation of his food. But they succeeded in convincing him of their innocence by calling to his attention that Esther and Haman shared his evening meal with him without feeling unpleasant after effects *(Midrash Lekach Tov).*

Some commentators say that this was the very first time Ahasuerus experienced insomnia, hence, his great concern *(Me'am Loez).*

סֵפֶר הַזִּכְרֹנוֹת דִּבְרֵי הַיָּמִים — *The record book, the annals.* [This is the

פֶּרֶק ו
ב-ד

ב וַיִּהְיוּ נִקְרָאִים לִפְנֵי הַמֶּלֶךְ: וַיִּמָּצֵא כָתוּב
אֲשֶׁר הִגִּיד מָרְדֳּכַי עַל־בִּגְתָנָא וָתֶרֶשׁ שְׁנֵי
סָרִיסֵי הַמֶּלֶךְ מִשֹּׁמְרֵי הַסַּף אֲשֶׁר בִּקְשׁוּ
ג לִשְׁלֹחַ יָד בַּמֶּלֶךְ אֲחַשְׁוֵרוֹשׁ: וַיֹּאמֶר
הַמֶּלֶךְ מַה־נַּעֲשָׂה יְקָר וּגְדוּלָּה לְמָרְדֳּכַי
עַל־זֶה וַיֹּאמְרוּ נַעֲרֵי הַמֶּלֶךְ מְשָׁרְתָיו לֹא־
ד נַעֲשָׂה עִמּוֹ דָּבָר: וַיֹּאמֶר הַמֶּלֶךְ מִי בֶחָצֵר

only place in תנ"ך, the Bible, that the phrase סֵפֶר זִכְרֹנוֹת — lit. 'the Book of Remembrance,' is used in conjunction with דִּבְרֵי הַיָּמִים, the annals.]

It is common for kings to have parables and official speeches read to them to help lull them to sleep (Rashi).

The king asked that the record book be read to him because he felt that his sleeplessness might be punishment for an unfulfilled oath (Ibn Ezra).

2. וַיִּמָּצֵא כָתוּב — *There it was found recorded.* [See our commentary to 2:23: וַיִּכָּתֵב — 'it was recorded.']

אֲשֶׁר הִגִּיד מָרְדֳּכַי — *That Mordechai had denounced.* In this record book it was mentioned that Mordechai denounced Bigsana and Teresh to the King *directly*, without the intercession of Esther *(Alshich).*

עַל־בִּגְתָנָא וָתֶרֶשׁ — *Bigsana and Teresh* — Previously [in 2:21] he is referred to as 'Bigsan'; why the addition of an *aleph* — א, at the end of his name? Haman's sons were the scribes who recorded the incident; they wished to make light of Mordechai's involvement so they wrote that Mordechai had denounced בִּגְתָן אוֹ תֶרֶשׁ — 'Bigsan or

Teresh' — not even knowing which was the guilty party. Thus, they implied an innocent man was executed as a result of Mordechai's vague suspicions — therefore Mordechai was unworthy of ány reward. When the incident was read now, the incriminating word "אוֹ — or" seemed separated. The *Aleph*, א moved to the end of 'Bigsan,' and the *Vav*, ו, [tHe prefix 'and'] to Teresh. Now the chronicle read, "בִּגְתָנָא וָתֶרֶשׁ" — *"Bigsana and Teresh"* i.e. Mordechai saved the King's life by denouncing both equally guilty plotters. He was eminently deserving of reward — which he never received (Alshich, M'nos Halevi).

According to the *Malbim*, the King had forgotten who was responsible for saving his life in the Bigsan-Teresh incident. All he remembered was that Esther had told him and, since Haman was responsible for his choosing a new Queen, the King promoted him and bestowed enormous power upon him. The *Malbim* differentiates between the דִּבְרֵי הַיָּמִים — *the book of records*, the official chronicle of the nation's history, which was kept under the jurisdiction of the prime minister, and the סֵפֶר הַזִּכְרֹנוֹת, *the annals*, [literally: book of remembrances] the King's personal diary

אסתר [92]

VI
2-4

Mordechai is
finally
rewarded

be read before the King. ² There it was found
recorded that Mordechai had denounced Bigsana and
Teresh, two of the King's chamberlains of the guardians of the threshold, who had plotted to lay hands
on King Ahasuerus. ³ 'What honor or dignity has
been conferred on Mordechai for this?' asked the
King. 'Nothing has been done for him,' replied the
King's pages. ⁴ The King said: 'Who is in the court?'

which was kept in the monarch's personal possession. Haman had rewritten *the book of records* and inserted his own name to conform with his self-serving version. Now, however, when the King had his personal diary read to him, he discovered that Mordechai, not Haman, was responsible for saving his life. Thus becoming aware of Haman's fraud in the Bigsan-Teresh affair, Ahasuerus was quite willing to accept the even more damning accusation that Esther would make against Haman the next day. This teaches a great lesson about Divine intervention — precisely at the crucial moment when Haman built a gallows to hang Mordechai — G-d reversed the course of events.

3. מַה־נַּעֲשָׂה...לְמָרְדֳּכַי — *What ...has been conferred on Mordechai?* Knowing that his kingdom's greatest honor had been bestowed upon Haman, and that as Esther's foster parent, Mordechai had been elevated to a position at the King's gate, — the King wanted to know if Mordechai had been given any form of special recognition for *this* particular good deed *(Yosef Lekach; Alshich; M'nos Halevi).*

לֹא־נַעֲשָׂה עִמּוֹ דָּבָר — *Nothing has been done for him.*

The Talmud comments: they answered him, not because they loved Mordechai but because they hated Haman. *(Megillah 16b)*

The servants said that nothing was done עִמּוֹ, 'with *him.*' — They meant to imply that rewards were indeed given, but not to *him* who was deserving of them. Instead of showering Mordechai with symbols of his gratitude, Ahasuerus rewarded the undeserving Haman *(Me'am Loez).*

Quoting the commentary *Tehillah L'Dovid* the *Me'am Loez* states that in the midst of this conversation the servants heard Haman approaching and they used the word עִמּוֹ — *with 'him'* [not specifically mentioning Mordechai] so Haman wouldn't understand the implication that was so unfavorable to his fortunes.

4. מִי בֶחָצֵר — *who is in the court?* The *Midrash Abba Gorion* relates that upon hearing Mordechai's name, the King finally dozed off. He dreamt that Haman was hovering above him with sword in hand ready to kill him. The King awoke, terrified, and asked 'Who is in the court?' When he heard it was Haman, he exclaimed, "My dream is coming true!" [See commentary on verse 6].

וְהָמָן בָּא לַחֲצַר בֵּית־הַמֶּלֶךְ הַחִיצוֹנָה
לֵאמֹר לַמֶּלֶךְ לִתְלוֹת אֶת־מָרְדֳּכַי עַל־
ה הָעֵץ אֲשֶׁר־הֵכִין לוֹ: וַיֹּאמְרוּ נַעֲרֵי הַמֶּלֶךְ
אֵלָיו הִנֵּה הָמָן עֹמֵד בֶּחָצֵר וַיֹּאמֶר הַמֶּלֶךְ
ו יָבוֹא: וַיָּבוֹא הָמָן וַיֹּאמֶר לוֹ הַמֶּלֶךְ מַה־
לַעֲשׂוֹת בָּאִישׁ אֲשֶׁר הַמֶּלֶךְ חָפֵץ בִּיקָרוֹ
וַיֹּאמֶר הָמָן בְּלִבּוֹ לְמִי יַחְפֹּץ הַמֶּלֶךְ
ז לַעֲשׂוֹת יְקָר יוֹתֵר מִמֶּנִּי: וַיֹּאמֶר הָמָן אֶל־
הַמֶּלֶךְ אִישׁ אֲשֶׁר הַמֶּלֶךְ חָפֵץ בִּיקָרוֹ:
ח יָבִיאוּ לְבוּשׁ מַלְכוּת אֲשֶׁר לָבַשׁ־בּוֹ
הַמֶּלֶךְ וְסוּס אֲשֶׁר רָכַב עָלָיו הַמֶּלֶךְ

According to the *Alshich* the intent of the King's question was: 'Who in my court bears the responsibility of reminding me to distribute rewards to deserving parties?''

וְהָמָן בָּא — *Haman had just come* — 'While it was still night' (*Alshich*).

[Haman was so anxious to rid himself of Mordechai that he didn't follow the sensible advice of Zeresh to wait until morning to approach the King. His entering the scene at so inopportune a time is the beginning of his downfall].

אֲשֶׁר־הֵכִין לוֹ — *which he had prepared for him.* [the word לוֹ, *for him,* is seemingly superfluous.] According to the Talmud: 'A Tanna stated: He had prepared it for himself' (*Meg. 16a*).

The Talmud tells us that Haman, without realizing it, was divinely influenced to prepare the gallows for ultimate use on himself. Elsewhere in the Megillah, the Heavenly decree that was originally against the Jews was reversed and turned against their enemies. The preparation of the gallows was different. The Talmud tells us that from the moment of its preparation, its intended victim was Haman (*Vilna Gaon*).

Traditionally, every Mitzvah requires הֲכָנָה — previous preparation; unlike sins, which are committed spontaneously. Therefore, our Sages [Meg.16a] commented that "Haman prepared the gallows *for himself.*" If there was הֲכָנָה, *preparation,* it follows that a Mitzvah was being readied. The Mitzvah was the destruction of the memory of Amalek [of whom Haman was a descendant] (*Belzer Rebbe*).

6. One analysis of the situation is as follows: Ahasuerus dreamt that Haman, sword in hand, was hovering above him to slay him and he awoke, unable to return to sleep. He ordered his servants to read to him and they related how Mordechai

VI

5-8

(Now Haman had just come into the outer court of the palace to speak to the King about hanging Mordechai on the gallows he had prepared for him.) ⁵ So the King's servants answered him: 'It is Haman standing in the court.' And the King said: 'Let him enter.' ⁶ When Haman came in the King said unto him: 'What should be done for the man whom the King especially wants to honor? (Now Haman reasoned to himself: 'Whom would the King especially want to honor besides me?') ⁷ So Haman said to the King: 'For the man whom the King especially wants to honor, ⁸ have them bring a royal robe that the King has worn and a horse that the King has rid-

---

saved the King in the Bigsan-Teresh incident. Haman entered the scene just then, in the middle of the night when the King never received callers. Ahasuerus was convinced that Haman had come at an hour when most people are asleep for only one reason — to kill him. 'Haman, who appears to be my intimate friend wants to assasinate me,' thought Ahasuerus, 'and he even wants to be rid of Mordechai — my real friend — who saved my life.' The King was determined to establish the facts. He began his plan by ordering Haman to personally bestow royal honors upon his arch-enemy, Mordechai *(Even Shoham).*

חָפֵץ בִּיקָרוֹ — *especially wants to honor or dignity.* Why, in his Ahasuerus mentioned יְקָר וּגְדוּלָה — *honor and greatness.* Why, in his question to Haman did he mention only יְקָר — *honor?* Had the King mentioned גְדוּלָה — *greatness,* Haman would have instantly infer-

red that the King couldn't mean him; what more greatness could Haman possibly get? The King had already גִדַּל, *promoted,* Haman (3:1) and *set his seat above all the officers who were with him.* But יְקָר — honor, knows no bounds. Ahasuerus knew full well that there is hardly a person alive — and surely not a vain man like Haman — who doesn't crave more honor than he already has. *(Vilna Gaon).*

וַיֹּאמֶר הָמָן בְּלִבּוֹ —*Haman reasoned to himself.* The writer of the Book of Esther was divinely inspired and knew what Haman was thinking by means of רוּחַ הַקּוֹדֶשׁ — the Holy Spirit *(Meg. 7a).*

7. אִישׁ אֲשֶׁר הַמֶּלֶךְ חָפֵץ בִּיקָרוֹ — *For the man whom the King especially wants to honor.* Haman said that there is no greater honor for any man than to know that the King wants to honor him publicly *(Malbim).*

וַאֲשֶׁר נָתַן כֶּתֶר מַלְכוּת בְּרֹאשׁוֹ: וְנָתוֹן
הַלְּבוּשׁ וְהַסּוּס עַל־יַד־אִישׁ מִשָּׂרֵי הַמֶּלֶךְ
הַפַּרְתְּמִים וְהִלְבִּישׁוּ אֶת־הָאִישׁ אֲשֶׁר
הַמֶּלֶךְ חָפֵץ בִּיקָרוֹ וְהִרְכִּיבֻהוּ עַל־הַסּוּס
בִּרְחוֹב הָעִיר וְקָרְאוּ לְפָנָיו כָּכָה יֵעָשֶׂה
לָאִישׁ אֲשֶׁר הַמֶּלֶךְ חָפֵץ בִּיקָרוֹ: וַיֹּאמֶר
הַמֶּלֶךְ לְהָמָן מַהֵר קַח אֶת־הַלְּבוּשׁ וְאֶת־
הַסּוּס כַּאֲשֶׁר דִּבַּרְתָּ וַעֲשֵׂה־כֵן לְמָרְדֳּכַי
הַיְּהוּדִי הַיּוֹשֵׁב בְּשַׁעַר הַמֶּלֶךְ אַל־תַּפֵּל
דָּבָר מִכֹּל אֲשֶׁר דִּבַּרְתָּ: וַיִּקַּח הָמָן אֶת־
הַלְּבוּשׁ וְאֶת־הַסּוּס וַיַּלְבֵּשׁ אֶת־מָרְדֳּכָי
וַיַּרְכִּיבֵהוּ בִּרְחוֹב הָעִיר וַיִּקְרָא לְפָנָיו

ינ"א וְהִלְבִּישׁוּ

8. כֶּתֶר מַלְכוּת בְּרֹאשׁוֹ—*Royal crown on his head.* At the very mention of the word 'crown', Ahasuerus' face reddened; Haman did not refer to it again during the conversation (*Alshich; Rashi*).

בְּרֹאשׁוֹ — *His head.* The commentators differ as to *whose* head is referred to: According to *Rashi* Haman suggested the crown be placed on the honoree's head; *Ibn Ezra* comments that in his opinion the *his* definitely refers to the horse because it is common knowledge that a crown is sometimes placed on the King's horse while the King is riding it, and that no one else may ever ride the crowned royal horse; *Alshich, Vilna Gaon* and *Malbim* understand Haman's suggestion to refer to the horse that the King himself rode *on the day of his coronation.*

9. הַפַּרְתְּמִים — *The most noble* [or: 'Royal descendants'; see commentary on 1:3].

וְקָרְאוּ לְפָנָיו — *Proclaiming before him.* Haman shrewdly suggested this proclamation in order to make sure that his attempt at self-aggrandizement did not backfire by inciting the King's jealousy. The King might respond that if the suggestion is implemented, and someone is dressed royally and paraded on the King's horse, then people might think this man is second to the throne! Anticipating this response, Haman suggested that whoever leads this person should loudly proclaim that this honor was bestowed upon this man by beneficence of the King in gratitude for a good deed — and not because of the recipient's governmental status (*Rav Arama*)

10. מַהֵר — *Hurry.* The King had a reason for rushing Haman so. Ahasuerus was going to meet Esther that day at the banquet. He wanted to make sure that in case Esther should ask him why Mordechai,

*den, one with a royal crown on his head. ⁹ Then
let the robe and horse be entrusted to one of the
King's most noble officers, and let them attire the
man whom the King especially wants to honor, and
parade him on horseback through the city square
proclaiming before him: 'This is what is done for the
man whom the King especially wants to honor.'*

Haman's
humiliation

¹⁰ *Then the King said to Haman: 'Hurry, then, get the
robe and the horse as you have said and do all this for
Mordechai the Jew, who sits at the King's gate. Do
not omit a single detail that you have suggested!' ¹¹So
Haman took the robe and the horse and attired
Mordechai, and led him through the city square
proclaiming before him: 'This is what is done for the*

who had saved the King's life, was
never rewarded, he would be able to
tell her that the oversight had
already been remedied (*Yosef
Lekach*).

Ahasuerus rushed Haman so
much because he wanted Haman to
be finished in time for Esther's banquet. It is indicative from here that
all of Ahasuerus' deeds — this one,
the execution of Vashti, the selection of Esther, the edict — were done
hastily and impetuously. Ahasuerus' behavior was typical of the
fool he was (*Me'am Loez*).

לְמָרְדְּכַי הַיְּהוּדִי — *For Mordechai the
Jew.* 'Haman said to him: Who is
Mordechai? He answered: הַיְּהוּדִי —
The Jew. He said: There are many
Mordechais among the Jews. He
answered: הַיּוֹשֵׁב בְּשַׁעַר הַמֶּלֶךְ —
Who sits at the King's gate (Meg.
16a).

כַּאֲשֶׁר דִּבַּרְתָּ —*As you have said.*
Human nature is such that when a

person is compelled to do something against his will, he tends to
omit details. Ahasuerus, therefore,
enumerated every detail of the
reward and let Haman know clearly
that he insisted on full compliance
(*Me'am Loez*).

Ahasuerus wanted to publicly
demonstrate that the reward given
to someone who reveals a conspiracy to the King is greater even
than Haman's. Thus, anyone with
similar information about a conspiracy between Haman or Esther —
a haunting suspicion that preyed on
the King's mind —would be en-
couraged to come forward and
reveal it to the King (*Alshich*).

11. וַיַּרְכִּיבֵהוּ בִּרְחוֹב הָעִיר — *And
led him through the city square.* 'As
he was leading Mordechai through
the streets, Haman's daughter saw
them from an overhanging roof.
She thought the man on the horse
was her father and the man leading

בָּכָה יַעֲשֶׂה לָאִישׁ אֲשֶׁר הַמֶּלֶךְ חָפֵץ
בִּיקָרוֹ: וַיָּשָׁב מָרְדֳּכַי אֶל־שַׁעַר הַמֶּלֶךְ יב
וְהָמָן נִדְחַף אֶל־בֵּיתוֹ אָבֵל וַחֲפוּי רֹאשׁ:
וַיְסַפֵּר הָמָן לְזֶרֶשׁ אִשְׁתּוֹ וּלְכָל־אֹהֲבָיו יג
אֵת כָּל־אֲשֶׁר קָרָהוּ וַיֹּאמְרוּ לוֹ חֲכָמָיו
וְזֶרֶשׁ אִשְׁתּוֹ אִם מִזֶּרַע הַיְּהוּדִים מָרְדֳּכַי
אֲשֶׁר הַחִלּוֹתָ לִנְפֹּל לְפָנָיו לֹא־תוּכַל לוֹ
כִּי־נָפוֹל תִּפּוֹל לְפָנָיו: עוֹדָם מְדַבְּרִים יד

him was Mordechai. So she took a chamber pot and emptied it on the head of her father. He looked up at her, and when she realized it was her father, she threw herself from the roof to the ground and killed herself *(Meg. 16a)*.

12. וַיָּשָׁב מָרְדֳּכַי אֶל־שַׁעַר הַמֶּלֶךְ — *And Mordechai returned to the King's gate.* 'This teaches us that he returned to his sackcloth and fasting [because he went, only *to* the gate but did not enter]. *(Midrash)*

He returned to the Sanhedrin which convened at the King's gate *(Targum)*.

Mordechai returned to the gate and gathered the children of Israel in prayer. He told them that he had hoped to beg the King to annul the decree in reward for his having saved the King's life; now that the King had already rewarded him, that opportunity was lost forever. 'Now we can rely only on G-d to save us from Haman' *(Me'am Loez)*.

וְהָמָן ... אָבֵל וַחֲפוּי רֹאשׁ — *But Haman ... despondent and with his head covered.* [אָבֵל — despondent, literally 'mourning.']

He was '*mourning*' for his daughter [see commentary on verse 11], *and with his head covered* [i.e. humiliated] on account of what had happened to him *(Meg. 16a)*.

13. וַיְסַפֵּר הָמָן—*[And] Haman told.* In 5:10, the verse tells us; וַיִּשְׁלַח וַיָּבֵא, '*he sent for*' his wife and friends and brought them to his house. They had remained in his house to learn the outcome of their advice and to see if he was successful in pursuading the King to hang Mordechai *(Ibn Ezra)*.

אֲשֶׁר קָרָהוּ — *Everything that had happened.* Haman was still not dissuaded from seeking revenge against Mordechai. The word קָרָהוּ — 'happened' implies a *coincidental* happening. This is how Haman viewed the situation: '*It was just a matter of bad luck* in my going to the King to hang Mordechai on the day the King decided to repay Mordechai some old debt of gratitude. Now that the debt has been paid, I am sure the King will listen to my advice and hang Mordechai.' His wife and advisors, however, did not share Haman's confidence and they so advised him *(Yosef Lekach, Malbim)*.

man whom the King especially wants to honor.'

¹² *Mordechai returned to the King's gate; But Haman hurried home, despondent and with his head covered.* ¹³ *Haman told his wife, Zeresh, and all his friends everything that had happened to him, and his advisors and his wife, Zeresh, said to him: 'If Mordechai, before whom you have begun to fall, is of Jewish descent, you will not prevail against him, but will undoubtedly fall before him.'*

Haman's
doom is
forecast

וַיֹּאמְרוּ לוֹ חֲכָמָיו — *His advisors said to him.* [חֲכָמָיו literally 'his wise men'].

'First they are called 'his friends' and then they are called 'his wise men.' Rav Yochanan said 'Whoever says a wise thing ... is called 'wise.' (Meg. 16a).

When Haman began to tell them his troubles they are called אֹהֲבָיו, 'his friends', now, when they reply they are called 'his wise men'. Their friendship was dependent upon his power. Now that they foresaw his downfall their love for him waned (Sfas Emes).

חֲכָמָיו, *His wise men;* i.e. those of אֹהֲבָיו, *his friends,* who were wise (Rav Galico).

Last time [5:10] Zeresh had answered first, now the חֲכָמִים, *advisors* answered first. Haman now blamed her for what seemed to be her ineffectual advice — after all it was she who advised him to go to the King early in the morning — so he now asked her to remain silent and let the advisors speak first (D'na Pashra).

אִם מִזֶּרַע הַיְּהוּדִים — *If he is of Jewish descent.* [הַיְּהוּדִים, lit. THE *Jewish* i.e. with the ה הַיְדִיעָה — the

definitive article ה] 'If Mordechai is a descendant of the saintly Jews ...' (Targum).

לֹא תוּכַל לוֹ — *You will not prevail against him.*

Seemingly, all they were doing was adding salt to his open wounds. What kind of advice was that? They knew that the Jews are compared both to the dust of the earth and the stars in heaven. When they begin to fall, they fall all the way down to the dust; but when they begin to rise they can reach the stars. (Meg. 16a) Having seen that Mordechai the Jew was beginning to rise — and with him the Jews — they knew that the King's command that Haman lead Mordechai was not coincidental; it meant the beginning of the Jews' rise — and of Haman's downfall. Therefore, Haman's only hope was כִּי־נָפוֹל תִּפּוֹל לְפָנָיו — to prostrate himself before Mordechai — beg his forgiveness, and dismantle the gallows (Yosef Lekach; Rashi; Vilna Gaon).

14. עוֹדָם מְדַבְּרִים עִמּוֹ — *While they were still talking with him.* i.e. while he was considering their advice that he dismantle the gallows.

עָמוֹ וְסָרִיסֵי הַמֶּלֶךְ הִגִּיעוּ וַיַּבְהִלוּ לְהָבִיא
אֶת־הָמָן אֶל־הַמִּשְׁתֶּה אֲשֶׁר־עָשְׂתָה
אֶסְתֵּר:

פֶּרֶק ז א וַיָּבֹא הַמֶּלֶךְ וְהָמָן לִשְׁתּוֹת עִם־אֶסְתֵּר
א־ד ב הַמַּלְכָּה: וַיֹּאמֶר הַמֶּלֶךְ לְאֶסְתֵּר גַּם בַּיּוֹם
הַשֵּׁנִי בְּמִשְׁתֵּה הַיַּיִן מַה־שְּׁאֵלָתֵךְ אֶסְתֵּר
הַמַּלְכָּה וְתִנָּתֵן לָךְ וּמַה־בַּקָּשָׁתֵךְ עַד־חֲצִי
ג הַמַּלְכוּת וְתֵעָשׂ: וַתַּעַן אֶסְתֵּר הַמַּלְכָּה
וַתֹּאמַר אִם־מָצָאתִי חֵן בְּעֵינֶיךָ הַמֶּלֶךְ
וְאִם־עַל־הַמֶּלֶךְ טוֹב תִּנָּתֶן לִי נַפְשִׁי
ד בִּשְׁאֵלָתִי וְעַמִּי בְּבַקָּשָׁתִי: כִּי נִמְכַּרְנוּ אֲנִי

G-d's plan caused the chamberlains to take him away to the party before he could implement their suggestion. This was because of the divine intention that the gallows was destined for Haman (Vilna Gaon).

VII

1. לִשְׁתּוֹת עִם־אֶסְתֵּר — *to feast with Esther*. [lit: to drink with Esther] This phrase is not mentioned at the first banquet [5:5] Her three days of fasting were now completed and, unlike the previous feast where Esther did not join them in partaking of the food, now she, too, ate (Alshich; Yosef Lekach).

Haman was embittered at his misfortune; the King, too, was disturbed at the unfolding turn of events and by his frightening dreams. They immersed themselves in drink to forget their bitterness (D'na Pashra).

It was one of G-d's miracles that, as disturbed as Ahasuerus was, He caused him to come to the feast, be cheered by the wine, and regain his good cheer to the extent that he was prepared to fulfill Esther's every wish (Rav Galico).

2. גַּם בַּיּוֹם הַשֵּׁנִי — Again the second day. The word גַּם, 'again' indicates that the King was as well-disposed on the second day as he was on the first. (Rav Galico)

— מַה־שְּׁאֵלָתֵךְ אֶסְתֵּר הַמַּלְכָּה וְתִנָּתֵן לָךְ *What is your request, Queen Esther, it shall be granted you*. This

14 *While they were still talking with him, the King's chamberlains arrived, and they hurried to bring Haman to the banquet which Esther had arranged.*

VII
1-4

The second banquet: Esther presents her request

1 *So the King and Haman came to feast with Queen Esther.* 2 *The King asked Esther again on the second day at the wine feast: 'What is your request, Queen Esther?—it shall be granted you. And what is your petition?— Even if it be up to half the kingdom, it shall be fulfilled'* 3 *So Queen Esther answered and said: 'If I have won Your Majesty's favor and if it pleases the King, let my life be granted to me as my request and my people's as my petition.* 4 *For we have*

time he referred to her as הַמַּלְכָּה, *the Queen*, i.e. "As my Queen who reigns over the Kingdom with me, you may request anything and it will be granted you" (*Yosef Lekach; Rav Galico; Malbim*). [See also commentary on 5:6 for the difference between שְׁאֵלָה, '*request*' and בַּקָשָׁה, '*petition*'.]

3. בְּעֵינֶיךָ הַמֶּלֶךְ...הַמֶּלֶךְ טוב, '*If I have won Your Majesty's* [lit. '*the King's*] *favor and if it pleases the King.* The first הַמֶּלֶךְ *King* is taken to refer to G-d, the second to Ahasuerus. 'Esther cast her eyes heavenward and said: "If I have found favor in Your sight, O Supreme King, and if it pleases thee, O King Ahasuerus, let my life be given me, and let my people be rescued out of the hands of the enemy'" (*Targum*).

תִּנָּתֶן לִי נַפְשִׁי בִּשְׁאֵלָתִי—*Let my life be granted to me as my request.* i.e. That I be not killed on the 13th day of Adar, the date on which your decree orders the annihilation for my people. (*Rashi*)

וְעַמִּי בְּבַקָשָׁתִי — *And my people's as my petition.* i.e. Let my petition be granted that the life of my people be spared because אֵיכָכָה אוּכַל....'*How can I bear witness to the disaster which will befall my people* [8:6] (*Rashi*).

G-d forbid that the sequence of Esther's request indicated that she placed her personal safety before her people's!

Rather, she showed great tact in arousing the King by first making a plea for her own life. The word בַּקָשָׁה '*petition*' is stronger than שְׁאֵלָה '*request*.' She requested her

פרק ז
ה-ז

וְעַמִּי לְהַשְׁמִיד לַהֲרוֹג וּלְאַבֵּד וְאִלּוּ
לַעֲבָדִים וְלִשְׁפָחוֹת נִמְכַּרְנוּ הֶחֱרַשְׁתִּי כִּי
אֵין הַצָּר שֹׁוֶה בְּנֵזֶק הַמֶּלֶךְ: וַיֹּאמֶר הַמֶּלֶךְ
אֲחַשְׁוֵרוֹשׁ וַיֹּאמֶר לְאֶסְתֵּר הַמַּלְכָּה מִי
הוּא זֶה וְאֵי־זֶה הוּא אֲשֶׁר־מְלָאוֹ לִבּוֹ
לַעֲשׂוֹת כֵּן: וַתֹּאמֶר אֶסְתֵּר אִישׁ צַר
וְאוֹיֵב הָמָן הָרָע הַזֶּה וְהָמָן נִבְעַת מִלִּפְנֵי
הַמֶּלֶךְ וְהַמַּלְכָּה: וְהַמֶּלֶךְ קָם בַּחֲמָתוֹ

ה

ו

ז

own life in terms of a שְׁאֵלָה — request. When the King immediately
responded that he would go to any
ends to save her life, she said that
her life was secondary to her. She
had something far more important
to ask — בַּקָּשָׁה — petition — the
salvation of her people. If her people were to be destroyed, then her
own life would matter little to her;
she would die a slow death from ut-
ter despair (Yosef Lekach).

4. לַעֲבָדִים וְלִשְׁפָחוֹת — as slaves and
servant-girls. Esther said to the
King: Had my people been en-
slaved, I would not have objected,
for the Jews were warned in the
Torah that if they sin they will be
sold to their enemies. Your punishment, Ahasuerus, would not have
been great, for you would have been
instrumental in fulfilling the prophecy. But now you have decreed
the complete extermination of the
Jews, something the Torah never
prophesied. For such a deed, your
punishment would have been enormous. The צָר — enemy who instigated the decree did not concern
himself with נֵזֶק הַמֶּלֶךְ — the damage
to the King that would result in the
form of Divine retribution. (Yosef
Lekach)

כִּי אֵין הַצָּר שֹׁוֶה בְּנֵזֶק הַמֶּלֶךְ — The
adversary is not worthy of the
King's damage, i.e. he is not concerned with the King's damage. Had
he been concerned with the King's
welfare he would have advised him
to sell the Jews and keep the money,
or keep them — and their descendants — as perpetual slaves (Rashi).

Of course, Esther wasn't suggesting that her people should be
sold as slaves! She merely wanted to
stress the evil intent of the adversary in not having originally made
this better suggestion to the King
(Yosef Lekach).

The Ibn Ezra comments that the
adversary was not concerned with
the financial damage to the King
resultant from the enormous loss of
tax revenue.

5. מִי הוּא זֶה — Who is it...? The
King was agitated and he mumbled
these words quickly. (Ibn Ezra).

[Ahasuerus had obviously not
forgotten his grant to Haman; why
did he ask for identification of the
adversary?

[The commentators differ: Some
say that when Haman originally
asked the King to issue the decree of
annihilation [3:8-9], he never inden-
tified the Jewish people as the in-

been sold, I and my people, to be destroyed, slain, and annihilated. Had we been sold as slaves and servant-girls, I would have kept quiet, for the adversary is not worthy of the King's damage.'

⁵ Thereupon, King Ahasuerus exclaimed and said to Queen Esther: 'Who is it? Where is the one who dared to do this?' ⁶ And Esther said: 'An adversary and an enemy! This wicked Haman!' Haman trembled in terror before the King and Queen. ⁷ The

tended victims, hence Ahasuerus' ignorance when Esther made the veiled reference to Haman. Other commentators say that at this point, Ahasuerus still did not realize that she was a Jewess and he did not know to what she referred. Others say that Ahasuerus had never given Haman permission לְאַבֵּד — to annihilate them, merely לַעֲשׂוֹת בּוֹ כַּטּוֹב בְּעֵינֶיךָ — 'to do with it as you see fit', i.e., to do what is good for the country, a course Haman obviously did not follow.]

6. אִישׁ צַר וְאוֹיֵב הָמָן הָרָע הַזֶּה — 'An adversary and and enemy! This wicked Haman.' Esther accused Haman, not of being a perpetrator of a sinful act, but of being *intrinsically* evil. Rather than concerning himself with the welfare of the State, he was involving Ahasuerus in a monstrous crime merely to seek revenge for his own petty hatreds (*Rav Galico*).

וְהָמָן נִבְעַת מִלִּפְנֵי הַמֶּלֶךְ וְהַמַּלְכָּה — *Haman trembled in terror before the King and Queen.* In the presence of both of them, together, he trembled. Had he been confronted by either of them privately, he could have

talked his way out of the bind. To the Queen he could have innocently pleaded that he did not know the Jews were her people, and had he known he would never have issued the decree. To the King he could have claimed that, although the Jews were Esther's people, they were nevertheless worthy of extinction. But since both the King and Queen were there he couldn't defend himself: How could he tell the King — in the Queen's presence — that her people were evil? And how could he say to the Queen — in the King's presence — that, had he known they were her people, he never would have condemned them? Having said they were thoroughly evil it would have been traitorous for him to allow their survival! Therefore, he trembled in terror, for in their joint presence he was unable to defend himself (*Vilna Gaon*).

7. וְהַמֶּלֶךְ קָם בַּחֲמָתוֹ —*The King rose in a rage.* He went out to "cool off" from his anger, part of G-d's master plan, to give Haman the opportunity to incriminate himself even further in the King's absence (*Rav Galico*).

The King, in his drunkenness

מִמִּשְׁתֵּה הַיַּיִן אֶל־גִּנַּת הַבִּיתָן וְהָמָן עָמַד
לְבַקֵּשׁ עַל־נַפְשׁוֹ מֵאֶסְתֵּר הַמַּלְכָּה כִּי
רָאָה כִּי־כָלְתָה אֵלָיו הָרָעָה מֵאֵת הַמֶּלֶךְ:
וְהַמֶּלֶךְ שָׁב מִגִּנַּת הַבִּיתָן אֶל־בֵּית|מִשְׁתֵּה
הַיַּיִן וְהָמָן נֹפֵל עַל־הַמִּטָּה אֲשֶׁר אֶסְתֵּר
עָלֶיהָ וַיֹּאמֶר הַמֶּלֶךְ הֲגַם לִכְבּוֹשׁ אֶת־
הַמַּלְכָּה עִמִּי בַּבָּיִת הַדָּבָר יָצָא מִפִּי
הַמֶּלֶךְ וּפְנֵי הָמָן חָפוּ: וַיֹּאמֶר חַרְבוֹנָה
אֶחָד מִן־הַסָּרִיסִים לִפְנֵי הַמֶּלֶךְ גַּם הִנֵּה־

ח

ט

---

acted most unwisely in leaving the Queen alone with Haman at such a time. This is why the verse says that he left בַּחֲמָתוֹ — in a rage; had he been more composed, he certainly would not have run out (Yad Hamelech).

לְבַקֵּשׁ עַל־נַפְשׁוֹ — To beg for his life. When the King left, Haman seized the opportunity to beg for his life by telling Esther that he didn't know the Jews were her people. Before he had a chance to get very far, however, the King returned (Vilna Gaon).

8. [In the garden, the King remembered that the incident resulting in Vashti's execution happened in that very same place! And the very same Haman — who was now alone with Esther — was responsible for Vashti's death just as he had been scheming to murder Esther and her people! Ahasuerus grew even more angry and he rushed back to the room only to see Haman נֹפֵל falling over Esther on her couch ('constantly falling' — having been pushed by an angel into this compromising position in order to infuriate the King —

Midrash) and the King misinterprets Haman's intention, perhaps deliberately, to add to Haman's misery—(M'nos Halevi).]

נֹפֵל עַל־הַמִּטָּה—Was prostrated [lit. 'falling'] on the couch.

They used to recline on couches during the meal, as it is written earlier [1:6] מִטּוֹת זָהָב וָכֶסֶף, couches of gold and silver (Rashi).

Another interpretation: Haman, by putting himself in this compromising position tried to implicate Esther and have her killed along with him. This plan, too, ended in failure as Esther screamed for help (Ma'amar Mordechai).

הַדָּבָר יָצָא מִפִּי הַמֶּלֶךְ — As soon as the King uttered this — The moment Ahasuerus uttered so serious a charge against Haman, it was obvious to the servants present that Haman was doomed (Rav Galico).

וּפְנֵי הָמָן חָפוּ — They covered Haman's face. The servants covered his face in deference to the King's displeasure so that Ahasuerus would not see the face of his enemy ever again (Ibn Ezra).

It was the common practice in

VII
8-9

King rose in a rage from the wine feast and went into the palace garden while Haman remained to beg Queen Esther for his life; for he saw that the King's evil determination against him was final. 8 When the King returned from the palace garden to the banquet room, Haman was prostrated on the couch upon which Esther was; so the King exclaimed: 'Would he actually assault the Queen while I'm in the house?'

Haman is executed

As soon as the King uttered this, they covered Haman's face. 9 Then Charbonah, one of the chamberlains in attendance of the King, said:

Persia to cover the face of a prisoner who was condemned to death (*Alshich*).

The *Vilna Gaon* and some other commentators understand חָפוּ, 'covered', in the sense of 'despondent' as in חֲפוּי רֹאשׁ [in 6:12].

9. וַיֹּאמֶר חַרְבוֹנָה — *Then Charbonah . . . said.* [The *Midrashim* all point out how Charbonah painted an evil picture of a Haman who did not have the welfare of the King in mind when he conceived his evil plans against a Mordechai whose only sin it was that he saved the King from death at the hands of Bigsan and Teresh, in whose plot Haman was undoubtedly a co-conspirator.]

Charbonah was one of the chamberlains who went to fetch Haman to the banquet [6:14]. While waiting in Haman's home, he overheard the plot to hang Mordechai, and saw the gallows (*Yosef Lekach*).

The Talmud says that Charbonah was among the conspirators to hang Mordechai (*Meg. 16a*). Now that he saw that the plot had failed and that

Haman was in disfavor, he became his enemy and, before Haman could open his mouth and implicate Charbonah, he advised the King to hang Haman (*Yad Hamelech*).

'Charbonah said: This is not the only crime committed by Haman, for he was an accomplice of the conspirators, Bigsan and Teresh. His enmity against Mordechai dates back to the time when he bared that assassination attempt. Haman erected the gallows to avenge himself against Mordechai for his loyalty to the King.' Charbonah's words illustrate the saying: 'Once the ox has been cast aground, slaughtering knives can readily be found.' Knowing that Haman had fallen from his high estate, Charbonah was intent upon winning the friendship of Mordechai' (*Panim Acherim*).

[Our Sages ordained that one should always say חַרְבוֹנָה זָכוּר לַטוֹב — 'Charbonah of blessed memory', because it was Charbonah's swift advice that prevented Haman from possibly talking — or bribing — his way back into the King's good graces].

פרק ז

י הָעֵץ אֲשֶׁר־עָשָׂה הָמָן לְמָרְדֳּכַי אֲשֶׁר
דִּבֶּר־טוֹב עַל־הַמֶּלֶךְ עֹמֵד בְּבֵית הָמָן
גָּבֹהַּ חֲמִשִּׁים אַמָּה וַיֹּאמֶר הַמֶּלֶךְ תְּלֻהוּ
עָלָיו: וַיִּתְלוּ אֶת־הָמָן עַל־הָעֵץ אֲשֶׁר־
הֵכִין לְמָרְדֳּכָי וַחֲמַת־הַמֶּלֶךְ שָׁכָכָה:

פרק ח

א־ב

א בַּיּוֹם הַהוּא נָתַן הַמֶּלֶךְ אֲחַשְׁוֵרוֹשׁ
לְאֶסְתֵּר הַמַּלְכָּה אֶת־בֵּית הָמָן צֹרֵר
הַיְּהוּדִיּים וּמָרְדֳּכַי בָּא לִפְנֵי הַמֶּלֶךְ כִּי־
ג הִגִּידָה אֶסְתֵּר מָה הוּא־לָהּ: וַיָּסַר הַמֶּלֶךְ
אֶת־טַבַּעְתּוֹ אֲשֶׁר הֶעֱבִיר מֵהָמָן וַיִּתְּנָהּ

יתיר י'

גַּם — *Furthermore.* Charbonah told the King — not only did Haman do the things Esther accused him of, he is גַּם, also, guilty of preparing a gallows to hang a friend of the King, one who saved the King's life (Rashi).

הִנֵּה־הָעֵץ ... — *Furthermore ... the gallows ...* Charbonah said: Haman's additional affront to the King is the fact that Haman dared to build a gallows on which, he boasted, he would hang the man of whom it was proclaimed [6:11] הַמֶּלֶךְ חָפֵץ בִּיקָרוֹ *'this is the man whom the King especially wants to honor.'* (Malbim).

וַיֹּאמֶר הַמֶּלֶךְ תְּלֻהוּ עָלָיו — *And the King said 'Hang him on it.'* [The King rendered this judgment independently, without consulting anyone. See Commentary on 1:19 s.v. יֵצֵא — *Let there go forth.*]

10. וַחֲמַת־הַמֶּלֶךְ שָׁכָכָה — *And the King's anger abated.*

The Talmud asks: Why does the letter כ [chaf] appear twice in שָׁכָכָה — *'abated'*? [The Hebrew word שָׁכָה — with one כ, as it is usually spelled in the Bible, would have sufficed.] The reply is given: There were two angers — the anger of the King of the Universe [G-d, against Israel for bowing down to the image] — and the other of Ahasuerus against Haman [for having condemned the Jews]. Others say, Ahasuerus was doubly angry at Haman, first on account of Esther [(i.e., Haman's plot against Esther — (Rashi)] and, second, on account of Vashti [for the King still remembered that he had allowed himself to be persuaded to act impetuously in having her executed. His anger was not abated until now, when Haman, who instigated Vashti's death also, was finally hanged (Maharsha)].

אסתר [106]

VII
10

'Furthermore, the fifty-cubit-high gallows which Haman made for Mordechai — who spoke good for the King — is standing in Haman's house.' And the King said: 'Hang him on it.' ¹⁰ *So they hanged Haman on the gallows which he had prepared for Mordecai, and the King's anger abated.*

VIII
1-2

Mordechai is appointed Prime Minister

¹*That very day, King Ahasuerus gave the estate of Haman, the enemy of the Jews, to Queen Esther. Mordechai presented himself to the King (for Esther had revealed his relationship to her).* ² *The King slipped off his signet ring, which he had removed from Haman, and gave it to Mordechai; and*

VIII

1. בַּיּוֹם הַהוּא — *That very day,* i.e., on which Haman was hanged (*Alshich*).

נָתַן...לְאֶסְתֵּר הַמַּלְכָּה — *Gave...to Queen Esther.* The decree was still in effect — not to be revoked — and the King wanted to demonstrate that Esther and Mordechai were not included in that decree (*Alshich*). G-d made everything happen so quickly to prevent Ahasuerus from reconsidering and perhaps changing his mind. (*Ma'amar Mordechai*).

וּמָרְדְּכַי בָּא — *And Mordechai presented himself.* i.e. of his own volition, without permission (*Rav Eleazer of Worms*). With the death of Haman, the law he instituted (to prevent Esther free access to the King) that no one may

approach the King unsummoned [4:11] was annulled (*M'nos Halevi*).

לִפְנֵי הַמֶּלֶךְ — *To the King.* Till now, his place was at the King's gate. This did not reflect an improvement of the status of the Jews in general, just of Mordechai (*Alshich*).

2. טַבַּעְתּוֹ אֲשֶׁר הֶעֱבִיר מֵהָמָן—*His sig-net ring which he had removed from Haman.* At one time the custom was that the King himself wore the signet ring. When he gave it מֵעַל יָדוֹ *'from his hand'* [3:10] to Haman he thereby instituted the custom that the prime minister would wear the signet. Therefore, the verse here specifically states that *'he removed it from Haman'* i.e. that the King did not remove it from his own hand but rather from his prime minister's hand — as the precedent

פֶּרֶק ח

ג־ו

לְמָרְדֳּכָי וַתָּשֶׂם אֶסְתֵּר אֶת־מָרְדֳּכַי עַל־
בֵּית הָמָן: וַתּוֹסֶף אֶסְתֵּר וַתְּדַבֵּר לִפְנֵי
הַמֶּלֶךְ וַתִּפֹּל לִפְנֵי רַגְלָיו וַתֵּבְךְּ וַתִּתְחַנֶּן־
לוֹ לְהַעֲבִיר אֶת־רָעַת הָמָן הָאֲגָגִי וְאֵת
מַחֲשַׁבְתּוֹ אֲשֶׁר חָשַׁב עַל־הַיְּהוּדִים:
וַיּוֹשֶׁט הַמֶּלֶךְ לְאֶסְתֵּר אֵת שַׁרְבִט הַזָּהָב
וַתָּקָם אֶסְתֵּר וַתַּעֲמֹד לִפְנֵי הַמֶּלֶךְ:
וַתֹּאמֶר אִם־עַל־הַמֶּלֶךְ טוֹב וְאִם־מָצָאתִי
חֵן לְפָנָיו וְכָשֵׁר הַדָּבָר לִפְנֵי הַמֶּלֶךְ
וְטוֹבָה אֲנִי בְּעֵינָיו יִכָּתֵב לְהָשִׁיב אֶת־
הַסְּפָרִים מַחֲשֶׁבֶת הָמָן בֶּן־הַמְּדָתָא
הָאֲגָגִי אֲשֶׁר כָּתַב לְאַבֵּד אֶת־הַיְּהוּדִים
אֲשֶׁר בְּכָל־מְדִינוֹת הַמֶּלֶךְ: כִּי אֵיכָכָה
אוּכַל וְרָאִיתִי בָּרָעָה אֲשֶׁר־יִמְצָא אֶת־
עַמִּי וְאֵיכָכָה אוּכַל וְרָאִיתִי בְּאָבְדָן

had already been so established (Yosef Lekach).

וַיִּתְּנָהּ לְמָרְדֳּכָי — And he gave it to Mordechai. [As a sign of power to act in the King's name].

וַתָּשֶׂם אֶסְתֵּר אֶת מָרְדֳּכַי — And Esther put Mordechai ... i.e., she appointed him superintendent and administrator over Haman's estate. Having received this property as a gift from the King, she could not very well have belittled the King's gift by transferring it outright to Mordechai; rather, she appointed him administrator (M'nos Halevi).

3. וַתּוֹסֶף אֶסְתֵּר — Esther ... again. Even though Mordechai had been appointed Prime Minister, his influence with the King was as yet untested. Having been so effective

previously, Esther again took the initiative to attempt to influence the King, this time to find a way to override Haman's evil decree. She and Mordechai were all too painfully aware that, despite the King's fury at Haman, her specific request regarding her own safety and her people's survival had not yet been answered by the King for the edict decreeing Israel's extermination was still in full force. She was apprehensive that the King, having hung Haman and advanced Mordechai, would not be concerned with the fate of her people. She spoke out (Rav Galico; Yosef Lekach; M'nos Halevi).

4. וַיּוֹשֶׁט הַמֶּלֶךְ...אֶת שַׁרְבִט הַזָּהָב — The King extended the gold scepter not as a sign of clemency, but as a

Esther put Mordechai in charge of Haman's estate.

³ *Esther yet again spoke to the King, collapsed at his feet, and cried and begged him to avert the evil in-*

tention of Haman the Agagite, and his scheme which he had plotted against the Jews. ⁴ *The King extended the gold scepter to Esther, and Esther arose and stood before the King.* ⁵ *She said: 'If it pleases the King, and if I have won his favor, and the proposal seems proper in the King's opinion, and I be pleasing to him, let a decree be written to countermand those dis-*

patches devised by Haman the son of Hammedasa, the Agagite, which he wrote ordering the destruction of the Jews who are in all the King's provinces. ⁶ *For how can I bear to witness the disaster which will befall my people! How can I bear to witness the destruction of my relatives!'*

sign of encouragement that Esther might rise and speak without tears (*Rav Galico; Yosef Lekach; M'nos Halevi*).

5. אִם־עַל־הַמֶּלֶךְ טוֹב — *If it pleases the King...* There are three prerequisites that assure the success of a request: it must please the respondent; the petitioner must be liked by the respondent; the proposal, itself, must be a proper one. Therefore Esther prefaced her request with these three criteria (*Vilna Gaon*).

יִכָּתֵב — *Let a decree be written,* because a verbal decree is not sufficiently permanent and long-lasting (*Maamar Mordechai*).

לְהָשִׁיב אֶת־הַסְּפָרִים — *To counter-mand* [lit. 'to return'; 'to recall'] *those dispatches.* Haman's decree did not end with his death. Esther proposed the recall of the sealed

letters as the best possible course. By ordering the return of the original letters instead of sending a second letter contradicting the first one, Ahasuerus would avoid the embarrassment of having two conflicting letters in the hands of the officers at the same time (*Malbim*).

[Most commentators, however, understand the word לְהָשִׁיב in the sense of 'nullify'. It was well established Persian law that a royal decree could not be revoked. Esther, however, represented the decree as being מַחֲשֶׁבֶת הָמָן — devised by Haman, not the King. In that case, she tried to persuade him, the decree *was* revocable — *see Yosef Lekach; M'nos Halevi.*]

6. כִּי אֵיכָכָה אוּכַל וְרָאִיתִי — *For how can I bear to witness.* Esther impressed upon the King that her own personal and emotional well being was

מוֹלַדְתִּי: וַיֹּאמֶר הַמֶּלֶךְ אֲחַשְׁוֵרֹשׁ
לְאֶסְתֵּר הַמַּלְכָּה וּלְמָרְדֳּכַי הַיְּהוּדִי הִנֵּה
בֵית־הָמָן נָתַתִּי לְאֶסְתֵּר וְאֹתוֹ תָּלוּ עַל־
הָעֵץ עַל אֲשֶׁר־שָׁלַח יָדוֹ בַּיְּהוּדִיִּים:

וְאַתֶּם כִּתְבוּ עַל־הַיְּהוּדִים כַּטּוֹב בְּעֵינֵיכֶם
בְּשֵׁם הַמֶּלֶךְ וְחִתְמוּ בְּטַבַּעַת הַמֶּלֶךְ כִּי־
כְתָב אֲשֶׁר־נִכְתָּב בְּשֵׁם־הַמֶּלֶךְ וְנַחְתּוֹם
בְּטַבַּעַת הַמֶּלֶךְ אֵין לְהָשִׁיב: וַיִּקָּרְאוּ
סֹפְרֵי־הַמֶּלֶךְ בָּעֵת־הַהִיא בַּחֹדֶשׁ
הַשְּׁלִישִׁי הוּא־חֹדֶשׁ סִיוָן בִּשְׁלוֹשָׁה
וְעֶשְׂרִים בּוֹ וַיִּכָּתֵב כְּכָל־אֲשֶׁר־צִוָּה
מָרְדֳּכַי אֶל־הַיְּהוּדִים וְאֶל הָאֲחַשְׁדַּרְפְּנִים

---

dependent on his favorable response to her plea. She would die of aggravation if her people were slaughtered. Even if they were left alive, but were constantly harassed, she would know no peace (Rav Galico; M'nos Halevi; Yosef Lekach).

7. הִנֵּה בֵית־הָמָן נָתַתִּי לְאֶסְתֵּר — *I have given Haman's estate to Esther* ... The King said: 'By my recent actions everyone will know that I am well disposed to you both, and anything you say will have royal force. Therefore, there is no need to annul the first decree; simply write a new decree as you see fit'(Rashi).

'Don't worry about the people in the environs of Shushan; since the word is out that Haman is dead and I transferred his estate to you and his power to Mordechai, you have nothing to fear. It is the far-away provinces you must reach' (Alshich; D'na Pashra).

8. כַּטּוֹב בְּעֵינֵיכֶם — *Whatever you*

desire. [The King gave them *carte blanche* permission not to annul, but to override Haman's decree by wording a new decree in any manner they thought effective. This, of course, faced Mordechai and Esther with the dilemma of framing an edict that would not challenge the legal standing of Haman's decree but that would effectively neutralize it.]

The Holy One, blessed be He, now performed an unprecedented miracle. Was there ever in history such a miracle that Israel should wreak vengeance on the other nations and do with their enemies as they pleased? (Midrash).

The King had told them to adjust the first decree in a manner favorable to the Jews. The original edict (sent to אֲחַשְׁדַּרְפְּנֵי־הַמֶּלֶךְ וְאֶל־הַפַּחוֹת ... וְאֶל שָׂרֵי עַם וָעָם *the satraps, governors and officials'* — which clearly spelled out the destruction) could not be revoked. Their hope was to modify the vaguely worded פַּתְשֶׁגֶן הַכְּתָב —

VIII
7-9

Permission
is granted to
override the
decree

⁷ *Then King Ahasuerus said to Queen Esther and
Mordechai the Jew: 'Behold, I have given Haman's
estate to Esther, and he has been hanged on the gallows because he plotted against the Jews.* ⁸ *You may
write concerning the Jews whatever you desire, in the
King's name, and seal it with the royal signet, for an
edict which is written in the King's name and sealed
with the royal signet may not be revoked.'* ⁹ *So the
King's secretaries were summoned at that time, on
the twenty-third day of the third month, that is, the
month of Sivan, and it was written exactly as
Mordechai had dictated to the Jews and to the
satraps, the governors and officials of the provinces*

the public copy of the decree — in a
way that would specifically allow
the Jews to kill their enemies *(Vilna
Gaon, Malbim)*...

And when the rulers of each
country received this new document
allowing the Jews to avenge
themselves on their enemies, they
would unquestionably destroy the
earlier decree because by then they
would certainly have heard of
Haman's hanging and the rise of
Mordechai indicating that the King
now sided with the Jews. Therefore,
they could write whatever they
wished without actually *contradicting* the first decree *(M'nos
Halevi)*.

9. [The events described in the
first eight verses of this chapter
took place on the 13th of Nissan.
The narrative of the events of that
day resumes in verse 15. Verses 9-
14 describe the writing and the dispatching of the second decree, all of
which took place on the 23rd of
Sivan. The reason for this five-

verse, parenthetical insert is to continue the train of thought begun in
verse 8 when Ahasuerus gave instructions that a second decree be
composed.]

Although Mordechai and Esther
were insistent upon immediate permission to countermand Haman's
decree, they waited over two
months before writing the all-
important edict without which
death still hovered over the head of
the Jews. One reason for the delay is
that Mordechai was waiting for the
return to Shushan of Haman's
couriers. He felt that it was essential
that his letters be delivered by the
same couriers. That would add
legitimacy to the contents of the second letter despite the fact that it
apparently contradicted the intent
of Haman's royal decree *(Yosef
Lekach)*.

אֶל הַיְּהוּדִים וְאֶל הָאֲחַשְׁדַּרְפְּנִים וְהַפַּחוֹת
וְשָׂרֵי הַמְּדִינוֹת — *To the Jews, and to
the satraps, the governors and officials.* Haman had sent three docu-

וְהַפַּחוֹת וְשָׂרֵי הַמְּדִינוֹת אֲשֶׁר|מֵהֹדּוּ וְעַד־
כּוּשׁ שֶׁבַע וְעֶשְׂרִים וּמֵאָה מְדִינָה מְדִינָה
וּמְדִינָה כִּכְתָבָהּ וְעַם וָעָם כִּלְשֹׁנוֹ וְאֶל־
הַיְּהוּדִים כִּכְתָבָם וְכִלְשׁוֹנָם: וַיִּכְתֹּב בְּשֵׁם
הַמֶּלֶךְ אֲחַשְׁוֵרֹשׁ וַיַּחְתֹּם בְּטַבַּעַת הַמֶּלֶךְ
וַיִּשְׁלַח סְפָרִים בְּיַד הָרָצִים בַּסּוּסִים
רֹכְבֵי הָרֶכֶשׁ הָאֲחַשְׁתְּרָנִים בְּנֵי הָרַמָּכִים:
אֲשֶׁר נָתַן הַמֶּלֶךְ לַיְּהוּדִים|אֲשֶׁר|בְּכָל־
עִיר־וָעִיר לְהִקָּהֵל וְלַעֲמֹד עַל־נַפְשָׁם
לְהַשְׁמִיד לַהֲרֹג וּלְאַבֵּד אֶת־כָּל־חֵיל עַם
וּמְדִינָה הַצָּרִים אֹתָם טַף וְנָשִׁים וּשְׁלָלָם
לָבוֹז: בְּיוֹם אֶחָד בְּכָל־מְדִינוֹת הַמֶּלֶךְ
אֲחַשְׁוֵרֹשׁ בִּשְׁלוֹשָׁה עָשָׂר לְחֹדֶשׁ שְׁנֵים־
עָשָׂר הוּא־חֹדֶשׁ אֲדָר: פַּתְשֶׁגֶן הַכְּתָב

י

יא

יב

יג

ments to each province — one each
to the satrap, governor, and officials
as evidenced by the Hebrew וְאֶל,
"and to the," separating the various
categories [in 3:12]. Mordechai,
however, sent two to each province:
One to the Jews, וְאֶל and one to, the
satraps, governors and officials
(Yosef Lekach).

10. וַיַּחְתֹּם בְּטַבַּעַת הַמֶּלֶךְ —And
sealed it with the King's signet
[which was in Mordechai's posses-
sion].

In this verse we see the verbs
וַיִּכְתֹּב...וַיַּחְתֹּם...וַיִּשְׁלַח, 'He wrote...he
sealed... he sent,' Haman allowed
others to attend to the mechanics of
preparing and dispatching the
decree. Mordechai, who wanted the
Mitzvah of being instrumental in
saving the Jews, took care of every
detail himself (M'nos Halevi).

בְּיַד הָרָצִים בַּסּוּסִים—He sent couriers on horseback. Having just
returned from their first mission,
they were tired. Mordechai wanted
the new letters to be delivered as
soon as possible even though there
were eight and one-half months
remaining before the 13th of Adar.
Therefore, he supplied them with
the swiftest animals available (Vilna
Gaon).

הָאֲחַשְׁתְּרָנִים בְּנֵי הָרַמָּכִים—(here
translated:) riders of swift mules
bred of mares. The Sages do not
know what these words mean
(Megillah 18a). Rashi suggests that
הָאֲחַשְׁתְּרָנִים are a species of swift
camels; according to Ibn Ezra
הָאֲחַשְׁתְּרָנִים are a species of mules,
and הָרַמָּכִים are mares.
[The word רֶמֶךְ — mare — is
found in the Mishnah Kilayim 8:5

from Hodu to Cush, a hundred and twenty-seven provinces, to each province in its own script, and each people in its own language, and to the Jews in their own script and language. 10 He wrote in the name of King Ahasuerus and sealed it with the King's signet. He sent letters by couriers on horseback; riders of swift mules bred of mares, 11 to the effect that the King had permitted the Jews of every single city to organize and defend themselves; to destroy, slay, and exterminate every armed force of any people or province that threaten them, along with their children and women, and to plunder their possessions, 12 on a single day in all the provinces of King Ahasuerus, namely, upon the thirteenth day of the twelfth month, that is, the month of Adar. 13 The contents of the document were to be promulgated in

where the meaning is a mule whose dam is known to be a mare].

11. לְהִקָּהֵל — *To organize.* Only by organizing and unifying themselves in begging for G-d's assistance could the Jews be victorious despite being seriously outnumbered (*D'na Pashra, Yosef Lekach*).

הַצָּרִים אֹתָם — *That threaten them.* The King gave them the right of organized self-defense only against *the forces that threatened them,* but they were permitted to be aggressive against descendants of Amalek (*Rav Galico; Alshich*).

12. בְּיוֹם אֶחָד — *On a single day.* It was Mordechai's wish that the Jews avoid taking spoils in order to

demonstrate that self-defense was their only motivation. He, therefore, worded the edict that the *assembly, defense, destruction, extermination, and taking of spoils* must all be accomplished on the same day so that there would no time for the gathering of spoils. This was in contrast to Haman, who ordered the wholesale destruction to take place in one day, with the following day being left for looting (*Malbim*).

13. פַּתְשֶׁגֶן הַכְּתָב — *The contents of the document.* Unlike the contents of Haman's decree which were vague and secret [see Commentary on 3:14], Mordechai's decree was specific and גָּלוּי לְכָל - הָעַמִּים *published to all peoples* that the Jews were to be ready on that day to avenge themselves (*Kad haKemach*)

לְהִנָּתֵן דָּת בְּכָל־מְדִינָה וּמְדִינָה גָּלוּי
לְכָל־הָעַמִּים וְלִהְיוֹת הַיְּהוּדִיים עֲתוּדִים
לַיּוֹם הַזֶּה לְהִנָּקֵם מֵאֹיְבֵיהֶם: הָרָצִים
רֹכְבֵי הָרֶכֶשׁ הָאֲחַשְׁתְּרָנִים יָצְאוּ
מְבֹהָלִים וּדְחוּפִים בִּדְבַר הַמֶּלֶךְ וְהַדָּת
נִתְּנָה בְּשׁוּשַׁן הַבִּירָה: וּמָרְדֳּכַי יָצָא
מִלִּפְנֵי הַמֶּלֶךְ בִּלְבוּשׁ מַלְכוּת תְּכֵלֶת
וָחוּר וַעֲטֶרֶת זָהָב גְּדוֹלָה וְתַכְרִיךְ בּוּץ
וְאַרְגָּמָן וְהָעִיר שׁוּשָׁן צָהֲלָה וְשָׂמֵחָה:
לַיְּהוּדִים הָיְתָה אוֹרָה וְשִׂמְחָה וְשָׂשֹׂן
וִיקָר: וּבְכָל־מְדִינָה וּמְדִינָה וּבְכָל־עִיר

14. וּדְחוּפִים מְבֹהָלִים יָצְאוּ— *Went forth in urgent haste.* [Lit. *'bewildered and pushed'*].

Even though they rode swift animals, they nevertheless rode *in urgent haste (Ma'amar Mordechai).*

When Haman's decree was dispatched [3:15], the word מְבֹהָלִים— *'bewildered'* — is not used. The couriers were not at all bewildered by a decree calling for the annihilation of Jews because Jews are frequently massacred. So when Haman issued his decree וּדְחוּפִים יָצְאוּ — they dutifully *went hurriedly.* But here, when Mordechai's decree in favor of, and protecting, the Jews was issued — an act without precedent — יָצְאוּ מְבֹהָלִים — they went forth *'bewildered'* — not understanding the King's intentions *(M'nos Halevi).*

וְהַדָּת נִתְּנָה בְּשׁוּשַׁן הַבִּירָה — *And the edict was distributed in Shushan the capitol.* Only after the couriers were urgently dispatched and well on their way — too late for the anti-

Semites in the capitol to influence the King against sending them — was the edict distributed in the capitol itself *(Malbim).*

[See Commentary on 1:2 for difference between שׁוּשַׁן הַבִּירָה — *Shushan the capitol,* and עִיר שׁוּשָׁן—*the city of Shushan.*]

15. וּמָרְדֳּכַי יָצָא — *And Mordechai left...* This verse is a chronological continuation of verse 8 after the parenthetical break of verses 9-14 [see Commentary on verse 9] *(M'nos Halevi).*

Only when Mordechai was completely assured that the Jews would be saved did he allow himself to appear in royal attire *(Alshich).*

[This verse is one of the four verses said aloud in the synagogue by the congregation during the public reading of the *Megillah.* See Commentary on 2:5].

וְהָעִיר שׁוּשָׁן צָהֲלָה וְשָׂמֵחָה—*And the city of Shushan was cheerful and was happy.* 'The city of Shushan' i.e., the residence of the Jews *(Ibn Ezra).*

VIII
14-17

every province, and be published to all peoples so that the Jews should be ready on that day to avenge themselves on their enemies. **14** *The couriers, riders of swift mules, went forth in urgent haste by order of the King, and the edict was distributed in Shushan the capitol.*

Shushan rejoices; the Jews have gladness

15 *Mordechai left the King's presence clad in royal apparel of blue and white with a large gold crown and a robe of fine linen and purple, then the city of Shushan was cheerful and glad.* **16** *The Jews had light and gladness, and joy and honor.* **17** *Likewise, in every province, and in every city, wherever the*

Because Mordechai stumbled about in sackcloth and ashes, he merited promenading about in such grandeur; having torn his clothing for the sake of his people, he merited donning the robes of a monarch; for having put dust on his forehead, he merited wearing a large gold crown; because the city of Shushan had been bewildered, it was filled with cheer and joy (*Rav Galico*).

The joy was so complete that even the stones, so to speak, of Shushan rejoiced (*D'na Pashra*).

16. לַיְהוּדִים הָיְתָה אוֹרָה — *The Jews had light.* Like one who emerges into bright light after having stayed in total darkness for a long time. [So stark was the 'darkness' of the Jewish nation facing impending doom and so brilliant the sudden miracle of the salvation, that the Jews were as blinded as a person emerging from darkness into sunlight.] (*Ibn Ezra; M'nos Halevi*).

'Rav Yehudah said: אוֹרָה — *light*, refers to Torah; שִׂמְחָה — *gladness*,

refers to holiday; שָׂשׂוֹן — *joy*, refers to circumcision; and יְקָר — *honor*, refers to תְּפִילִין — *tefillin* (phylacteries) [i.e. they were finally able to resume the study of Torah without hinderance; so with the holidays, circumcision and tefillin] (*Megillah 16b*).

Why, then, didn't the *Megillah* specifically mention that the Jews had 'Torah, holidays, circumcision and *tefillin*'? The essence of the redemption was that the Jews attained a heightened realization of the true nature of light, gladness, joy, and honor. They once thought that the true source of light is the sun; after the miracle, they realized that Torah is the only true light. Even the most brilliant material light is but a faint approximation in allegorical terms of spiritual light. So it was with the other commandments. The Jews felt gladness, joy, and honor only in the performance of mitzvos (*S'fas Emes*).

[This verse is one of the four verses read aloud in the Synagogue by the Congregation during the

וָעִיר מָקוֹם אֲשֶׁר דְּבַר־הַמֶּלֶךְ וְדָתוֹ מַגִּיעַ
שִׂמְחָה וְשָׂשׂוֹן לַיְּהוּדִים מִשְׁתֶּה וְיוֹם טוֹב
וְרַבִּים מֵעַמֵּי הָאָרֶץ מִתְיַהֲדִים כִּי־נָפַל
פַּחַד־הַיְּהוּדִים עֲלֵיהֶם:

פרק ט ‬א‭ וּבִשְׁנֵים֩ עָשָׂר חֹדֶשׁ הוּא־חֹדֶשׁ אֲדָר
א־ג‭ בִּשְׁלוֹשָׁה עָשָׂר יוֹם בּוֹ אֲשֶׁר הִגִּיעַ דְּבַר־
הַמֶּלֶךְ וְדָתוֹ לְהֵעָשׂוֹת בַּיּוֹם אֲשֶׁר שִׂבְּרוּ
אֹיְבֵי הַיְּהוּדִים לִשְׁלוֹט בָּהֶם וְנַהֲפוֹךְ הוּא
אֲשֶׁר יִשְׁלְטוּ הַיְּהוּדִים הֵמָּה בְּשֹׂנְאֵיהֶם:
ב‭ נִקְהֲלוּ הַיְּהוּדִים בְּעָרֵיהֶם בְּכָל־מְדִינוֹת
הַמֶּלֶךְ אֲחַשְׁוֵרוֹשׁ לִשְׁלֹחַ יָד בִּמְבַקְשֵׁי
רָעָתָם וְאִישׁ לֹא־עָמַד בִּפְנֵיהֶם כִּי־נָפַל
ג‭ פַּחְדָּם עַל־כָּל־הָעַמִּים: וְכָל־שָׂרֵי

public reading of the *Megillah*. See Commentary on 2:5].

17. מִתְיַהֲדִים — *Professed themselves Jews.* They were not accepted as true proselytes because their conversion, motivated by fear, was not genuine. Therefore the verse says מִתְיַהֲדִים —i.e. *'feigned Jewishness'* when they really weren't and had no intention of becoming serious proselytes (*Vilna Gaon*).

[Some commentators say that the amusing Purim custom of masquerading in outlandish costumes is derived from this verse. Just as non-Jews 'masqueraded' as proselytes in order to curry favor, so we masquerade merrily to commemorate the miracle].

IX

1. אֹיְבֵי הַיְּהוּדִים ... הֵמָּה בְּשֹׂנְאֵיהֶם — *The enemies of the Jews ... over their adversaries.* אוֹיֵב, *'enemy'* is one who seeks to personally inflict harm on someone he dislikes; שׂוֹנֵא, *'adversary'* is one who rejoices at

*King's command and his decree reached, the Jews
had gladness and joy, a feast and a holiday.
Moreover, many from among the people of the land
professed themselves Jews; for the fear of the Jews
had fallen upon them.*

IX
1-3

¹ **A**nd so, on the the thirteenth day of the twelfth
month, which is the month of Adar, when the
King's command and edict were about to be en-
forced—on the very day that the enemies of the Jews
expected to gain the upper hand over them—and it
was turned about: The Jews gained the upper hand
over their adversaries; ² the Jews organized
themselves in their cities throughout all the provinces
of King Ahasuerus, to attack those who sought their
hurt; and no one stood in their way, for fear of them
had fallen upon all the peoples. ³ Moreover, all the

The
turnabout:
the Jews
avenge
themselves

the ill-fortune of someone he dislikes even though he himself may
not be inclined to inflict it personally. This is the meaning of the verse:
On the very day when *the enemies*
[אֹויְבִים] of the Jews, planned to inflict bodily harm on the Jews to gain
the upper hand, the tables were
turned and *the Jews prevailed.* So
total was the Jewish victory that
they prevailed even over their
שֹׂונְאִים, lesser enemies, the *adversaries* who did not themselves seek
to inflict bodily harm (*Vilna Gaon*).

[See Commentary on verse 5 for
further distinctions between אֹויֵב,
enemy and שֹׂונֵא, *adversary*].

2. נִקְהֲלוּ הַיְּהוּדִים — *The Jews
organized themselves.* Many Jews
who, under fear of Haman's edict
fled to the anonymity of the smaller
villages where the decree was not
well known and where they could
safely hide, now returned and assembled בְּעָרֵיהֶם — in their cities
(*Rav Arama*).

בִּמְבַקְשֵׁי רָעָתָם — *Who sought their
hurt.* The Jews limited their
vengeance to those who would hurt
them, that is why וְאִישׁ לֹא עָמַד
בִּפְנֵיהֶם — *no one withstood them,*
for fear of them had fallen on all the
peoples (*Yad Hamelech*).

הַמְּדִינוֹת וְהָאֲחַשְׁדַּרְפְּנִים וְהַפַּחוֹת וְעֹשֵׂי
הַמְּלָאכָה אֲשֶׁר לַמֶּלֶךְ מְנַשְּׂאִים אֶת־
הַיְּהוּדִים כִּי־נָפַל פַּחַד־מָרְדֳּכַי עֲלֵיהֶם:
כִּי־גָדוֹל מָרְדֳּכַי בְּבֵית הַמֶּלֶךְ וְשָׁמְעוֹ
הוֹלֵךְ בְּכָל־הַמְּדִינוֹת כִּי־הָאִישׁ מָרְדֳּכַי
הוֹלֵךְ וְגָדוֹל: וַיַּכּוּ הַיְּהוּדִים בְּכָל־אֹיְבֵיהֶם
מַכַּת־חֶרֶב וְהֶרֶג וְאַבְדָן וַיַּעֲשׂוּ בְשֹׂנְאֵיהֶם
כִּרְצוֹנָם: וּבְשׁוּשַׁן הַבִּירָה הָרְגוּ הַיְּהוּדִים
וְאַבֵּד חֲמֵשׁ מֵאוֹת אִישׁ: וְאֵת|

ד

ה

ו

ז

3. כִּי־נָפַל פַּחַד־מָרְדֳּכַי עֲלֵיהֶם —
*Because the fear of Mordechai had
fallen upon them.* The previous
verse refers to פַּחְדָּם —*The fear (of
the Jews);* this verse indicates פַּחַד
מָרְדֳּכַי — *the fear of Mordechai.* To
the general public (verse 2) — who
did not know Mordechai personally
— the "fear of the Jews" sufficed as
a deterrent; but for the officials etc.,
to whom Mordechai was an intimate, familiar personality — and,
even more , who knew him as prime
minister of the entire kingdom—*the
fear of Mordechai,* as an individual,
was the deterrent *(Vilna Gaon).*

There was no lack of people who
were quite ready, as per Haman's
decree — to go out and fight the
Jews, but they did not go, *for the
fear of Mordechai had fallen upon
them.*

4. כִּי גָדוֹל מָרְדֳּכַי — *For Mordechai
was now preeminent* [lit. 'great.']

A government usually has three
high officials: one in charge of the
palace; one for matters of state; and
one for war and foreign affairs.
Mordechai dominated all three
areas. Therefore, the verse tells us
that *Mordechai grew influential*

בְּבֵית הַמֶּלֶךְ — *in the royal palace; his
fame was spreading* בְּכָל־הַמְּדִינוֹת —
throughout all the provinces [i.e. in
matters of state]; *for the man
Mordechai* הוֹלֵךְ וְגָדוֹל — *grew increasingly greater* [in matters of war
and foreign conquests] *(Targum;
Malbim).*

The Commentators remark how,
at first, people assumed that Mordechai's promotion was entirely due
to his role in having saved the King
from assassination. Later they came
to realize what a great man he was
in his own right, and his fame
spread.

5. [After the parenthetical break of
the last two verses, this verse continues the description of what the
assembled Jews did on the 13th of
Adar].

בְּכָל־אֹיְבֵיהֶם — *At all their enemies.*
The Jews tried to establish who
were אוֹיְבִים — *enemies,* and who
were שׂוֹנְאִים — *adversaries.* An אוֹיֵב
— *enemy* is one who openly profes-
ses his hatred while a שׂוֹנֵא — *adversary* is one whose hatred is within
(M'nos Halevi).
According to the *Malbim* the
שׂוֹנְאִים were the outspoken anti-

provincial officials, satraps, and governors and those that conduct the King's affairs, deferred to the Jews because the fear of Mordechai had fallen upon them. ⁴ *For Mordechai was now preeminent in the royal palace and his fame was spreading throughout all the provinces, for the man Mordechai grew increasingly greater.* ⁵ *And the Jews struck at all their enemies with the sword, slaughtering and annihilating; they treated their enemies as they pleased.* ⁶ *In Shushan the capitol, the Jews slew and annihilated five hundred men.* ⁷ *including*

Semites who were slain, and the אוֹיְבִים were those with hatred in their hearts, who were merely subject to humiliation.

6. וּבְשׁוּשָׁן הַבִּירָה — *In Shushan the capitol.* Shushan was divided into two parts [see Commentary on 1:2 s.v. שׁוּשַׁן — 'Shushan'.] The gentiles — many of whom had been staunch supporters of Haman as well as enemies of the Jews — resided in עִיר שׁוּשָׁן — the City of Shushan. The Jews were, therefore, afraid to assemble in the hostile atmosphere of the city of Shushan. Instead they assembled in the palace compound — שׁוּשָׁן הַבִּירָה, *Shushan the capitol* — near to the King and Mordechai where they felt relatively safe. Nevertheless, many gentiles came to avenge Haman's death in arrogant disregard of the close proximity of the King to Mordechai (*M'nos Halevi; Yad Hamelech*).

אִישׁ—*Men.* The emphatic word "אִישׁ" man, [a title of honor used for such great figures as Moses and Mordechai] implies that these five hundred men were prominent people of renown (*Yosef Lekach*).

7⁻10. וְאֵת פַּרְשַׁנְדָּתָא ... עֲשֶׂרֶת בְּנֵי הָמָן— *Including Parshandasa ... the ten sons of Haman.* The names of Haman's ten sons are listed because each one was esteemed and prominent (*Targum*).

The ten sons of Haman and the word עֲשֶׂרֶת, 'ten', which follows, should be said [by one reading the Megillah on Purim] in one breath ... because they all died together (*Megilla 16b*).

'The letter Vav [ו] of *Vayzasa* is enlarged in the Megillah like a long pole to indicate that they were all strung [one underneath the other] on one long pole (*Megilla 16b*).

Each son's name along with the word וְאֵת ["and"] is written on a separate line, one on top of the other in the form of a half brick over a half brick, and a whole brick over a whole brick unlike the other poetic portions in the Torah which are written 'in the form of a half brick over a whole brick. The half brick over whole brick construction (overlapping bricks in the form of all brick structures) adds strength whereas the whole over whole will be weak. Haman's sons are written

וְאֵת |	פַּרְשַׁנְדָּתָא
וְאֵת |	דַּלְפוֹן
וְאֵת |	אַסְפָּתָא:
וְאֵת |	פּוֹרָתָא
וְאֵת |	אֲדַלְיָא
וְאֵת |	אֲרִידָתָא:
וְאֵת |	פַּרְמַשְׁתָּא
וְאֵת |	אֲרִיסַי
וְאֵת |	אֲרִידַי
עֲשֶׂרֶת	וַיְזָתָא:

·סי״א ש׳ זעירא
ת׳ זעירא

·סי״א ר׳ זעירא
ש׳ זעירא

· ו׳ רבתי
· ז׳ זעירא

בְּנֵי הָמָן בֶּן־הַמְּדָתָא צֹרֵר הַיְּהוּדִים הָרָגוּ
יא וּבַבִּזָּה לֹא שָׁלְחוּ אֶת־יָדָם: בַּיּוֹם הַהוּא
בָּא מִסְפַּר הַהֲרוּגִים בְּשׁוּשַׁן הַבִּירָה לִפְנֵי
יב הַמֶּלֶךְ: וַיֹּאמֶר הַמֶּלֶךְ לְאֶסְתֵּר הַמַּלְכָּה
בְּשׁוּשַׁן הַבִּירָה הָרְגוּ הַיְּהוּדִים וְאַבֵּד
חֲמֵשׁ מֵאוֹת אִישׁ וְאֵת עֲשֶׂרֶת בְּנֵי־הָמָן

in this manner so that 'They should never rise again from their downfall' *(Megillah 16a).*

Names of important people are usually written prominently on a separate line. Hence, the ten sons of Haman were so listed, each on an individual line *(Yosef Lekach).*

[Their prominence could not save them from death, thus pointing up to the greatness of the triumph].

The word וְאֵת ['and'] preceding each name is a continuation of חֲמֵשׁ מֵאוֹת אִישׁ 'five hundred men ... and ...' It tells us that each one of Haman's sons was equal in prominence to all the other five hundred enemies of the Jews who were slain in Shushan *(Rav Galico).*

10. עֲשֶׂרֶת בְּנֵי הָמָן — *Haman's ten sons.* These were the ones who had instigated the decree by which Ahasuerus halted the building of the Temple soon after he ascended to the throne *(Meg. 16a; Rashi quoting Seder Olam).*

וּבַבִּזָּה לֹא שָׁלְחוּ אֶת־יָדָם — *But they did not lay their hands on the spoils.* Even though Mordechai's decree seemingly permitted it, the Jews, in unison, did not lay their hands on the spoils. Rather, the spoils went directly to the royal treasuries in order to pacify the King and to make it obvious that the Jews entertained no financial considerations in selecting those they killed *(Rashi;*

IX	*Parshandasa*	*and*
8-12	*Dalphon*	*and*
	Aspasa	[8] *and*
	Porasa	*and*
	Adalia	*and*
	Aridasa	[9] *and*
	Parmashta	*and*
	Arisai	*and*
	Aridai	*and*
	Vaizasa	[10] *the ten*

sons of Haman, son of Hammedasa, the Jews' enemy; but they did not lay their hand on the spoils.

That same day the number of those killed in Shushan the capitol was reported to the King. [12] *The King said unto Queen Esther: 'In Shushan the Capitol the Jews have slain and annihilated five hundred men as well as the ten sons of Haman; what*

Ibn Ezra; D'na Pashra; Megilas Sesarim).

In not enjoying the spoils of its victory, Israel remedied the sin of its ancestors in the days of Saul. Then, they were commanded by Samuel to wage war against Amalek and not to plunder the spoils. They won the war, but ignored the command to desist from looting [see I Samuel 15]. In the time of Mordechai and Esther, that sin was atoned for because the people were permitted to enjoy the spoils, but refrained from doing it (Nachal Eshkol).

[Mordechai was a descendant of King Saul and he corrected Saul's iniquity of allowing Agag to live long enough to beget a son who was the forefather of Haman.]

It was obviously most difficult for poor Jews to restrain themselves from taking spoils. In reward for their restraint, it was established that, throughout all generations, the poor — without exception and investigation as to need — will be the recipients of מַתָּנוֹת לָאֶבְיוֹנִים — 'gifts to the poor' (Gerer Rebbe).

11. מִסְפַּר הַהֲרוּגִים — The number of those killed.

The enemies of the Jews reported the number of prominent Shushanites killed by the Jews that day hoping to kindle the King's anger. But, miraculously, the King did not stop the Jews from continuing on the next day (Rav Galico).

The only Jews who participated in the fighting in Shushan the capitol were those Jews who resided there. Those Jews who resided in the city and were in the capitol only

בִּשְׁאָר מְדִינוֹת הַמֶּלֶךְ מֶה עָשׂוּ וּמַה־
שְׁאֵלָתֵךְ וְיִנָּתֵן לָךְ וּמַה־בַּקָּשָׁתֵךְ עוֹד
יג וְתֵעָשׂ: וַתֹּאמֶר אֶסְתֵּר אִם־עַל־הַמֶּלֶךְ
טוֹב יִנָּתֵן גַּם־מָחָר לַיְּהוּדִים אֲשֶׁר בְּשׁוּשָׁן
לַעֲשׂוֹת כְּדָת הַיּוֹם וְאֵת עֲשֶׂרֶת בְּנֵי־הָמָן
יד יִתְלוּ עַל־הָעֵץ: וַיֹּאמֶר הַמֶּלֶךְ לְהֵעָשׂוֹת
כֵּן וַתִּנָּתֵן דָּת בְּשׁוּשָׁן וְאֵת עֲשֶׂרֶת בְּנֵי־
טו הָמָן תָּלוּ: וַיִּקָּהֲלוּ הַיְּהוּדִיִּים אֲשֶׁר־
בְּשׁוּשָׁן גַּם בְּיוֹם אַרְבָּעָה עָשָׂר לְחֹדֶשׁ
אֲדָר וַיַּהַרְגוּ בְשׁוּשָׁן שְׁלֹשׁ מֵאוֹת אִישׁ
טז וּבַבִּזָּה לֹא שָׁלְחוּ אֶת־יָדָם: וּשְׁאָר
הַיְּהוּדִים אֲשֶׁר בִּמְדִינוֹת הַמֶּלֶךְ נִקְהֲלוּ

temporarily did not participate (Me'am Loez).

12. בִּשְׁאָר מְדִינוֹת הַמֶּלֶךְ מֶה עָשׂוּ—What must they have done in the rest of the King's provinces? The Talmud says that his mode of expression indicates the King was angry, but an angel forced him to speak kindly.

The King said: 'The Jews have slain five hundred men in Shushan the capitol along with Haman's ten sons. I never realized that there were so many violent anti-Semites right here in the capitol. Now I can imagine how many there must have been in other parts of the kingdom, and with what danger you people were faced. Tell me what else you request and it will be granted' (Malbim).

13. וַתֹּאמֶר אֶסְתֵּר — Esther said. By requesting of the King that he officially allow the Jews to avenge themselves in the city of Shushan on the 14th of Adar and to publicly hang Haman's ten sons — requests which were not contained in the King's decree — Esther wanted to make it obvious to everyone that the Jews' actions were in keeping with the King's pleasure, thereby freeing the Jews from all danger of later persecution (Vilna Gaon).

[The Jews avenged themselves in the *capitol* on the first day, but not in the *city* (Commentary 9:6). Esther now sought permission to extend the battle to the city on the next day].

Esther requested that a powerful example be set in Shushan to frighten the enemies of Jewry throughout the realm (Malbim), and to destroy Haman's staunchest supporters. She claimed that this was the only guarantee that the surviving enemies would not attempt to avenge their comrades on the following day (M'nos Halevi).

יִתְלוּ עַל־הָעֵץ — *Be hanged on the gallows.* And thereby make a public spectacle out of them and frighten

must they have done in the rest of the King's provinces! What is your petition now? It shall be granted you. What is your request further? It shall be fulfilled.' ¹³ Esther replied: 'If it pleases His Majesty, allow the Jews who are in Shushan to act tomorrow as they did today, and let Haman's ten sons be hanged on the gallows.' ¹⁴ The King ordered that this be done. A decree was distributed in Shushan, and they hanged Haman's ten sons. ¹⁵ The Jews that were in Shushan assembled again on the fourteenth day of the month of Adar, and slew three hundred men in Shushan; but they did not lay their hand on the spoils.

¹⁶ The rest of the Jews throughout the King's

The Jews in Shushan are granted a second day

all who see them (Megilas Sesarim).

14. וַתִּנָּתֵן דָּת בְּשׁוּשָׁן — A decree was distributed in Shushan. To ensure that the Jews would not be afraid to assemble on the following day, Ahasuerus legalized Esther's request by issuing a formal decree (Alshich).

וְאֵת עֲשֶׂרֶת בְּנֵי־הָמָן תָּלוּ — And they hanged Haman's ten sons. As soon as the decree was issued, Haman's sons were hanged (Maamar Mordechai), and Haman's wife, Zeresh, fled (Targum).

15. שְׁלֹשׁ מֵאוֹת אִישׁ — Three hundred men. Having witnessed the destruction of the previous day, the enemies of the Jews were afraid to show their faces. The Jews, therefore, killed less men that day in the entire city of Shushan than they killed the day before in the capitol alone (Yad Hamelech). Nevertheless, the Jews killed 300 Amalekites who were brazen enough to seek

vengeance for the death of those killed the day before (Ma'amar Mordechai).

וּבַבִּזָּה לֹא שָׁלְחוּ אֶת־יָדָם — But they did not lay their hands on the spoils, on the second day, as well, so they could not be accused of having mercenary interests (Yad Hamelech).

There were those who said that the Jews refrained from looting on 13 Adar only because the number of bodies was overwhelming. On 14 Adar, however, when less were involved, the Jews would surely give way to looting. On this day too, however, they refrained from taking spoils (Ma'amar Mordechai).

16⁻17. [These verses expand upon verse 5 and tell us that שְׁאָר הַיְּהוּדִים — the rest of the Jews; i.e., those who resided outside of Shushan, had organized themselves on the thirteenth of Adar, killing 75,000 of their enemy and abstain-

וְעָמֹד עַל־נַפְשָׁם וְנוֹחַ מֵאֹיְבֵיהֶם וְהָרוֹג
בְּשֹׂנְאֵיהֶם חֲמִשָּׁה וְשִׁבְעִים אֶלֶף וּבַבִּזָּה
לֹא שָׁלְחוּ אֶת־יָדָם: בְּיוֹם־שְׁלוֹשָׁה עָשָׂר   יז
לְחֹדֶשׁ אֲדָר וְנוֹחַ בְּאַרְבָּעָה עָשָׂר בּוֹ
וְעָשֹׂה אֹתוֹ יוֹם מִשְׁתֶּה וְשִׂמְחָה:
וְהַיְּהוּדִיים אֲשֶׁר־בְּשׁוּשָׁן נִקְהֲלוּ   יח
בִּשְׁלוֹשָׁה עָשָׂר בּוֹ וּבְאַרְבָּעָה עָשָׂר בּוֹ
וְנוֹחַ בַּחֲמִשָּׁה עָשָׂר בּוֹ וְעָשֹׂה אֹתוֹ יוֹם
מִשְׁתֶּה וְשִׂמְחָה: עַל־כֵּן הַיְּהוּדִים   יט
הַפְּרוֹזִים הַיֹּשְׁבִים בְּעָרֵי הַפְּרָזוֹת עֹשִׂים
אֵת יוֹם אַרְבָּעָה עָשָׂר לְחֹדֶשׁ אֲדָר
שִׂמְחָה וּמִשְׁתֶּה וְיוֹם טוֹב וּמִשְׁלֹחַ מָנוֹת

יתיר י'   (verse 18 margin)
יתיר ו'   (verse 19 margin)

ing from taking spoils. Unlike the Jews of Shushan who were engaged in battle for two days, the other Jews of the kingdom gained relief from their enemies on the fourteenth of Adar and devoted that day to celebration of the miracle.]

18. [This verse expands upon verses 6 and 15. The Jews of Shushan — the capitol and the city — fought on both the thirteenth and fourteenth of Adar, gained relief from their enemies on the fifteenth, and celebrated on that day.]

וְעָשֹׂה אֹתוֹ יוֹם מִשְׁתֶּה — *Making it a day of feasting.* Despite their exhaustion from a two-day battle, the Jews of Shushan celebrated on the next day because it was clear that there would be no reprisals (*Rav Galico*).

19. הַפְּרָזוֹת — *Unwalled.* [Lit. 'unfortified.'

שִׂמְחָה — *Gladness.* i.e., [a day] on which eulogizing the dead is prohibited (*Meg. 5b*)

וּמִשְׁתֶּה — *And feasting.* i.e., [a day] on which fasting is prohibited (*ibid.*)

וְיוֹם טוֹב — *And holiday-making.* [Lit. 'A holiday']. i.e., [a day] on which מְלָאכָה, 'work' is prohibited (*ibid.*)

[Cessation from מְלָאכָה, work, is the one facet of the Purim observance not instituted by Mordechai nor undertaken for posterity. See commentary to verse 22 s.v. יְמֵי מִשְׁתֶּה 'days of feasting.']

וּמִשְׁלֹחַ מָנוֹת — *Sending delicacies.* The plural מָנוֹת, *ready-to-eat foods,* is used, say the Sages, because each gift must consist of at least two kinds of food (*Megillah 7a*).

[The law of 'Shushan Purim' — celebrating Purim on the 15th day of Adar in walled cities in commemoration of the victory in Shushan — is not specifically stated in the Megillah. It is implied in

provinces organized and defended themselves gaining relief from their foes slaying seventy-five thousand of their enemies — but they did not lay their hand on the spoils. ¹⁷ That was the thirteenth day of the month of Adar; and they gained relief on the fourteenth day, making it a day of feasting and gladness. ¹⁸ But the Jews that were in Shushan assembled on both the thirteenth and fourteenth, and they gained relief on the fifteenth, making it a day of feasting and gladness. ¹⁹ That is why Jewish villagers who live in unwalled towns, celebrate the fourteenth day of the month of Adar as an occasion of gladness and feasting, for holiday-making and for sending delicacies to one another.

verses 19 and 21 and so established by the Rabbis.]

The historical sequence is as follows: The Sanhedrin wanted to establish Purim as a holiday לְפִּירְסוּמֵי נִיסָא to celebrate the miracle of the deliverance. Since the spontaneous celebration throughout the Empire originally took place on the fourteenth of Adar — the day the Jews gained relief from their enemies — Mordechai, as head of the Sanhedrin, proclaimed that day as a festival. Shushan, however, had a miracle all its own and its original celebration was the fifteenth of Adar. Rather than limit the celebration of the fifteenth to Shushan — a city that could hardly be expected to remain Jewish for all time — the Rabbis ordained that the fifteenth, Shushan-Purim, should be celebrated in all cities which, like Shushan, had walls around them. However, this created a problem: Israel lay in ruins at that time, and Jerusa-

lem was unwalled; its status would be inferior to other walled cities throughout the world, and Jerusalem would have to celebrate its Purim on the fourteenth like an ordinary unwalled city. To accord honor to Jerusalem, and to Israel, and to attach the remembrance of Israel in some way to the miracle, the Rabbis decreed that all cities that were walled מִימוֹת יְהוֹשֻׁעַ בֶּן־נוּן — 'from the days of Joshua son of Nun' (who led the conquest of Israel) would celebrate Purim on the fifteenth of Adar, thus including Jerusalem in the celebration. Shushan itself, which was unwalled in the time of Joshua, was accorded a special status 'because the miracle was performed there' (Megillah 2b; Rambam; M'nos Halevi; Torah T'mimah).

There were, of course, many walled cities during the days of Joshua. All of them were destroyed during the course of history, however, and,

פֶּרֶק ט
כ-כב

כ אִישׁ לְרֵעֵהוּ: וַיִּכְתֹּב מָרְדֳּכַי אֶת־הַדְּבָרִים הָאֵלֶּה וַיִּשְׁלַח סְפָרִים אֶל־כָּל־הַיְּהוּדִים אֲשֶׁר בְּכָל־מְדִינוֹת הַמֶּלֶךְ אֲחַשְׁוֵרוֹשׁ כא הַקְּרוֹבִים וְהָרְחוֹקִים: לְקַיֵּם עֲלֵיהֶם לִהְיוֹת עֹשִׂים אֵת יוֹם אַרְבָּעָה עָשָׂר לְחֹדֶשׁ אֲדָר וְאֵת יוֹם־חֲמִשָּׁה עָשָׂר בּוֹ כב בְּכָל־שָׁנָה וְשָׁנָה: כַּיָּמִים אֲשֶׁר־נָחוּ בָהֶם הַיְּהוּדִים מֵאֹיְבֵיהֶם וְהַחֹדֶשׁ אֲשֶׁר נֶהְפַּךְ לָהֶם מִיָּגוֹן לְשִׂמְחָה וּמֵאֵבֶל לְיוֹם טוֹב לַעֲשׂוֹת אוֹתָם יְמֵי מִשְׁתֶּה וְשִׂמְחָה

even though they may have been rebuilt, there is no way of knowing whether they stand today on their original sites. This applies even to Shushan itself. As a result, the only city in the world that definitely celebrates its Purim only on the fifteenth is Jerusalem. The other ancient walled cities read the Megillah with a blessing on the fourteenth and again, without a blessing, on the fifteenth. Those cities are Ashdod, Ashkelon, Beer Sheva, Beit Sha'an, Gush Khalav, Hebron, Haifa, Tiberias, Jaffa, Lod, Gaza, Acco, Safed, Ramleh, and Shechem (Ziv Haminhagim).

20. וַיִּכְתֹּב מָרְדֳּכַי אֶת־הַדְּבָרִים הָאֵלֶּה — *Mordechai recorded these events.* i.e. He wrote this Megillah exactly as it appears in its present text (Rashi).

Mordechai himself recorded these events to ensure the continued annual celebration of the festival of Purim (Ibn Ezra).

It was Mordechai's aim to firmly establish Purim as a festival so that the Jews would never forget the

miracle. He therefore ordained that the Megillah be read annually and that the observance take place on the 14th of Adar in all unwalled cities and on the 15th in the walled cities. He also established that there need not be a cessation from מְלָאכָה — *work* on that festival (Rav Galico).

הַקְּרוֹבִים וְהָרְחוֹקִים — *Near and far.* Mordechai committed these instructions to writing and sent them to all the provinces, the near and far-away villages and walled cities throughout Ahasuerus' empire, and throughout the world (Me'am Loez).

21. לְקַיֵּם עֲלֵיהֶם — *Charging them.* Mordechai's intention was to unify all Jews throughout the world in the celebration — even those Jews who had tried to escape Haman's decree by fleeing, and who, therefore, thought their own personal safety had not been jeopardized (D'na Pashra)

אֵת יוֹם אַרְבָּעָה עָשָׂר לְחֹדֶשׁ אֲדָר וְאֵת יוֹם חֲמִשָּׁה עָשָׂר בּוֹ — *The fourteenth*

IX
20-22

²⁰ *Mordechai recorded these events and sent letters to all the Jews throughout the provinces of King Ahasuerus, near and far,* ²¹ *charging them that they should observe annually the fourteenth and fifteenth days of Adar,* ²² *as the days on which the Jews gained relief from their enemies, and the month which had been transformed for them from one of sorrow to gladness, and from mourning to festivity. They were to observe them as days of feasting and gladness, and*

and fifteenth. . . [i.e. the fourteenth in walled and the fifteenth in unwalled cities].

בְּכָל־שָׁנָה וְשָׁנָה — *Annually.* The festival of Purim will never be abolished even in the days of the Messiah *(Talmud Yerushalmi, Meg. 1:4)*

22. כַּיָּמִים אֲשֶׁר־נָחוּ בָהֶם הַיְּהוּדִים — *As the days on which the Jews gained relief.* The celebration was not to commemorate the *downfall* of our enemies; It is written בִּנְפֹל אוֹיִבְךָ אַל תִּשְׂמָח, *rejoice not at the downfall of your enemy* (Proverbs 24:17). Rather, the celebration is in commemoration of the *redemption and salvation* of the Jews. This is the intent of *'as the days on which the Jews gained relief'.* For this reason the celebration is made — not on the day of victory — but on the day of 'relief' — אֲשֶׁר־נָחוּ. *(Me'am Loez)*

On a leap year — when there are two Adars — Purim is celebrated in the Adar closest to Nissan (i.e., the second Adar) just as the original miracle of Purim occurred on the Adar closest to Nissan and because Nissan is the historic month of Jewish redemption [see commentary

on verse 27] *(M'nos Halevi).*

יְמֵי מִשְׁתֶּה וְשִׂמְחָה . . . וכו׳ — *Days of feasting and gladness . . .* etc. Feasting — eating and drinking and merry-making — was instituted on Purim because the miracles in the Megillah occurred through feasting: the death of Vashti, the coronation of Esther, Haman's downfall. Mordechai permitted work on Purim because it is forbidden to proclaim new holidays similar to those given by the Torah. Instead, he instituted מִשְׁלֹחַ מָנוֹת — *sending delicacies,* and מַתָּנוֹת לָאֶבְיֹנִים — *gifts to the poor (Me'am Loez).*

'As physical life was threatened here and physical life saved; so, apart from the public recital of the story handed down to us perpetuating the event, Purim stresses the enjoyment of festivities, mutual gifts and consideration for our poorer brethren. Together with this we should joyfully remember how life was given to us again, and in this feeling of joy we should each revive the spirit of our common brotherhood and give it greater scope by bringing cheer to our less fortunate ones' *(Rav S. R. Hirsch, Horeb, trans. Dayan Dr. I. Grunfeld).*

פֶּרֶק ט וּמִשְׁלֹחַ מָנוֹת אִישׁ לְרֵעֵהוּ וּמַתָּנוֹת כג־כו
כג לָאֶבְיוֹנִים: וְקִבֵּל הַיְּהוּדִים אֵת אֲשֶׁר־
הֵחֵלּוּ לַעֲשׂוֹת וְאֵת אֲשֶׁר־כָּתַב מָרְדֳּכַי
כד אֲלֵיהֶם: כִּי הָמָן בֶּן־הַמְּדָתָא הָאֲגָגִי צֹרֵר
כָּל־הַיְּהוּדִים חָשַׁב עַל־הַיְּהוּדִים לְאַבְּדָם
וְהִפִּיל פּוּר הוּא הַגּוֹרָל לְהֻמָּם וּלְאַבְּדָם:
כה וּבְבֹאָהּ לִפְנֵי הַמֶּלֶךְ אָמַר עִם־הַסֵּפֶר
יָשׁוּב מַחֲשַׁבְתּוֹ הָרָעָה אֲשֶׁר־חָשַׁב עַל־
הַיְּהוּדִים עַל־רֹאשׁוֹ וְתָלוּ אֹתוֹ וְאֶת־בָּנָיו
כו עַל־הָעֵץ: עַל־כֵּן קָרְאוּ לַיָּמִים הָאֵלֶּה
פוּרִים עַל־שֵׁם הַפּוּר עַל־כֵּן עַל־כָּל־

וּמִשְׁלוֹחַ מָנוֹת אִישׁ לְרֵעֵהוּ — *Sending delicacies to one another* 'At least two gifts [מָנוֹת — *gifts*, being plural] to one man' (*Megillah 7a*).

'The more friends one sends gifts to, the more praiseworthy he is' (*Rambam*).

וּמַתָּנוֹת לָאֶבְיוֹנִים — *And gifts to the poor.* 'That means two gifts to two men', [one gift to each of the two. The minimum number of the plural אֶבְיוֹנִים 'poor' being two] (*Megillah 7a*).

Since everyone, rich and poor alike, had been rescued from mortal danger, Mordechai wanted to ensure that even the poor would have the means to make a feast on this holiday. He, therefore, ordained that alms be given so that all Jews everywhere — regardless of financial capabilites — would be able to celebrate Purim amidst joy (*D'r.a Pashra*).

No investigation should be made of applicants for such Purim money, rather it should be given to anyone who stretches out his hand.

Nor may Purim money be diverted to any other charitable purpose (*Rambam*)

It is preferable to spend more on gifts to the poor than on the Purim meal or on presents to friends. For no joy is greater or more glorious than the joy of gladdening the hearts of the poor, the orphans, the widows, the strangers (*Rambam*).

23. וְקִבֵּל הַיְּהוּדִים — The verb קִבֵּל — 'undertook' [lit. 'accept'] here is in singular form to indicate that all of Jewry united as one in undertaking to continue the celebration yearly (*M'nos Halevi*).

אֲשֶׁר־הֵחֵלּוּ לַעֲשׂוֹת — *To continue the practice they had begun,* [lit. as they had spontaneously begun to do in the year of their deliverance].

אֲשֶׁר־כָּתַב מָרְדֳּכַי — *As Mordechai had prescribed.* The Jews had undertaken to celebrate Purim annually. מִשְׁלוֹחַ מָנוֹת, *sending delicacies,* and מַתָּנוֹת לָאֶבְיוֹנִים, *and gifts to the poor,* however, were not part of the undertaking. They were instituted

for sending delicacies to one another, and gifts to the
poor. ²³ The Jews undertook to continue the practice
they had begun, just as Mordechai had prescribed to
them.

²⁴ For Haman the son of Hammedasa, the Agagite,
enemy of all the Jews, had plotted to destroy the Jews
and had cast a pur (that is, the lot) to terrify and
destroy them; ²⁵ but when she appeared before the
King, he commanded by means of letters that the
wicked scheme, which [Haman] had devised against
the Jews, should recoil on his own head; and they
hanged him and his sons on the gallows. ²⁶ That is
why they called these days "Purim" from the word

by Mordechai and undertaken at his
insistence (M'nos Halevi).

24. הָמָן ... צֹרֵר כָּל־הַיְּהוּדִים —
Haman ...the enemy of all the Jews.
Mordechai wanted to make it
manifestly clear that Haman's
grudge was not a personal one
against him. Like Agag, his
ancestor, Haman was the enemy of
all the Jews, man, woman, and child
(Alshich).

Haman even exceeded Pharaoh in
his cruelty, for Pharaoh's decree
was directed only at the males;
Haman's was against all the Jews
(Me'am Loez).

וְהִפִּל פּוּר . . . לְהֻמָּם וּלְאַבְּדָם — And
had cast a pur to terrify and destroy
them. Haman had been quite confident that he would be able to
destroy the Jews. He cast the lots
only to determine the date that
would be most auspicious for utterly obliterating them from the face of
the earth (Yosef Lekach, M'nos
Halevi).

25. וּבְבֹאָהּ לִפְנֵי הַמֶּלֶךְ — But when
she appeared. i.e. when Esther appeared before the King to beg for
mercy (Rashi).

26. עַל־כֵּן קָרְאוּ — That is why they
called. 'They' i.e. the Sanhedrin
who lived in Mordechai's time
(Alshich).

פּוּרִים — "Purim". Many reasons are
offered for naming the holiday after
the "pur." Among them:

Were it not for the Pur — which
delayed Haman from carrying out
his decree for eleven months, thus
giving Mordechai the opportunity
to pray and abolish the decree,
Haman would have executed his
scheme immediately, and he might
ח"ו have been able to accomplish
his goal (Me'am Loez).

These days were called Purim,
after the lots, as a reminder that the
bad fortune which the stars had dictated for Jewry on those days was
turned into good fortune (Malbim).

The throwing of lots represented

פרק ט
כז־כח

דִּבְרֵי הָאִגֶּרֶת הַזֹּאת וּמָה־רָאוּ עַל־כָּכָה
וּמָה הִגִּיעַ אֲלֵיהֶם: קִיְּמוּ וְקִבֵּל הַיְּהוּדִים |
עֲלֵיהֶם | וְעַל־זַרְעָם וְעַל כָּל־הַנִּלְוִים
עֲלֵיהֶם וְלֹא יַעֲבוֹר לִהְיוֹת עֹשִׂים אֵת־
שְׁנֵי הַיָּמִים הָאֵלֶּה כִּכְתָבָם וְכִזְמַנָּם בְּכָל־
שָׁנָה וְשָׁנָה: וְהַיָּמִים הָאֵלֶּה נִזְכָּרִים
וְנַעֲשִׂים בְּכָל־דּוֹר וָדוֹר מִשְׁפָּחָה
וּמִשְׁפָּחָה מְדִינָה וּמְדִינָה וְעִיר וָעִיר וִימֵי
הַפּוּרִים הָאֵלֶּה לֹא יַעַבְרוּ מִתּוֹךְ

כז
*וְקִבְּלוּ ק׳

only a minor happening in the entire perspective of events. According to the *Gaon Harav Moshe Feinstein* שליט"א, the message of the name "Purim" is that a person should never be over-joyous about his good fortunes. He should never feel so content, safe, and guaranteed in his position that he is no longer in need of praying to G-d or following His precepts. Rather, he must always regard himself as uncertain of his 'lot' and he should recognize the need to communicate to Hashem even after he has attained good fortune. This is evidenced by the fate of Haman: the 'lots' were on his side, but events turned out against him and in favor of the Jews (*Bastion of Faith*).

וּמָה־רָאוּ — *what they had experienced* [lit. 'what they had seen; i.e. from personal experience, as much as Mordechai's decree, made them anxious to accept Purim as a permanent feast].

27. קִיְּמוּ וְקִבְּלוּ הַיְּהוּדִים — *The Jews confirmed and undertook.*

The Talmud explains the verse: וַיִּתְיַצְּבוּ בְּתַחְתִּית הָהָר — *And they stood under the mount* [Exodus

19:17 — in reference to the Jews' receiving the Torah at Mount Sinai] 'Rav Avdimi ben Chama ben Chasa said: This teaches that the Holy One, blessed be He, overturned the mountain over them like a cask, and said to them: "If you accept the Torah, it is well; if not, *there* shall be your grave." Rav Acha ben Jacob observed: This furnishes a strong protest against the Torah [i.e., this provides an excuse for non-observance, since the Torah was imposed by threat of death thus rendering its acceptance invalid.] Said Rava: Yet, even so, they re-accepted it in the days of Ahasuerus, for it is written: קִיְּמוּ וְקִבְּלוּ they confirmed and undertook — i.e., they confirmed what they had undertaken long before' (*Shabbos* 88a).

The *S'fas Emes* pointed out that just as the first acceptance of the Torah followed a victorious war with Amalek, here, too, the war with Amalek's descendant, Haman was followed by a re-acceptance of the Torah (see introduction).

Now, [even though the *spelling* of וְקִבֵּל is in the singular, the pronunciation] קִיְּמוּ וְקִבְּלוּ is in plural

אסתר [130]

IX
27-28

"pur". Therefore, because of all that was written in this letter, and because of what they had experienced, and what had happened to them, ²⁷ the Jews confirmed and undertook upon themselves, and their posterity, and upon all who might join them, to observe these two days, without fail, in the manner prescribed, and at the proper time each year: ²⁸ Consequently, these days should be remembered and celebrated by every single generation, family, province, and city; and these days of Purim should never cease among the Jews, nor shall their

---

form to demonstrate that the Jews confirmed and undertook to celebrate the holiday upon themselves and their children [This is indicated by the contrast between this and the earlier reference to Jewish acceptance of Purim (verse 23) which is entirely in the singular.] *(Yosef Lekach).*

הַנִּלְוִים עֲלֵיהֶם — *Who might join them.* i.e. future גֵּרִים - *proselytes.* They, too, were indirectly affected by the decree of annihilation because Haman wanted to unroot the faith they would some day embrace *(Vilna Gaon).*

כִּכְתָבָם — *in the manner prescribed* [lit. 'in accordance with their writing']. The Sages interpret this to include the law of reading the Megillah on the evening and morning of Purim and its various details *(Megillah 19a).*

בְּכָל־שָׁנָה וְשָׁנָה — *each year.* [lit. 'each and every year']. According to the Talmud *(Meg. 6b)* in a leap year when there is a second Adar, Purim is observed in the second Adar. בְּכָל שָׁנָה וְשָׁנָה — *'each and every*

year': Just as in most years Adar adjoins Nissan, so in a leap year, as well, Purim is celebrated in the Adar adjoining Nissan. 'But,' the Talmud asks, 'Adar also adjoins Shevat?' To which the answer given is: מְסָמֵךְ גְּאוּלָה לִגְאוּלָה עֲדִיף, more weight is to be attached to bringing one period of redemption close to another [i.e. Purim to Passover].

28. נִזְכָּרִים—*Remembered.* By reading the Megillah *(Rashi).*

וְנַעֲשִׂים — *And celebrated.* With feast, gladness, delicacies, and gifts *(Rashi).*

מִשְׁפָּחָה וּמִשְׁפָּחָה — *By every single family,* who assemble to eat and drink together, thus undertaking that the days of Purim לֹא יַעַבְרוּ — *should never cease (Rashi).*

The verse specified *every single generation, family, province, and city,* to make clear that no one may claim that he resides in a country that didn't exist or where no Jews lived at the time of the miracle, and is, therefore, free from the obligation to observe Purim . . .

Rather, *the days of Purim should*

פֶּרֶק ט הַיְּהוּדִים וְזִכְרָם לֹא־יָסוּף מִזַּרְעָם: כט־לא
כט וַתִּכְתֹּב אֶסְתֵּר הַמַּלְכָּה בַת־אֲבִיחַיִל יֵת רבתי
וּמָרְדֳּכַי הַיְּהוּדִי אֶת־כָּל־תֹּקֶף לְקַיֵּם אֵת
ל אִגֶּרֶת הַפֻּרִים הַזֹּאת הַשֵּׁנִית: וַיִּשְׁלַח
סְפָרִים אֶל־כָּל־הַיְּהוּדִים אֶל־שֶׁבַע
וְעֶשְׂרִים וּמֵאָה מְדִינָה מַלְכוּת
לא אֲחַשְׁוֵרוֹשׁ דִּבְרֵי שָׁלוֹם וֶאֱמֶת: לְקַיֵּם

never cease from among the Jews and no one is exempt from its observance (Ibn Ezra, M'nos Halevi).

לֹא יַעַבְרוּ — Should never cease. 'Even if all the festivals should be annulled, Purim will never be annulled' (Midrash).

The Talmud [taking the words לֹא יַעַבְרוּ, should not cease, and לֹא יָסוּף, not perish, as a prophetic promise rather than an injunction] quotes this verse as further proof that the Book of Esther was composed under the inspiration of רוּחַ הַקֹּדֶשׁ — the holy spirit [for how else could the authors of the Megillah know that 'Purim will never cease from among the Jews?] (Megillah 7a).

29. וַתִּכְתֹּב — Wrote. The letter ת in this word is enlarged to indicate that just as the ת is the last letter of the alphabet, so is the story of Esther the end of all the miracles to be included in the Bible ([Yoma 29a]; Me'am Loez).

וַתִּכְתֹּב אֶסְתֵּר — Then Esther wrote. Esther elaborated upon all that Mordechai had written earlier, making clear that the apparently natural events leading up to Haman's downfall and the Jewish salvation were but manifestations of the hand of G-d, and that they were brought

about by prayers, fasting, and supplication (Alshich, Yosef Lekach)

בַת־אֲבִיחַיִל — Daughter of Avichail. Having finally been able to reveal her identity as a Jewess after having had to conceal it for so long, Esther is proud to mention her father's name publicly (Me'am Loez)

אֶת־כָּל־תֹּקֶף — With full authority. [lit. 'all the power'].

According to Rashi:, תּוֹקְפּוֹ שֶׁל נֵס — all the power of the miracle: of Ahasuerus, of Haman, of Mordechai and of Esther. [i.e. that each one of these were instrumental on the miracle].

'Hitherto they had not used Esther's authority, for they preferred that the people accept voluntarily the practice of Purim without the power of government to overawe them. But after the nation had voluntarily accepted Purim as an eternal practice, Esther and Mordechai supported it with the royal authority' (Torah Nation).

לְקַיֵּם — to ratify. Once Esther and Mordechai were assured that the Jews had accepted Purim, they wrote this second letter with "all their authority to ensure that the Jews would never — even in later generations — abolish observance of this festival out of fear of their

remembrance perish from their descendants.
²⁹ Then Queen Esther, daughter of Avichail, and Mordechai the Jew, wrote with full authority to ratify this second letter of Purim. ³⁰ Dispatches were sent to all the Jews, to the hundred and twenty-seven provinces of the kingdom of Ahasuerus — with words of peace and truth — ³¹ to establish these days

rulers, wherever they might be (M'nos Halevi)

The Megillah spans a history of nine years, from the third to the twelfth year of Ahasuerus' reign. A layman could never recognize that the Jews' refusal to obey Mordechai's plea not to attend Ahasuerus' feast would result in a dramatic, but seemingly unconnected, series of events over the next nine years.

The common people 'knew' that Haman's decree was caused by Mordechai's obstinate refusal to bow. They held him responsible for the mortal danger to the nation. Mordechai knew better. He knew that the decree was in punishment for the Jews' weakness in enjoying the forbidden feast. He knew that refusal to bow was the first step in a chain of courage and repentance that, alone, could save his people.

When he and Esther wrote the Megillah, he began the story with the feast of Ahasuerus because their participation was the cause of the evil decree, which, was annulled as a result of their sincere repentance — a full nine years later.

The Megillah teaches us that our leaders discern much more than we; ultimate salvation lies in submission to their authority (Rav Eliyahu Dessler).

30. דִּבְרֵי שָׁלוֹם וֶאֱמֶת — with words of peace and truth. According to the Talmud, the Torah is called 'Truth' and the Megillah is compared to it in its ritual requirements. 'This shows that the Megillah must be written with ruled lines, like the 'true essence' of the Torah (Meg. 16b).

Just as the Torah is open to interpretation [to uncover its deeper meaning — (Torah T'mimah)], so is the Megillah open to interpretation (Yerushalmi, Megillah 1:1)

Another meaning is: Esther began her letter to the 127 provinces with greetings of peace as one usually begins a letter (D'na Pashra).

At the same time she admonished the Jews to live a life of שָׁלוֹם וֶאֱמֶת — peace and truth — and thus ensure the rebuilding of the Temple (Me'am Loez).

31. Mordechai and Esther realized that people might ask by what right they instituted a new festival and made it binding on all future generations without direct Biblical precedent. Esther and Mordechai tell us in this verse that it was their aim that Purim be accepted by future generations 'just as they undertook upon themselves and their posterity the matter of

אֶת־יְמֵי הַפֻּרִים הָאֵלֶּה בִּזְמַנֵּיהֶם
כַּאֲשֶׁר קִיַּם עֲלֵיהֶם מָרְדֳּכַי הַיְּהוּדִי
וְאֶסְתֵּר הַמַּלְכָּה וְכַאֲשֶׁר קִיְּמוּ עַל־נַפְשָׁם
וְעַל־זַרְעָם דִּבְרֵי הַצּוֹמוֹת וְזַעֲקָתָם:

לב וּמַאֲמַר אֶסְתֵּר קִיַּם דִּבְרֵי הַפֻּרִים הָאֵלֶּה
וְנִכְתָּב בַּסֵּפֶר:

א וַיָּשֶׂם הַמֶּלֶךְ אֲחַשְׁ׳ֵרֹשׁ|מַס עַל־הָאָרֶץ
ב וְאִיֵּי הַיָּם: וְכָל־מַעֲשֵׂה תָקְפּוֹ וּגְבוּרָתוֹ
וּפָרָשַׁת גְּדֻלַּת מָרְדֳּכַי אֲשֶׁר גִּדְּלוֹ הַמֶּלֶךְ
הֲלוֹא־הֵם כְּתוּבִים עַל־סֵפֶר דִּבְרֵי הַיָּמִים
ג לְמַלְכֵי מָדַי וּפָרָס: כִּי|מָרְדֳּכַי הַיְּהוּדִי
מִשְׁנֶה לַמֶּלֶךְ אֲחַשְׁוֵרוֹשׁ וְגָדוֹל לַיְּהוּדִים

---

fasts and their lamentations, i.e., just as the Jews undertook to observe the four fasts instituted by the Prophets (Tenth of Teves, Seventeenth of Tammuz, Ninth of Av, and the Fast of Gedaliah) — even though there is no direct Torah authority for their imposition. In a like manner, should the Jews undertake the celebration of Purim for themselves and their

children (M'nos Halevi).

32. וּמַאֲמַר אֶסְתֵּר קִיַּם — Esther's ordinance validated. Esther requested from the Sages of her time to commemorate her [lit. 'fix' her] and to include this book among the other [sacred] Writings. This is the meaning of וְנִכְתָּב בַּסֵּפֶר, and it was recorded in the book (Rashi) [See introduction].

X

1. וַיָּשֶׂם...מַס — Levied taxes. [This verse tells us that with the salvation of the Jews, affairs of state returned to normal. Under Mordechai, the empire grew stronger.]

'These words, inserted to accord honor to the Persian government, were necessary to demonstrate that the Megillah does not deal solely with the triumph of the Jews. This

IX
32

of Purim on their proper dates just as Mordechai the Jew and Queen Esther had enjoined them, and as they had undertook upon themselves and their posterity the matter of the fasts and their lamentations. ³² Esther's ordinance validated these regulations for Purim; and it was recorded in the book.

X
1-3

¹ King Ahasuerus levied taxes on both the mainland and the islands. ² All his mighty and powerful acts, and a full account of the greatness of Mordechai, whom the King had promoted, are recorded in the book of chronicles of the Kings of Media and Persia. ³ For Mordechai the Jew was viceroy to King Ahasuerus; he was a great man

demonstrates clearly that the Megillah *was completed* in the early days of the Great Assembly, when Persia was still powerful and all the Jews were still its subjects. (Thus is demolished the fantasy of the "Bible-critics" that the book of Esther was composed in the time of the Hasmoneans, long after the Persians had lost their power to the Greeks)' (*Torah Nation*).

מַס ... וְאִיֵּי הַיָּם — *taxes ... the islands.* This verse supports the Midrashic statement that Ahasuerus' 127 provinces consisted of 100 provinces on the mainland, and 27 on islands. The *Vilna Gaon* ingeniously points out that the גִּימַטְרִיָא — numerical value of מַס,

taxes (which were imposed on the mainland), is 100; the numerical value of וְאִיֵּי (*the islands*) is 27!

2. גְּדֻלַת מָרְדְּכַי — *The greatness of Mordechai:* It was made clear that Ahasuerus' newly gained stature was the result of Mordechai's service to him (*Ibn Ezra*)

3. לְרֹב אֶחָיו — *With the multitude of his brethren.* [lit. 'with the majority of his brethren']. It is impossible for someone to achieve *universal* acceptance because of jealousy and rivalry (*Ibn Ezra*).

The Talmud states: 'Of the *majority* of his brethren, but not *all* of his brethren; this informs us that

[135]   *Esther*

פֶּרֶק י וְרָצוּי לְרֹב אֶחָיו דֹרֵשׁ טוֹב לְעַמּוֹ וְדֹבֵר
שָׁלוֹם לְכָל־זַרְעוֹ:

some members of Sanhedrin parted from him [because, having become close to the government, he neglected his study of Torah, — (Rashi)] (Megillah 16b).

דֹרֵשׁ טוֹב לְעַמּוֹ — He sought the good of his people. He did not wait until asked; he actively sought opportunities to do good (Ibn Ezra).

He appropriated the monies he took from Haman's house toward the eventual re-construction of the Temple (Midrash Lekach Tov).

X   among the Jews, and popular with the multitude of
his brethren; he sought the good of his people and
was concerned for the welfare of all his posterity.

וְדֹבֵר שָׁלוֹם לְכָל־זַרְעוֹ — *And was
concerned for the welfare of all
his posterity. [lit. 'Speaking peace
to all his seed'].* Thus, with the

blessing of peace, and a picture of
the stature and security of the
Jews under Mordechai, the Megillah closes.

תם ונשלם שבח לאל בורא עולם

Bibliography
of Authorities Cited in the Commentary

Italics are used to denote the name of a work. **Bold italics** *within the biography indicate the specific book of that particular author cited in the commentary.*

An asterisk (*) precedes the names of contemporary figures

Abba Gorion:
See *Midrash Abba Gorion*

Abudarham, David ben Joseph:
[also pronounced 'Abudraham.']
Born in Seville, Spain in 1340. According to some, he was a student of R. Yaakov ben Asher, author of the *Turim.* Author of *Sefer Abudarham,* a collection of Halachos based on the order of prayers in the *Siddur.* He commented on the prayers in great detail and traced the variations in customs of different countries. The book was first published in 1490, and is quoted many times in the *Shulchan Aruch.*

Akedas Yitzchak:
See Arama, Rav Yitzchak b. Moshe.

Alkabetz, Rav Shlomo Halevi:
[b. 1505-Salonica; d. 1576 Safed]
One of the greatest Kaballists and mystical poets of his day. Author of the Piyyut 'L'cha Dodi' recited every Friday evening. He was a contemporary and friend of Rav Yosef Karo, author of *Shulchan Aruch.*

Rav Shlomo sent his father-in-law his commentary on Megillas Esther, *M'nos Halevi,* which he had finished that year, in lieu of 'Mishloach Manos.' They received the gift warmly and treasured it 'more than they would gifts of silver and gold.'

In his Piyyut, 'L'cha Dodi,' he speaks of the sufferings of the Jewish people and their aspirations for Redemption. Probably no other Piyyut has reached the popularity of 'L'cha Dodi;' it is recited every Friday by all Jewish congregations throughout the world.

Alshich, Rav Moshe:
[Also spelled Alshekh]
Rav, Posek, and Bible Commentator. Born in Andrionople in 1508, studied Torah there in Yeshiva of Rav Yosef Karo. Settled in Safed where he spent most of his life and was ordained there by Rav Karo with the full Semichah reintroduced by Rav Yaakov Berav. Died while travelling in Damascus in 1600

He wrote Commentaries on most of the Bible. His *Mas'as Moshe* on Esther was published by his son in 1601.

Alter, Rav Yehudah Leib:
(1847-1905)
Gerrer Rebbe; son of Rav Avraham Mordechai, the eldest son the 'Chidushei HaRim'. He was orphaned as a child and was brought up and educated largely by his grandfather. In 1870, after the death of Rav Henach of Alexandrow, he became Rebbe of Ger.

The Rebbe devoted much energy promoting Torah study and attracted many youths. His writings are collected under the title *S'fas Emes,* by which name he is also known.

Alter, Rav Yitzchak Meir:
(1789-1866)
Gerrer Rebbe; founder of the Gerrer Chassidic dynasty. Rav Yitzchak Meir was a disciple of the Maggid of Koznitz, and later of Rav Simcha Bunem of Pshyscha, and of Rav Menachem Mendel of Kotzk.

After the Kotzker's death in 1859, Rav Yitzchak Meir was acknowledged Rebbe by the majority of Kotzk Chassidim.

His influence was far-reaching. Although his leadership lasted only seven years, he had a formative influence on the development of Chassidus in Poland. Gerrer Chassidus became a powerful element in Orthodox Polish Jewry.

He wrote *Chiddushei haRim,* novellae on the Talmud and *Shulchan Aruch,* and was frequently referred to by the name of his work, "The Chiddushei haRim."

Arama, R. Meir b. Yitzchak:

[1460?-c.1545] Spanish Rabbi, born in Saragossa. Expelled from Spain by inquisition in 1492. Moved to Naples and in 1495 settled and became Rabbi in Salonica. Wrote a commentary to *Esther* falsely attributed to his father, Rav Yitzchak, author of *Akedas Yitzchak,* and which appears in almost all editions of that book.

Arama, Rav Yitzchak b. Moshe:

(1420-1494) Spanish Rav, philosopher and preacher. He was Rav of Calatayud where he wrote most of his works. After expulsion of Jews from Spain, in 1492, he settled in Naples, where he died.

He is best known for his book *Akedas Yitzchak,* a collection of allegorical commentaries on the Torah. First published in 1522, it has been reprinted many times and has exercised great influence on Jewish thought.

It should be noted that the commentary to *Megillas Esther,* extant in all editions of *Akedas Yitzchak* since Venice, 1573, is actually the work of his son, Meir. [See above.]

Yitzchak's own **Commentary on Esther** was published in Constantinople, 1518.

Ashkenazy, Rav Eliezer b. Eliyahu Harofe:

Born 1513 (?). Died 1586 in Cracow. Considered one of the leaders of his generation. He was a student of Rav Yosef Caro, author of *Shulchan Aruch,* and a close friend of Rav Moshe Alshich. For 22 years he was the Torah leader in Egypt, and was greatly known for his piety and learning.

His first work, **Yosef Lekach** on *Megillas Esther* was published in 1566 and brought him much praise from his contemporaries. He wrote *Maasei Hashem* on the deeper meanings of the stories in the Torah, and wrote many Responsa, his answers to Halachic query having been accepted as authoritative.

Attar, Rav Chaim b. Moshe, Ibn:

(1696-1763)
Rav and Kabbalist. Born in Morocco, moved to Leghorn en route to Israel In 1741, he reached Israel and established a Yeshivah in Jerusalem, 'Midrash Knesses Israel Yeshivah.' Rav Chaim ibn Attar died a year after settling in Jerusalem.

His best known and most important work is the **Or Hachaim,** his commentary on the Torah, often published in most large editions of the Bible.

Rav Avraham Ibn Ezra:

(Born 1089 in Toledo; died 1164).

Famous poet, philosopher, grammarian, scientist, astronomer, — and above all — Biblical commentator. He also wrote a commentary on the *Megillos* — including Esther. In all his Bible commentaries he strived for the plain, literal meaning of the verse. His aim was to explain the etymology of difficult words within their grammatical context. Next to Rashi, his commentary on the Torah is most widely studied, and appears in almost all large editions of the Bible.

In France, he met Rav Yaakov Tam ['Rabbeinu Tam' — grandson of Rashi] and a deep friendship between the two followed.

According to some, he married the daughter of Rav Yehudah Halevi, and had five sons.

Legend has it that he once met the Rambam [Maimonides] and dedicated a poem to him that he wrote on the day of his death.

Azulai, Rav Chaim Yosef David:

Known by his Hebrew acronym CHIDA. Born in Jerusalem in 1724; died in Leghorn in 1806. Halachist, Kabbalist, and bibliographer/historian, he possessed great intellectual powers and many-faceted talents.

He went abroad as an emissary and he would send large sums of money back to Israel. He ended his mission in 1778 in Leghorn where he spent the rest of his life.

His fame as a halachist rest on his glosses to *Shulchan Aruch,* contained in his *Birkei Yosef,* a work constantly quoted by later authorities.

He was the author of the famous bibliographic work *Shem-Hagedolim.* Among his many works was the homiletic *Nachal Eshkol.*

Rav Bachya ben Asher:

(also pronounced B'chayai):
(Lived in Saragossa, Spain, mid 13th century.) He was one of the foremost students of R. Shlomo ben Aderes *(Rashba).* His most famous work was his commentary on the Torah written in 1291. His *Kad Hakemach* on the foundations of faith had wide circulation. Among his many other works was a commentary on the *Book of Esther* based on the interpretation of the Ibn Ezra "who wrote the most accurate commentary of all on the Megillah. He died in 1340.

Bastion of Faith:

by Rav Avraham Fishelis. (See Feinstein, Rav Moshe.)

Belzer Rebbe:

See — Rokeach, Rav Aharon.

Chidushei HaRim:

See Alter, Rav Yitzchak Meir .

Chortkover, Rebbe:

See Friedmann, Rav Shlomo.

Chullin:

Talmudic tractate in *Seder Kodashim.*

Dessler, Rav Eliyahu Eliezer:

(1891-1954)

One of the outstanding personalities of the Mussar movement. He was born in Homel, Russia.

In 1929 he settled in London and became the Rav of several synagogues. He exercised a profound influence on the teaching of Mussar, not only because of the profundity of his ideas, but also on account of his personal, ethical conduct.

In 1941 he became director of the Kollel of Gateshead Yeshiva in London.

In 1947, at the invitation of Rav Yosef Kahaneman, he became Mashgiach of Ponovez Yeshiva in Bnei Brak, Israel, and there he remained until his death.

His teachings reflect a harmonious mixture of Mussar, Kaballah, and Chassidus. Some of his ideas were published by his pupils in *Michtav Me-Eliyahu* (3 vols. 1955-64).

D'na Pashra:

See Rav Eliyahu Shlomo Avraham haKohen.

Eidels, Rav Shmuel Eliezer b. Yehudah haLevi

(Known as MaHaRSHA — Moreinu Ha Rav Shmuel Eliezer.)

1555-1631. One of the foremost Talmud commentators, whose commentary is included in almost every edition of Talmud.

Born in Cracow, he moved to Posen in his youth. In 1614 he became Rav of Lublin and in 1625 of Ostrog, where he founded a large Yeshivah.

Rav Eleazar b. Yehudah of Worms:

[*Heb.* Eleazar of Germeiza]. Also known as *Baal HaRokeach.* 1160-1237.

Scholar in the fields of Halachah, Kaballah, and Paytan in midieval Germany. Student of Rav Yehudah haChassid the author of *Sefer Chasidim.*

Rav Eleazar is known primarily for his halachic work *Sefer Rokeach.* His students were many, among them Rav Yitzchak of Vienna, author of *Or Zarua.* Among his exegetical works are **Shaarei Binah.**

Rav Eliyahu Shlomo Avraham haKohen:

(d. 1729)

Born in Smyrna, he spent most of his life there as *Dayyan* and *Rav.*

His most famous works are *Shevet Mussar* on ethics and homiletics; *Midrash halttamari,* a homiletical work on ethical subjects. Because of this work, he became known as Rav Eliyahu halttamari. He also wrote *Midrash Talpiot,* novellae on various subjects arranged alphabetically; and **D'na Pashra** [abbreviated: *Perush SHir Hashirim, Ruth Esther*] commentary on three *Megillos* — *Song of Songs, Ruth, and Esther.*

Rav Eliyahu ben Shlomo Zalman of Vilna:

Also known as the "Vilna Gaon;" acronym haGRA = haGaon Rav Eliyahu. Born, 1st day of Passover 1720; died 3rd day of Chol Hamoed Sukkos 1797.

One of the greatest spiritual leaders of Jewry in modern times. A child prodigy and man of phenominal genius, his knowledge of every facet of Torah learning was without equal. His glosses and commentaries encompassed nearly every one of the important classical writings.

Epstein, Rav Baruch haLevi:

(1860-1940). Born in Bobruisk, Russia. received early education from his father, Rav Yechiel Michel Epstein, author of *Aruch haShulchan.* Rav Baruch later studied under his uncle, Rav Naftali Zvi Yehudah Berlin [the 'Netziv']. He is best known for his brilliant commentary **Torah Temimah.**

Eshkol Hakofer:

See Sava, Rav Avraham b. Yaakov.

Even Shoham:

Commentary on *Megillah* by Rav Shlomo Chanoch Henoch.

Eybeschuetz, Rav Yonassan b. Nassan Nata:

Rav, and one of the greatest Torah scholars of his generation.

Born in 1690 in Cracow, served as Rosh Yeshiva in Prague. Served as Rav of the "Three Communities" — Altona, Hamburg, and Wandsbek until his death in 1796. Published extensively on Halachah and Bible. His most famous Halachic works were *Urim U'Tummim* on Choshen Mishpat (1775), and *K'resi Upleisi* on Yoreh Deah. His homiletic work, **Ya'aros D'vash,** published posthumously, was reprinted many times.

*Feinstein, Rav Moshe:

Contemporary Posek, and Rosh Yeshiva, Harav Feinstein is considered by many to be the *Gadol Hador* — Torah leader of this generation.

Born in Russia in 1895, Harav Feinstein was known as a child prodigy. He came to America in 1937 and became Dean of Mesivtha Tifereth Jerusalem in New York's lower East side. Harav Feinstein responds to Halachic inquiries from around the world daily. Author of *'Igrose Moshe'* — 5 volumes of his Halachic responsa; and an ongoing series of *Dibrose Moshe* — his novellae on Talmud.

Some of Rabbi Feinstein's homiletic lectures were collected and published by Rabbi Avraham Fishelis in *Kol Ram* (Hebrew; 2 vols.) and *Bastion of Faith* (English).

Friedmann, Rav Shlomo:

(1894-1959) Chortkkover Rebbe, of the illustrious Rizhiner dynasty. Resided in Israel. Member of Agudath Israel's Moetzes Gedolei Torah [Council of Rabbinic Sages]; Son of Rav Nachum Mordechai (1854-1934); author of *Tiferes Yisrael.*

Galico, Rav Elisha ben Gavriel:

Prominent Talmudist and Kaballist of the early 16th Century. Member of Rabbinical Court of Rav Yosef Karo in Safed.

Rav Galico's Halachic responsa are quoted in *Knesses Hagedolah*. His famous **Commentary on Megillas Esther** was published in Venice in 1582, the year of his death.

GRA:
See Eliyahu (ben Shlomo Zalman) of Vilna.

Hirsch, Rav Shamshon Raphael:
(1808-1888). The father of modern German Orthodoxy, he was a fiery leader, brilliant writer, and profound educator. His greatness as a Talmudic scholar was obscured by his other monumental accomplishments. After becoming Chief Rabbi and member of Parliament in Austria, he left to revitalize Torah Judaism in Frankfort-am-Main. He transformed it into Torah bastion. His best known works are the classic six-volume commentary on *Chumash*, and **Horeb**, a philosophical analysis of the mitzvos.

Ibn Ezra:
See Rav Avraham Ibn Ezra.

Imrei Moshe:
By Rav Moshe Rapaport.

Isserles, Rav Moshe:
(Known as RaMA).
(c. 1525-1572) Polish Rav and codifier, one of the great Halachic authorities. His contemporaries considered him to be "The Rambam of Polish Jewry," and he can be compared to the Rambam in many ways.

When Rav Yosef Caro published his *Bais Yoseph* on the *Tur*, Rav Moshe Isserles simultaneously had written his *Darkei Moshe* which he later condensed. He utilized the *Darkei Moshe* as a basis for his glosses on Rav Yosef Caro's *Shulchan Aruch*. Published as **'Hagahos'** or 'ha-Mappah,' it contained the custom of the Ashkenazi scholars ignored by the *Shulchan Aruch*. By spreading his *Mappah* ('Tablecloth'), so to speak, over the *Shulchan Aruch* ('Prepared Table') — which had codified Sephardic prac-

tice — Rav Moshe Isserles, in fact, made that work acceptable to Ashkenazim as well as Sephardim.

Generally, the rulings of Rav Moshe Isserles were accepted as binding on Ashkenazi Jewry.

Jaffe, Rav Mordechai:
(1535-1612). Talmudist, Kabbalist. Born in Prague, he was sent as a little boy to study under Rav Shlomo Luna (Ra-SHaL) and Rav Moshe Isserles (RaMA). Became Rosh Yeshivah in Prague in 1533.

When Rav Yosef Caro's *Beis Yosef* appeared, Rav Mordechai found it overlong, and so began to write his *"Levush Malchus."* Later, the *Shulchan Aruch* appeared with the gloss of Rav Moshe Isserles, and Rav Mordechai put aside his work only to re-consider many years later. He published his work — **The Levushim** encompassing all of *Shulchan Aruch*, as well as a commentary on Maimonides, Rashi, astronomy — "as a work that will be midway between the two extremes: the lengthy *Beis Yosef* of Rav Caro on the one hand, and on the other, Caro's *Shulchan Aruch* together with the *Mappah* of Rav Isserles, which is too brief."

Kad Hakemach:
See Rabbenu Bachya b. Asher.

*Kitov, Rav Eliyahu:
Contemporary Israeli scholar, and author. Famous for his *Ish Ubeiso*, ("The Jew and His Home"), **Sefer HaTodaah** ('-'The Book of Seasons"), both translated into English by Rav Nathan Bulman; and his ongoing series of *Sefer haParshiot* on the Five Books of the Bible.

Kol Bo:
Early work on Halacha. Quoted as authoritative by all later authorities and by *Shulchan Aruch*. Authorship uncertain.

Kol Rinah:
Commentary on *Megillas Esther* by Rav Moshe Chai Milul.

Lekach Tov:
See *Midrash Lekach Tov.*

Levush:
See Jaffe, Rav Mordechai.

Lorberbaum, Rav Yaakov b. Yaakov Moshe of Lissa:
(1760-1832). Polish Rav and Halachist. His father died before he was born. In 1809, he became Rav of Lissa, a long-time Torah-center in Poland. Together with Rav Akiva Eger and the Chassam Sofer, he vehemently opposed and attacked the *Maskilim* and reformers. After he published his *Chavas Da'as* on *Yosh De'ah,* he was acknowledged as an outstanding *Posek.* Among his writings were *Imre Yosher,* a comprehensive commentary on the Five Megillos, each published at a different place and time, the commentary on *Megillas Esther,* being called **Megillas Sesarim,** printed in large editions of the Bible.

Ma'amar Mordechai:
Commentary by Rav Shem Tov b. Yaakov Melamed. Mid. 16th Century.

Maharsha:
See Eidels, Rav Shmuel Eliezer b. Yehudah haLevi.

Maimonides:
See Rambam.

Malbim, Rav Meir Leibush:
(1809-1879). Rav, preacher, and Biblical commentator.

The name Malbim is an acronym of "Meir Leibush ben Yechiel Michel." The Malbim was also known as the 'illui [prodigy] from Volhynia.' He was Rav in several cities, but he suffered much persecution because of his uncompromising stand against Reform which led to his short-term imprisonment on a false accusation. He wandered much of his life, serving as Rav in various cities for several years at a time.

His fame and immense popularity rest upon his widely esteemed commentary on the Bible. His first published commentary was on **Megillas Esther** (1845). His commentaries on the remaining Books of the Bible were published between then and 1876.

Me'am Loez:
An 18th-Century homiletical Bible commentary in Ladino. The outstanding work of Judeo-Spanish literature. A commentary of an encyclopaedic nature begun by Rav Yaakov Culi (1685-1732) of whom the Chidah in *Shem Hagedolim* speaks in the most superlative of adjectives. No work designed to instruct the Jewish masses ever proved so popular. Rav Yaakov Culi died in 1732 with only *Breishis* having been published. He left many unfinished manuscripts, and his work was continued by others.

The all-encompassing Volume on **Megillas Esther** was edited by Rav Rafael Chiyah Pontremoli (1864).

A Hebrew translation of the entire work, entitled *Yalkot Me'am Loez,* was undertaken by Rav Shmuel Yerushalmi beginning in 1967. *Esther* was published, with additional commentaries, in 1974.

Megillah:
[As differentiated from 'Megillas Esther' — the Biblical Book of Esther.]
Talmudic tractate in Seder Moed.

Megillas Sesarim:
See Lorberbaum, Rav Yaakov b. Yaakov Moshe of Lissa.

Mesoras Habris:
See Posner, Rav David Tevele.

Michtav Me'Eliyahu:
See Dessler, Rav Eliyahu Eliezer.

Midrash:
See *Midrash Rabbah.*

Midrash Abba Gorion:
One of the 'smaller' early Midrashim on *Megillas Esther.* It begins with a statement of the Talmudic Sage Abba Gorion of Sidon, hence the name *Abba*

Gorion. This Midrash is quoted by Rashi, and is quoted extensively by the *Yalkut Shim'oni.*

Included — in incomplete form — by Yellinek in his *Beis HaMidrash* and reprinted in enlarged form by Buber in his *Sifrei D'Agad'ta al Megillas Esther.*

Midrash Lekach Tov:

A "small" early Midrash on *Megillas Esther* — very often referred to by Rav Shlomo Alkabetz in his *M'nos Halevi.* Published by Buber in his *Sifrei D'Agadta al Megilles Esther.*

Midrash Panim Acherim L'Esther:

One of the early "Smaller" Midrashim. Existing in two versions: *Nussach Aleph and Nussach Bais.* Quoted extensively by Rav Shlomo Alkabetz in his *M'nos Halevi.*

Published by Buber from a manuscript in the *Sifrei D'Agad'ta al Megillas Esther.*

Midrash Rabbah:

[Lit. 'The Great Midrash'] Denoting the oldest Amoraic, classical Midrashim. (Throughout the commentary of this work whenever 'Midrash' alone is quoted, the reference is to *Midrash Esther Rabbah.*)

*Miller, Rav Avigdor:

Contemporary Rav, noted lecturer and author. A dominant force on the American Yeshivah scene. Rav in Brooklyn. Author of *Rejoice O Youth!; Sing You Righteous; Torah Nation; Behold a People.*

M'nos Halevi:

(Also called: *Midrash Megillas Esther*). See Alkabetz, Rav Shlomo Halevi

Mishneh Brurah:

See Rav Yisrael Meir haKohen.

Nachal Eshkol:

See Azulai, Rav Chaim Yosef David.

Or Hachaim:

See Attar, Rav Chaim b. Moshe, ibn.

Panim Acherim:

See Midrash Panim Acherim.

Pirchei L'vanon:

Commentary. Quoted in the recently published anthology 'Yaynah Shel Torah' (Jerusalem, 1954).

Pirke Avos:

"Chapters" or "Ethics" of the Fathers. A Talmudic tractate in *Seder Nezikin.* Read in the synagogue Shabbos afternoon from Passover to Rosh Hashanah.

Posner, Rav David Tevele:

Rav and author, mid 17th Century. Born in Posen. A disciple of Rav Sheftel Horowitz.

He wrote *Shaarei Zion* — on Mussar, and *Mesoras Habris,* both published posthumously by his son. He died in 1690 near Altona.

Rabinowitz, Rav Shlomo haKohen of Radomsk:

(1803-1866).

Radomsker Rebbe. A follower of the Apta Rebbe after the death of the 'Chozeh' [The 'Seer'] of Lublin. In 1843 he became Rebbe of Radomsk. He attracted many Chassidim. He is known for his classical work, *Tiferes Shlomo.*

Rambam:

Acronym for Rav Moshe ben Maimon; Maimonides. (1135-1204).

One of the most illustrious figures in Judaism in the post-Talmudic era, and probably one of the greatest of all time. He was a rabbinic authority, codifier, philosopher, and royal physician. According to some, he was a descendant of Rav Yahuda HaNasi.

Born in Cordoba; moved to Israel and then to Fostat, the old city of Cairo, Egypt.

At the age of 23 he began his commentary on the Mishnah which he authored throughout his wanderings. His main work was *Mishneh-Torah, Yad ha-Chazaka,* his codification of the spectrum of halachah until his day. This was the only book he wrote in Hebrew. All his other works were written in Arabic, a fact he regretted later in life. He is also known for his *'Guide to the Perplexed,'* and for his many works in the field of medicine, hygiene, astronomy, etc. Truly it may be said 'from Moshe to Moshe there are none like Moshe.'

Rashi:
See Rav Shlomo b. Yitzchak.

RaMA:
See Isserles, Rav Moshe.

Rokeach, Rav Aharon:
(1880-1957)
Belzer Rebbe. Successor to his father, Rav Yissachar Dov, and Rebbe of one of the most important Chassidic dynasties of Galicia. After confinement in many ghettos in Europe during World War II, he was deported to Kashau and subsequently to Budapest. In 1944 he managed to reach Israel where he resided until his death. Universally considered one of the great and holy tzaddikim of the last generation.

Sava, Rav Avraham b. Yaakov:
Kabbalist and Preacher. Rav Avraham was among those expelled from Spain in 1492. He wrote many books, among them his commentary on the Five Megillos, *Eshkol haKofer.*

Seder Hadoros:
See Heilprin, Rav Yechiel b. Shlomo.

Seder Olam:
Early Midrashic-chronological work. *Seder Olam* is mentioned in the Talmud (Shab. 88a; Yev. 82b, *et al.*) and is ascribed to the *Tanna* Rav Yose ben Chalafta.

Sefas Emes:
See Alter, Rav Yehudah Aryah Leib.

Sefer HaTodaah:
See Kitov, Rav Eliyahu.

Shaar Bas Rabim:
Quoted in the recently published anonymous anthology *'Yaynah Shel Torah'* (Jerusalem, 1964).

Shaarei Binah:
See Rav Eleazar ben Judah of Worms.

Rav Shlomo ben Yitzchok (Rashi):
Leading commentator on the Bible and Talmud. He was born in Troyes, France in 1040 — the year in which Rabbeinu Gershom M'or HaGolah died. According to tradition, Rashi's ancestry goes back to Rav Yochanan haSandlar and to King David.

The summit of Rashi's commentaries was his commentary on the Talmud — an encyclopaedic and brilliant undertaking. Nothing can be compared to the impact this commentary has had upon all who study the Talmud. Rashi's commentary has opened to all what otherwise would have been a sealed book. Without his commentary, no one would dare navigate the 'Sea of Talmud.' Every word is precise and laden with inner meaning. Rashi's corrections of the Talmud text were, for the most part, introduced into the standard editions and became the accepted text.

Rashi's **Commentary to the Bible,** too, made a similar impact — and virtualy every Bible printed contains his commentary which is distinguished by its conciseness and clarity.

Many Halachic works from 'the School of Rashi' have come down to us: *Sefer Ha'orah; Sefer HaPardes; Machzor Vitry; Siddur Rashi;* and responsa.

He died on Tammuz 29, 1105. His burial place is not known.

* Singer, Rav Yehudah David:
Contemporary Rav and Author. Rav of Givat Shmuel, Israel. Author of *Ziv Hamitzvos* ['Splender of the Commandments']; and *Ziv Haminhagim* ['Splender of the Customs'], arranged according to the Hebrew calender; and *Ziv Hashabbos* ['Splendor of the Sabbath']; Israel, 1971.

Shabbos:
Talmudic tractate in *Seder Moed*.

Targum:
(Lit. 'Translation')
The ancient Aramaic translation of the Bible. Usually referring to the *Targum Onkelos*.

Targum Sheni:
(Lit. 'Second Translation')
An ancient, and extensive collection of homilies in Aramaic on *Megillas Esther*. The early Gaonim refer to it.

Teitelbaum, Rav Moshe:
(1759-1841). Founder of the Sigheter dynasty. A pupil of the Chozeh of Lublin. A renowned Tzaddik, he was among the first to spread Chassidus in the Northern and Central districts of Hungary in his capacity as Rav of Vjhely. Author of *Yismach Moshe*, considered one of the classic works of Chassidus.

Tiferes Shlomo:
See Rabinowitz, Rav Shlomo haKohen, of Radomsk.

Torah Nation:
See Miller, Rav Avigdor.

Torah T'mimah:
See Epstein, Rav Baruch haLevi.

Tosafos:
[Literally, 'additions'.] Collective term for the leading Talmudic scholars of France and Germany during the twelfth century. There were up to 200 of them. They compiled **novellae on the Talmud** which became the companion to Rashi as the standard commentary to the Talmud. Basing their work on Rashi, they broadened and deepened his interpretations.

Valerio, Rav Shmuel ben Yehudah:
Rav, physician and author who lived in Greece in the second half of the sixteenth century. He wrote *Yad-Hamelech* on Megillas Esther, published in Corfu in 1579.

Vilna Gaon:
See Rav Eliyahu ben Shlomo Zalman of Vilna.

Yaaros Devash:
See Eybeschuetz, Rav Yonasan ben Nassan Nata.

Yad Hamelech:
See Valerio, Rav Shmuel ben Yehudah.

Yalkut Shimoni:
The early classical anthology of Midrashim. Authorship uncertain.

Yismach Moshe:
See Teitelbaum, Rav Moshe.

Rav Yisrael Meir haKohen:
(1838-1933)
"Chafetz Chaim"
One of the greatest Tzadikim in modern Judaism. He became universally known as 'The Chafetz Chaim,' after the title of his first work which he published anonymously at the age of 35. He established the Radun Yeshivah.

Author of many works, he is best known for his **Mishneh B'rurah** (6 vols., 1894-1907), a comprehensive commentary on *Shulchan Aruch, Orach Chayim*, which has become the indispensible commentary used in studying the *Shulchan Aruch*.

He was a founder of Agudath Israel. He constantly stressed the fundamental belief in the *imminent* arrival of Mashiach, and, as a *Kohen*, he emphasized the study of the law of sacrifice and Temple worship and other related subjects.

His saintliness exercised a tremendous influence on all who knew him, and is the subject of many stories, all rich in morals, about him.

Yoma:
Talmudic tractate in *Seder Moed*.

Yosef Lekach:
See Rav Eliezer b. Eliyahu Ashkenazy Harofe.

Yismach Moshe:
See Teitelbaum, Rav Moshe.

Ziv Haminhagim:
See Singer, Rav Yehudah David.

סֵדֶר לֵיל פּוּרִים
Purim Evening Service

וְהוּא רַחוּם יְכַפֵּר עָוֹן וְלֹא יַשְׁחִית, וְהִרְבָּה לְהָשִׁיב אַפּוֹ וְלֹא יָעִיר כָּל חֲמָתוֹ. יְיָ הוֹשִׁיעָה הַמֶּלֶךְ יַעֲנֵנוּ בְיוֹם קָרְאֵנוּ.

The חַזָּן:

בָּרְכוּ אֶת יְיָ הַמְבֹרָךְ.

Congregation and חַזָּן

בָּרוּךְ יְיָ הַמְבֹרָךְ לְעוֹלָם וָעֶד.

בָּרוּךְ אַתָּה יְיָ אֱלֹהֵינוּ מֶלֶךְ הָעוֹלָם אֲשֶׁר בִּדְבָרוֹ מַעֲרִיב עֲרָבִים בְּחָכְמָה פּוֹתֵחַ שְׁעָרִים וּבִתְבוּנָה מְשַׁנֶּה עִתִּים וּמַחֲלִיף אֶת הַזְּמַנִּים וּמְסַדֵּר אֶת־הַכּוֹכָבִים בְּמִשְׁמְרוֹתֵיהֶם בָּרָקִיעַ כִּרְצוֹנוֹ בּוֹרֵא יוֹם וָלַיְלָה גּוֹלֵל אוֹר מִפְּנֵי־חֹשֶׁךְ וְחֹשֶׁךְ מִפְּנֵי־אוֹר וּמַעֲבִיר יוֹם וּמֵבִיא לַיְלָה וּמַבְדִּיל בֵּין יוֹם וּבֵין לַיְלָה יְיָ צְבָאוֹת שְׁמוֹ אֵל חַי וְקַיָּם תָּמִיד יִמְלוֹךְ עָלֵינוּ לְעוֹלָם וָעֶד. בָּרוּךְ אַתָּה יְיָ הַמַּעֲרִיב עֲרָבִים.

אַהֲבַת עוֹלָם בֵּית יִשְׂרָאֵל עַמְּךָ אָהָבְתָּ, תּוֹרָה וּמִצְוֹת חֻקִּים וּמִשְׁפָּטִים אוֹתָנוּ לִמַּדְתָּ. עַל כֵּן יְיָ אֱלֹהֵינוּ בְּשָׁכְבֵּנוּ וּבְקוּמֵנוּ נָשִׂיחַ בְּחֻקֶּיךָ וְנִשְׂמַח בְּדִבְרֵי תוֹרָתֶךָ וּבְמִצְוֹתֶיךָ לְעוֹלָם וָעֶד. כִּי הֵם חַיֵּינוּ וְאֹרֶךְ יָמֵינוּ וּבָהֶם נֶהְגֶּה יוֹמָם וָלַיְלָה וְאַהֲבָתְךָ אַל תָּסִיר מִמֶּנּוּ לְעוֹלָמִים. בָּרוּךְ אַתָּה יְיָ אוֹהֵב עַמּוֹ יִשְׂרָאֵל.

When praying in private, add:

אֵל מֶלֶךְ נֶאֱמָן

שְׁמַע יִשְׂרָאֵל יְיָ אֱלֹהֵינוּ יְיָ אֶחָד.

(In a whisper:)

בָּרוּךְ שֵׁם כְּבוֹד מַלְכוּתוֹ לְעוֹלָם וָעֶד.

וְאָהַבְתָּ אֵת יְיָ אֱלֹהֶיךָ בְּכָל לְבָבְךָ וּבְכָל נַפְשְׁךָ וּבְכָל מְאֹדֶךָ וְהָיוּ הַדְּבָרִים הָאֵלֶּה אֲשֶׁר אָנֹכִי מְצַוְּךָ הַיּוֹם עַל לְבָבֶךָ וְשִׁנַּנְתָּם לְבָנֶיךָ וְדִבַּרְתָּ בָּם בְּשִׁבְתְּךָ בְּבֵיתֶךָ וּבְלֶכְתְּךָ בַדֶּרֶךְ וּבְשָׁכְבְּךָ וּבְקוּמֶךָ וּקְשַׁרְתָּם לְאוֹת עַל יָדֶךָ וְהָיוּ לְטֹטָפֹת בֵּין עֵינֶיךָ וּכְתַבְתָּם עַל מְזֻזוֹת בֵּיתֶךָ וּבִשְׁעָרֶיךָ.

וְהָיָה אִם־שָׁמֹעַ תִּשְׁמְעוּ אֶל מִצְוֹתַי אֲשֶׁר אָנֹכִי מְצַוֶּה אֶתְכֶם הַיּוֹם לְאַהֲבָה אֶת יְיָ אֱלֹהֵיכֶם וּלְעָבְדוֹ בְּכָל לְבַבְכֶם וּבְכָל נַפְשְׁכֶם. וְנָתַתִּי מְטַר אַרְצְכֶם בְּעִתּוֹ יוֹרֶה וּמַלְקוֹשׁ וְאָסַפְתָּ דְגָנֶךָ

וְתִירשְׁךָ וְיִצְהָרֶךָ. וְנָתַתִּי עֵשֶׂב בְּשָׂדְךָ לִבְהֶמְתֶּךָ וְאָכַלְתָּ וְשָׂבָעְתָּ. הִשָּׁמְרוּ לָכֶם פֶּן־יִפְתֶּה לְבַבְכֶם וְסַרְתֶּם וַעֲבַדְתֶּם אֱלֹהִים אֲחֵרִים וְהִשְׁתַּחֲוִיתֶם לָהֶם. וְחָרָה אַף־יְיָ בָּכֶם וְעָצַר אֶת הַשָּׁמַיִם וְלֹא יִהְיֶה מָטָר וְהָאֲדָמָה לֹא תִתֵּן אֶת יְבוּלָהּ וַאֲבַדְתֶּם מְהֵרָה מֵעַל הָאָרֶץ הַטֹּבָה אֲשֶׁר יְיָ נֹתֵן לָכֶם. וְשַׂמְתֶּם אֶת דְּבָרַי אֵלֶּה עַל לְבַבְכֶם וְעַל נַפְשְׁכֶם וּקְשַׁרְתֶּם אֹתָם לְאוֹת עַל יֶדְכֶם וְהָיוּ לְטוֹטָפֹת בֵּין עֵינֵיכֶם. וְלִמַּדְתֶּם אֹתָם אֶת בְּנֵיכֶם לְדַבֵּר בָּם בְּשִׁבְתְּךָ בְּבֵיתֶךָ וּבְלֶכְתְּךָ בַדֶּרֶךְ וּבְשָׁכְבְּךָ וּבְקוּמֶךָ. וּכְתַבְתָּם עַל מְזוּזוֹת בֵּיתֶךָ וּבִשְׁעָרֶיךָ.

לְמַעַן יִרְבּוּ יְמֵיכֶם וִימֵי בְנֵיכֶם עַל הָאֲדָמָה אֲשֶׁר נִשְׁבַּע יְיָ לַאֲבֹתֵיכֶם לָתֵת לָהֶם כִּימֵי הַשָּׁמַיִם עַל הָאָרֶץ.

וַיֹּאמֶר יְיָ אֶל מֹשֶׁה לֵּאמֹר. דַּבֵּר אֶל בְּנֵי יִשְׂרָאֵל וְאָמַרְתָּ אֲלֵהֶם וְעָשׂוּ לָהֶם צִיצִת עַל כַּנְפֵי בִגְדֵיהֶם לְדֹרֹתָם וְנָתְנוּ עַל צִיצִת הַכָּנָף פְּתִיל תְּכֵלֶת. וְהָיָה לָכֶם לְצִיצִת וּרְאִיתֶם אֹתוֹ וּזְכַרְתֶּם אֶת כָּל מִצְוֹת יְיָ וַעֲשִׂיתֶם אֹתָם, וְלֹא תָתוּרוּ אַחֲרֵי לְבַבְכֶם וְאַחֲרֵי עֵינֵיכֶם אֲשֶׁר אַתֶּם זֹנִים אַחֲרֵיהֶם. לְמַעַן תִּזְכְּרוּ וַעֲשִׂיתֶם אֶת כָּל מִצְוֹתָי וִהְיִיתֶם קְדֹשִׁים לֵאלֹהֵיכֶם. אֲנִי יְיָ אֱלֹהֵיכֶם אֲשֶׁר הוֹצֵאתִי אֶתְכֶם מֵאֶרֶץ מִצְרַיִם לִהְיוֹת לָכֶם לֵאלֹהִים אֲנִי יְיָ אֱלֹהֵיכֶם —

אֱמֶת וֶאֱמוּנָה כָּל־זֹאת וְקַיָּם עָלֵינוּ כִּי הוּא יְיָ אֱלֹהֵינוּ וְאֵין זוּלָתוֹ וַאֲנַחְנוּ יִשְׂרָאֵל עַמּוֹ הַפּוֹדֵנוּ מִיַּד מְלָכִים מַלְכֵּנוּ הַגּוֹאֲלֵנוּ מִכַּף כָּל־הֶעָרִיצִים הָאֵל הַנִּפְרָע לָנוּ מִצָּרֵינוּ וְהַמְשַׁלֵּם גְּמוּל לְכָל אֹיְבֵי נַפְשֵׁנוּ הָעֹשֶׂה גְדֹלוֹת עַד אֵין חֵקֶר וְנִפְלָאוֹת עַד־אֵין מִסְפָּר. הַשָּׂם נַפְשֵׁנוּ בַּחַיִּים וְלֹא נָתַן לַמּוֹט רַגְלֵנוּ הַמַּדְרִיכֵנוּ עַל בָּמוֹת אֹיְבֵינוּ וַיָּרֶם קַרְנֵנוּ עַל כָּל־שֹׂנְאֵינוּ. הָעֹשֶׂה לָּנוּ נִסִּים וּנְקָמָה בְּפַרְעֹה אוֹתוֹת וּמוֹפְתִים בְּאַדְמַת בְּנֵי חָם. הַמַּכֶּה בְּעֶבְרָתוֹ כָּל־בְּכוֹרֵי מִצְרַיִם וַיּוֹצֵא אֶת־עַמּוֹ יִשְׂרָאֵל מִתּוֹכָם לְחֵרוּת עוֹלָם. הַמַּעֲבִיר בָּנָיו בֵּין גִּזְרֵי יַם סוּף אֶת רוֹדְפֵיהֶם וְאֶת שׂוֹנְאֵיהֶם בִּתְהוֹמוֹת טִבַּע. וְרָאוּ בָנָיו גְּבוּרָתוֹ שִׁבְּחוּ וְהוֹדוּ לִשְׁמוֹ וּמַלְכוּתוֹ בְּרָצוֹן קִבְּלוּ עֲלֵיהֶם מֹשֶׁה וּבְנֵי יִשְׂרָאֵל לְךָ עָנוּ שִׁירָה בְּשִׂמְחָה רַבָּה וְאָמְרוּ כֻלָּם.

מִי כָמֹכָה בָּאֵלִם יְיָ מִי כָּמֹכָה נֶאְדָּר בַּקֹּדֶשׁ נוֹרָא תְהִלֹּת עֹשֵׂה
פֶלֶא. מַלְכוּתְךָ רָאוּ בָנֶיךָ בּוֹקֵעַ יָם לִפְנֵי מֹשֶׁה זֶה אֵלִי עָנוּ
וְאָמְרוּ יְיָ יִמְלֹךְ לְעֹלָם וָעֶד.

וְנֶאֱמַר. כִּי־פָדָה יְיָ אֶת יַעֲקֹב וּגְאָלוֹ מִיַּד חָזָק מִמֶּנּוּ, בָּרוּךְ
אַתָּה יְיָ גָּאַל יִשְׂרָאֵל.

הַשְׁכִּיבֵנוּ יְיָ אֱלֹהֵינוּ לְשָׁלוֹם וְהַעֲמִידֵנוּ מַלְכֵּנוּ לְחַיִּים וּפְרֹשׂ
עָלֵינוּ סֻכַּת שְׁלוֹמֶךָ וְתַקְּנֵנוּ בְּעֵצָה טוֹבָה מִלְּפָנֶיךָ וְהוֹשִׁיעֵנוּ
לְמַעַן שְׁמֶךָ וְהָגֵן בַּעֲדֵנוּ וְהָסֵר מֵעָלֵינוּ אוֹיֵב דֶּבֶר וְחֶרֶב וְרָעָב
וְיָגוֹן וְהָסֵר שָׂטָן מִלְּפָנֵינוּ וּמֵאַחֲרֵינוּ וּבְצֵל כְּנָפֶיךָ תַּסְתִּירֵנוּ כִּי
אֵל שׁוֹמְרֵנוּ וּמַצִּילֵנוּ אָתָּה כִּי אֵל מֶלֶךְ חַנּוּן וְרַחוּם אָתָּה
וּשְׁמֹר צֵאתֵנוּ וּבוֹאֵנוּ לְחַיִּים וּלְשָׁלוֹם מֵעַתָּה וְעַד עוֹלָם. בָּרוּךְ
אַתָּה יְיָ שׁוֹמֵר עַמּוֹ יִשְׂרָאֵל לָעַד.

בָּרוּךְ יְיָ לְעוֹלָם אָמֵן וְאָמֵן בָּרוּךְ יְיָ מִצִּיּוֹן שֹׁכֵן יְרוּשָׁלָיִם
הַלְלוּיָהּ בָּרוּךְ יְיָ אֱלֹהִים אֱלֹהֵי יִשְׂרָאֵל עֹשֵׂה נִפְלָאוֹת לְבַדּוֹ,
וּבָרוּךְ שֵׁם כְּבוֹדוֹ לְעוֹלָם וְיִמָּלֵא כְבוֹדוֹ אֶת כָּל הָאָרֶץ אָמֵן
וְאָמֵן. יְהִי כְבוֹד יְיָ לְעוֹלָם יִשְׂמַח יְיָ בְּמַעֲשָׂיו יְהִי שֵׁם יְיָ מְבֹרָךְ
מֵעַתָּה וְעַד־עוֹלָם כִּי לֹא יִטֹּשׁ יְיָ אֶת־עַמּוֹ בַּעֲבוּר שְׁמוֹ הַגָּדוֹל כִּי
הוֹאִיל יְיָ לַעֲשׂוֹת אֶתְכֶם לוֹ לְעָם וַיַּרְא כָּל הָעָם וַיִּפְּלוּ עַל
פְּנֵיהֶם וַיֹּאמְרוּ יְיָ הוּא הָאֱלֹהִים. וְהָיָה יְיָ לְמֶלֶךְ עַל כָּל הָאָרֶץ
בַּיּוֹם הַהוּא יִהְיֶה יְיָ אֶחָד וּשְׁמוֹ אֶחָד. יְהִי חַסְדְּךָ יְיָ עָלֵינוּ כַּאֲשֶׁר
יִחַלְנוּ לָךְ הוֹשִׁיעֵנוּ יְיָ אֱלֹהֵינוּ וְקַבְּצֵנוּ מִן הַגּוֹיִם לְהוֹדוֹת לְשֵׁם
קָדְשֶׁךָ לְהִשְׁתַּבֵּחַ בִּתְהִלָּתֶךָ. כָּל גּוֹיִם אֲשֶׁר עָשִׂיתָ יָבוֹאוּ
וְיִשְׁתַּחֲווּ לְפָנֶיךָ אֲדֹנָי וִיכַבְּדוּ לִשְׁמֶךָ כִּי־גָדוֹל אַתָּה וְעֹשֵׂה
נִפְלָאוֹת אַתָּה אֱלֹהִים לְבַדֶּךָ וַאֲנַחְנוּ עַמְּךָ וְצֹאן מַרְעִיתֶךָ נוֹדֶה
לְךָ לְעוֹלָם לְדוֹר וָדוֹר נְסַפֵּר תְּהִלָּתֶךָ.

בָּרוּךְ יְיָ בַּיּוֹם בָּרוּךְ יְיָ בַּלָּיְלָה, בָּרוּךְ יְיָ בְּשָׁכְבֵנוּ בָּרוּךְ יְיָ
בְּקוּמֵנוּ, כִּי בְיָדְךָ נַפְשׁוֹת הַחַיִּים וְהַמֵּתִים אֲשֶׁר בְּיָדוֹ נֶפֶשׁ כָּל
חָי וְרוּחַ כָּל בְּשַׂר אִישׁ. בְּיָדְךָ אַפְקִיד רוּחִי פָּדִיתָה אוֹתִי יְיָ אֵל
אֱמֶת. אֱלֹהֵינוּ שֶׁבַּשָּׁמַיִם יַחֵד שִׁמְךָ וְקַיֵּם מַלְכוּתְךָ תָּמִיד וּמְלוֹךְ
עָלֵינוּ לְעוֹלָם וָעֶד.

יִרְאוּ עֵינֵינוּ וְיִשְׂמַח לִבֵּנוּ וְתָגֵל נַפְשֵׁנוּ בִּישׁוּעָתְךָ בֶּאֱמֶת
בֶּאֱמֹר לְצִיּוֹן מָלַךְ אֱלֹהָיִךְ. יְיָ מֶלֶךְ, יְיָ מָלָךְ, יְיָ יִמְלֹךְ לְעוֹלָם
וָעֶד. כִּי הַמַּלְכוּת שֶׁלְּךָ הִיא וּלְעוֹלְמֵי עַד תִּמְלֹךְ בְּכָבוֹד כִּי אֵין
לָנוּ מֶלֶךְ אֶלָּא אָתָּה בָּרוּךְ אַתָּה, יְיָ, הַמֶּלֶךְ בִּכְבוֹדוֹ תָּמִיד יִמְלֹךְ
עָלֵינוּ לְעוֹלָם וָעֶד וְעַל כָּל מַעֲשָׂיו.

The חַזָּן:
יִתְגַּדַּל וְיִתְקַדַּשׁ שְׁמֵהּ רַבָּא, בְּעָלְמָא דִי בְרָא כִרְעוּתֵהּ וְיַמְלִיךְ מַלְכוּתֵהּ,
בְּחַיֵּיכוֹן וּבְיוֹמֵיכוֹן וּבְחַיֵּי דְכָל בֵּית יִשְׂרָאֵל, בַּעֲגָלָא וּבִזְמַן קָרִיב וְאִמְרוּ
אָמֵן.
יְהֵא שְׁמֵהּ רַבָּא מְבָרַךְ לְעָלַם וּלְעָלְמֵי עָלְמַיָּא.
יִתְבָּרַךְ וְיִשְׁתַּבַּח וְיִתְפָּאַר וְיִתְרוֹמַם וְיִתְנַשֵּׂא וְיִתְהַדָּר וְיִתְעַלֶּה וְיִתְהַלָּל
שְׁמֵהּ דְּקֻדְשָׁא בְּרִיךְ הוּא. לְעֵלָּא מִן כָּל בִּרְכָתָא וְשִׁירָתָא תֻּשְׁבְּחָתָא
וְנֶחֱמָתָא דַּאֲמִירָן בְּעָלְמָא וְאִמְרוּ אָמֵן.

Shemoneh Esreh שְׁמוֹנֶה עֶשְׂרֵה:
יְיָ שְׂפָתַי תִּפְתָּח, וּפִי יַגִּיד תְּהִלָּתֶךָ.

בָּרוּךְ אַתָּה, יְיָ אֱלֹהֵינוּ וֵאלֹהֵי אֲבוֹתֵינוּ, אֱלֹהֵי אַבְרָהָם אֱלֹהֵי
יִצְחָק וֵאלֹהֵי יַעֲקֹב, הָאֵל הַגָּדוֹל הַגִּבּוֹר וְהַנּוֹרָא, אֵל עֶלְיוֹן,
גּוֹמֵל חֲסָדִים טוֹבִים, וְקוֹנֵה הַכֹּל וְזוֹכֵר חַסְדֵי אָבוֹת, וּמֵבִיא
גוֹאֵל לִבְנֵי בְנֵיהֶם לְמַעַן שְׁמוֹ בְּאַהֲבָה.
מֶלֶךְ עוֹזֵר וּמוֹשִׁיעַ וּמָגֵן: בָּרוּךְ אַתָּה יְיָ מָגֵן אַבְרָהָם:
אַתָּה גִּבּוֹר, לְעוֹלָם אֲדֹנָי, מְחַיֵּה מֵתִים אַתָּה, רַב לְהוֹשִׁיעַ.
מַשִּׁיב הָרוּחַ וּמוֹרִיד הַגָּשֶׁם

מְכַלְכֵּל חַיִּים בְּחֶסֶד מְחַיֵּה מֵתִים בְּרַחֲמִים רַבִּים, סוֹמֵךְ
נוֹפְלִים וְרוֹפֵא חוֹלִים, וּמַתִּיר אֲסוּרִים, וּמְקַיֵּם אֱמוּנָתוֹ לִישֵׁנֵי
עָפָר. מִי כָמוֹךָ בַּעַל גְּבוּרוֹת, וּמִי דוֹמֶה לָּךְ, מֶלֶךְ מֵמִית וּמְחַיֶּה
וּמַצְמִיחַ יְשׁוּעָה:
וְנֶאֱמָן אַתָּה לְהַחֲיוֹת מֵתִים: בָּרוּךְ אַתָּה יְיָ מְחַיֵּה הַמֵּתִים:
אַתָּה קָדוֹשׁ וְשִׁמְךָ קָדוֹשׁ. וּקְדוֹשִׁים בְּכָל־יוֹם יְהַלְלוּךָ סֶּלָה:
בָּרוּךְ אַתָּה, יְיָ, הָאֵל הַקָּדוֹשׁ:
אַתָּה חוֹנֵן לְאָדָם דַּעַת, וּמְלַמֵּד לֶאֱנוֹשׁ בִּינָה.

On Saturday night, מוֹצָאֵי שַׁבָּת, add:

(אַתָּה חוֹנַנְתָּנוּ לְמַדַּע תּוֹרָתֶךָ, וַתְּלַמְּדֵנוּ לַעֲשׂוֹת חֻקֵּי רְצוֹנֶךָ, וַתַּבְדֵּל יְיָ אֱלֹהֵינוּ, בֵּין קֹדֶשׁ לְחוֹל, בֵּין אוֹר לְחֹשֶׁךְ בֵּין יִשְׂרָאֵל לָעַמִּים, בֵּין יוֹם הַשְּׁבִיעִי לְשֵׁשֶׁת יְמֵי הַמַּעֲשֶׂה. אָבִינוּ מַלְכֵּנוּ הָחֵל עָלֵינוּ הַיָּמִים הַבָּאִים לִקְרָאתֵנוּ לְשָׁלוֹם, חֲשׂוּכִים מִכָּל־חֵטְא, וּמְנֻקִּים מִכָּל־עָוֹן, וּמְדֻבָּקִים בְּיִרְאָתֶךָ)

(וְ)חָנֵּנוּ מֵאִתְּךָ דֵּעָה בִּינָה וְהַשְׂכֵּל. בָּרוּךְ אַתָּה, יְיָ חוֹנֵן הַדָּעַת.

הֲשִׁיבֵנוּ אָבִינוּ לְתוֹרָתֶךָ, וְקָרְבֵנוּ מַלְכֵּנוּ לַעֲבוֹדָתֶךָ, וְהַחֲזִירֵנוּ בִּתְשׁוּבָה שְׁלֵמָה לְפָנֶיךָ. בָּרוּךְ אַתָּה, יְיָ הָרוֹצֶה בִּתְשׁוּבָה.

סְלַח לָנוּ אָבִינוּ כִּי חָטָאנוּ, מְחַל לָנוּ מַלְכֵּנוּ כִּי פָשָׁעְנוּ, כִּי מוֹחֵל וְסוֹלֵחַ אָתָּה. בָּרוּךְ אַתָּה, יְיָ, חַנּוּן הַמַּרְבֶּה לִסְלוֹחַ.

רְאֵה נָא בְעָנְיֵנוּ וְרִיבָה רִיבֵנוּ, וּגְאָלֵנוּ מְהֵרָה לְמַעַן שְׁמֶךָ, כִּי גוֹאֵל חָזָק אָתָּה. בָּרוּךְ אַתָּה יְיָ גּוֹאֵל יִשְׂרָאֵל.

רְפָאֵנוּ יְיָ וְנֵרָפֵא, הוֹשִׁיעֵנוּ וְנִוָּשֵׁעָה, כִּי תְהִלָּתֵנוּ אָתָּה, וְהַעֲלֵה רְפוּאָה שְׁלֵמָה לְכָל מַכּוֹתֵינוּ, כִּי אֵל מֶלֶךְ רוֹפֵא נֶאֱמָן וְרַחֲמָן אָתָּה. בָּרוּךְ אַתָּה יְיָ, רוֹפֵא חוֹלֵי עַמּוֹ יִשְׂרָאֵל.

בָּרֵךְ עָלֵינוּ, יְיָ אֱלֹהֵינוּ, אֶת־הַשָּׁנָה הַזֹּאת וְאֶת כָּל מִינֵי תְבוּאָתָהּ לְטוֹבָה, וְתֵן טַל וּמָטָר לִבְרָכָה עַל כָּל־פְּנֵי הָאֲדָמָה, וְשַׂבְּעֵנוּ מִטּוּבֶךָ וּבָרֵךְ שְׁנָתֵנוּ כַּשָּׁנִים הַטּוֹבוֹת. בָּרוּךְ אַתָּה, יְיָ, מְבָרֵךְ הַשָּׁנִים.

תְּקַע בְּשׁוֹפָר גָּדוֹל לְחֵרוּתֵנוּ, וְשָׂא נֵס לְקַבֵּץ גָּלֻיּוֹתֵינוּ, וְקַבְּצֵנוּ יַחַד מֵאַרְבַּע כַּנְפוֹת הָאָרֶץ. בָּרוּךְ אַתָּה, יְיָ, מְקַבֵּץ נִדְחֵי עַמּוֹ יִשְׂרָאֵל.

הָשִׁיבָה שׁוֹפְטֵינוּ כְּבָרִאשׁוֹנָה, וְיוֹעֲצֵינוּ כְּבַתְּחִלָּה, וְהָסֵר מִמֶּנּוּ יָגוֹן וַאֲנָחָה, וּמְלוֹךְ עָלֵינוּ אַתָּה יְיָ לְבַדְּךָ בְּחֶסֶד וּבְרַחֲמִים וְצַדְּקֵנוּ בַּמִּשְׁפָּט. בָּרוּךְ אַתָּה, יְיָ, מֶלֶךְ אוֹהֵב צְדָקָה וּמִשְׁפָּט.

וְלַמַּלְשִׁינִים אַל־תְּהִי תִקְוָה, וְכָל הָרִשְׁעָה כְּרֶגַע תֹּאבֵד, וְכָל אוֹיְבֶיךָ מְהֵרָה יִכָּרֵתוּ, וְהַזֵּדִים מְהֵרָה תְעַקֵּר וּתְשַׁבֵּר וּתְמַגֵּר וְתַכְנִיעַ בִּמְהֵרָה בְיָמֵינוּ. בָּרוּךְ אַתָּה, יְיָ, שׁוֹבֵר אוֹיְבִים וּמַכְנִיעַ זֵדִים.

עַל־הַצַּדִּיקִים וְעַל הַחֲסִידִים וְעַל זִקְנֵי עַמְּךָ בֵּית יִשְׂרָאֵל, וְעַל פְּלֵיטַת סוֹפְרֵיהֶם, וְעַל גֵּרֵי הַצֶּדֶק וְעָלֵינוּ, יֶהֱמוּ נָא רַחֲמֶיךָ יְיָ אֱלֹהֵינוּ, וְתֵן שָׂכָר טוֹב לְכָל־הַבּוֹטְחִים בְּשִׁמְךָ בֶּאֱמֶת, וְשִׂים חֶלְקֵנוּ עִמָּהֶם לְעוֹלָם וְלֹא נֵבוֹשׁ, כִּי בְךָ בָּטָחְנוּ. בָּרוּךְ אַתָּה, יְיָ, מִשְׁעָן וּמִבְטָח לַצַּדִּיקִים.

וְלִירוּשָׁלַיִם עִירְךָ בְּרַחֲמִים תָּשׁוּב וְתִשְׁכּוֹן בְּתוֹכָהּ כַּאֲשֶׁר דִּבַּרְתָּ, וּבְנֵה אוֹתָהּ בְּקָרוֹב בְּיָמֵינוּ בִּנְיַן עוֹלָם, וְכִסֵּא דָוִד מְהֵרָה לְתוֹכָהּ תָּכִין. בָּרוּךְ אַתָּה, יְיָ, בּוֹנֵה יְרוּשָׁלָיִם.

אֶת־צֶמַח דָּוִד עַבְדְּךָ מְהֵרָה תַצְמִיחַ, וְקַרְנוֹ תָּרוּם בִּישׁוּעָתֶךָ, כִּי לִישׁוּעָתְךָ קִוִּינוּ כָּל־הַיּוֹם. בָּרוּךְ אַתָּה, יְיָ, מַצְמִיחַ קֶרֶן יְשׁוּעָה.

שְׁמַע קוֹלֵנוּ יְיָ אֱלֹהֵינוּ, חוּס וְרַחֵם עָלֵינוּ, וְקַבֵּל בְּרַחֲמִים וּבְרָצוֹן אֶת תְּפִלָּתֵנוּ, כִּי אֵל שׁוֹמֵעַ תְּפִלּוֹת וְתַחֲנוּנִים אָתָּה. וּמִלְּפָנֶיךָ מַלְכֵּנוּ רֵיקָם אַל־תְּשִׁיבֵנוּ. כִּי אַתָּה שׁוֹמֵעַ תְּפִלַּת עַמְּךָ יִשְׂרָאֵל בְּרַחֲמִים. בָּרוּךְ אַתָּה, יְיָ, שׁוֹמֵעַ תְּפִלָּה.

רְצֵה יְיָ אֱלֹהֵינוּ בְּעַמְּךָ יִשְׂרָאֵל וּבִתְפִלָּתָם, וְהָשֵׁב אֶת הָעֲבוֹדָה לִדְבִיר בֵּיתֶךָ, וְאִשֵּׁי יִשְׂרָאֵל, וּתְפִלָּתָם בְּאַהֲבָה תְקַבֵּל בְּרָצוֹן, וּתְהִי לְרָצוֹן תָּמִיד עֲבוֹדַת יִשְׂרָאֵל עַמֶּךָ.

וְתֶחֱזֶינָה עֵינֵינוּ בְּשׁוּבְךָ לְצִיּוֹן בְּרַחֲמִים: בָּרוּךְ אַתָּה, יְיָ, הַמַּחֲזִיר שְׁכִינָתוֹ לְצִיּוֹן.

מוֹדִים אֲנַחְנוּ לָךְ שָׁאַתָּה הוּא יְיָ אֱלֹהֵינוּ וֵאלֹהֵי אֲבוֹתֵינוּ לְעוֹלָם וָעֶד, צוּר חַיֵּינוּ מָגֵן יִשְׁעֵנוּ אַתָּה הוּא לְדֹר וָדֹר, נוֹדֶה לְּךָ וּנְסַפֵּר תְּהִלָּתֶךָ, עַל־חַיֵּינוּ הַמְּסוּרִים בְּיָדֶךָ, וְעַל נִשְׁמוֹתֵינוּ הַפְּקוּדוֹת לָךְ, וְעַל־נִסֶּיךָ שֶׁבְּכָל־יוֹם עִמָּנוּ וְעַל נִפְלְאוֹתֶיךָ וְטוֹבוֹתֶיךָ שֶׁבְּכָל־עֵת, עֶרֶב וָבֹקֶר וְצָהֳרָיִם. הַטּוֹב, כִּי לֹא כָלוּ רַחֲמֶיךָ. וְהַמְרַחֵם, כִּי לֹא תַמּוּ חֲסָדֶיךָ, מֵעוֹלָם קִוִּינוּ לָךְ.

עַל־הַנִּסִּים וְעַל־הַפֻּרְקָן וְעַל־הַגְּבוּרוֹת וְעַל־הַתְּשׁוּעוֹת וְעַל־הַמִּלְחָמוֹת שֶׁעָשִׂיתָ לַאֲבוֹתֵינוּ בַּיָּמִים הָהֵם בַּזְּמַן הַזֶּה.

בִּימֵי מָרְדְּכַי וְאֶסְתֵּר בְּשׁוּשַׁן הַבִּירָה כְּשֶׁעָמַד עֲלֵיהֶם הָמָן הָרָשָׁע בִּקֵּשׁ לְהַשְׁמִיד לַהֲרֹג וּלְאַבֵּד אֶת־כָּל־הַיְּהוּדִים מִנַּעַר וְעַד זָקֵן טַף וְנָשִׁים בְּיוֹם אֶחָד בִּשְׁלוֹשָׁה עָשָׂר לְחֹדֶשׁ שְׁנֵים־

עָשָׂר הוּא־חֹדֶשׁ אֲדָר וְשָׁלָל לָבוֹז. וְאַתָּה בְּרַחֲמֶיךָ הָרַבִּים הֵפַרְתָּ אֶת־עֲצָתוֹ וְקִלְקַלְתָּ אֶת־מַחֲשַׁבְתּוֹ וַהֲשֵׁבוֹתָ גְּמוּלוֹ בְּרֹאשׁוֹ וְתָלוּ אֹתוֹ וְאֶת־בָּנָיו עַל־הָעֵץ.

וְעַל־כֻּלָּם יִתְבָּרַךְ וְיִתְרוֹמַם שִׁמְךָ מַלְכֵּנוּ תָּמִיד לְעוֹלָם וָעֶד.

וְכֹל הַחַיִּים יוֹדוּךָ סֶּלָה, וִיהַלְלוּ אֶת שִׁמְךָ בֶּאֱמֶת הָאֵל יְשׁוּעָתֵנוּ וְעֶזְרָתֵנוּ סֶּלָה: בָּרוּךְ אַתָּה יְיָ, הַטּוֹב שִׁמְךָ וּלְךָ נָאֶה לְהוֹדוֹת:

שָׁלוֹם רָב עַל יִשְׂרָאֵל עַמְּךָ תָּשִׂים לְעוֹלָם, כִּי אַתָּה הוּא מֶלֶךְ אָדוֹן לְכָל הַשָּׁלוֹם, וְטוֹב בְּעֵינֶיךָ לְבָרֵךְ אֶת עַמְּךָ יִשְׂרָאֵל בְּכָל עֵת וּבְכָל שָׁעָה בִּשְׁלוֹמֶךָ. בָּרוּךְ אַתָּה, יְיָ, הַמְבָרֵךְ אֶת עַמּוֹ יִשְׂרָאֵל בַּשָּׁלוֹם:

אֱלֹהַי, נְצוֹר לְשׁוֹנִי מֵרָע, וּשְׂפָתַי מִדַּבֵּר מִרְמָה, וְלִמְקַלְלַי נַפְשִׁי תִדּוֹם, וְנַפְשִׁי כֶּעָפָר לַכֹּל תִּהְיֶה. פְּתַח לִבִּי בְּתוֹרָתֶךָ, וּבְמִצְוֹתֶיךָ תִּרְדּוֹף נַפְשִׁי. וְכָל־הַחוֹשְׁבִים עָלַי רָעָה, מְהֵרָה הָפֵר עֲצָתָם וְקַלְקֵל מַחֲשַׁבְתָּם. עֲשֵׂה לְמַעַן שְׁמֶךָ, עֲשֵׂה לְמַעַן יְמִינֶךָ, עֲשֵׂה לְמַעַן קְדֻשָּׁתֶךָ, עֲשֵׂה לְמַעַן תּוֹרָתֶךָ, לְמַעַן יֵחָלְצוּן יְדִידֶיךָ, הוֹשִׁיעָה יְמִינְךָ וַעֲנֵנִי. יִהְיוּ לְרָצוֹן אִמְרֵי פִי, וְהֶגְיוֹן לִבִּי לְפָנֶיךָ, יְיָ צוּרִי וְגוֹאֲלִי. עוֹשֶׂה שָׁלוֹם בִּמְרוֹמָיו, הוּא יַעֲשֶׂה שָׁלוֹם עָלֵינוּ, וְעַל כָּל יִשְׂרָאֵל וְאִמְרוּ אָמֵן.

יְהִי רָצוֹן מִלְּפָנֶיךָ יְיָ אֱלֹהֵינוּ וֵאלֹהֵי אֲבוֹתֵינוּ שֶׁיִּבָּנֶה בֵּית־הַמִּקְדָּשׁ בִּמְהֵרָה בְיָמֵינוּ, וְתֵן חֶלְקֵנוּ בְּתוֹרָתֶךָ וְשָׁם נַעֲבָדְךָ בְּיִרְאָה כִּימֵי עוֹלָם וּכְשָׁנִים קַדְמוֹנִיּוֹת, וְעָרְבָה לַיְיָ מִנְחַת יְהוּדָה וִירוּשָׁלָיִם כִּימֵי עוֹלָם וּכְשָׁנִים קַדְמוֹנִיּוֹת:

The חַזָּן:
יִתְגַּדַּל וְיִתְקַדַּשׁ שְׁמֵהּ רַבָּא, בְּעָלְמָא דִּי בְרָא כִרְעוּתֵהּ וְיַמְלִיךְ מַלְכוּתֵהּ, בְּחַיֵּיכוֹן וּבְיוֹמֵיכוֹן וּבְחַיֵּי דְכָל בֵּית־יִשְׂרָאֵל, בַּעֲגָלָא וּבִזְמַן קָרִיב וְאִמְרוּ אָמֵן:
יְהֵא שְׁמֵהּ רַבָּא מְבָרַךְ לְעָלַם לְעָלְמֵי עָלְמַיָּא.
יִתְבָּרַךְ וְיִשְׁתַּבַּח וְיִתְפָּאַר וְיִתְרוֹמַם וְיִתְנַשֵּׂא, וְיִתְהַדָּר וְיִתְעַלֶּה וְיִתְהַלָּל שְׁמֵהּ דְּקֻדְשָׁא בְּרִיךְ הוּא. לְעֵלָּא מִן כָּל־בִּרְכָתָא וְשִׁירָתָא תֻּשְׁבְּחָתָא וְנֶחָמָתָא דַּאֲמִירָן בְּעָלְמָא וְאִמְרוּ אָמֵן:
תִּתְקַבֵּל צְלוֹתְהוֹן וּבָעוּתְהוֹן דְּכָל־בֵּית יִשְׂרָאֵל קֳדָם אֲבוּהוֹן דִּי בִשְׁמַיָּא וְאִמְרוּ אָמֵן:

יְהֵא שְׁלָמָא רַבָּא מִן שְׁמַיָּא, וְחַיִּים עָלֵינוּ וְעַל כָּל יִשְׂרָאֵל וְאִמְרוּ אָמֵן:
עוֹשֶׂה שָׁלוֹם בִּמְרוֹמָיו, הוּא יַעֲשֶׂה שָׁלוֹם עָלֵינוּ, וְעַל כָּל יִשְׂרָאֵל וְאִמְרוּ
אָמֵן:

בָּרוּךְ אַתָּה, יְיָ אֱלֹהֵינוּ, מֶלֶךְ הָעוֹלָם, אֲשֶׁר קִדְּשָׁנוּ בְּמִצְוֹתָיו
וְצִוָּנוּ עַל מִקְרָא מְגִלָּה.

בָּרוּךְ אַתָּה, יְיָ אֱלֹהֵינוּ, מֶלֶךְ הָעוֹלָם, שֶׁעָשָׂה נִסִּים לַאֲבוֹתֵינוּ
בַּיָּמִים הָהֵם בַּזְּמַן הַזֶּה.

בָּרוּךְ אַתָּה, יְיָ אֱלֹהֵינוּ, מֶלֶךְ הָעוֹלָם, שֶׁהֶחֱיָנוּ וְקִיְּמָנוּ
וְהִגִּיעָנוּ לַזְּמַן הַזֶּה.

[The Megillah is Read]

After the reading of the Megillah, say:

בָּרוּךְ אַתָּה, יְיָ אֱלֹהֵינוּ, מֶלֶךְ הָעוֹלָם, הָרָב אֶת רִיבֵנוּ וְהַדָּן
אֶת דִּינֵנוּ וְהַנּוֹקֵם אֶת נִקְמָתֵנוּ וְהַנִּפְרָע לָנוּ מִצָּרֵינוּ וְהַמְשַׁלֵּם
גְּמוּל לְכָל אֹיְבֵי נַפְשֵׁנוּ. בָּרוּךְ אַתָּה, יְיָ, הַנִּפְרָע לְעַמּוֹ יִשְׂרָאֵל
מִכָּל צָרֵיהֶם הָאֵל הַמּוֹשִׁיעַ.

At שַׁחֲרִית *Purim morning services, omit the following paragraph:*

אֲשֶׁר הֵנִיא עֲצַת גּוֹיִם וַיָּפֶר מַחְשְׁבוֹת עֲרוּמִים.
בְּקוּם עָלֵינוּ אָדָם רָשָׁע נֵצֶר זָדוֹן מִזֶּרַע עֲמָלֵק.
גָּאָה בְעָשְׁרוֹ וְכָרָה לוֹ בּוֹר וּגְדֻלָּתוֹ יָקְשָׁה לּוֹ לָכֶד.
דִּמָּה בְנַפְשׁוֹ לִלְכּוֹד וְנִלְכָּד בִּקֵּשׁ לְהַשְׁמִיד וְנִשְׁמַד מְהֵרָה.
הָמָן הוֹדִיעַ אֵיבַת אֲבוֹתָיו וְעוֹרֵר שִׂנְאַת אַחִים לַבָּנִים.
וְלֹא־זָכַר רַחֲמֵי שָׁאוּל כִּי בְחֶמְלָתוֹ עַל אֲגָג נוֹלַד אוֹיֵב.
זָמַם רָשָׁע לְהַכְרִית צַדִּיק וְנִלְכַּד טָמֵא בִּידֵי טָהוֹר.
חֶסֶד גָּבַר עַל־שִׁגְגַת אָב וְרָשָׁע הוֹסִיף חֵטְא עַל חֲטָאָיו.
טָמַן בְּלִבּוֹ מַחְשְׁבוֹת עֲרוּמָיו וַיִּתְמַכֵּר לַעֲשׂוֹת רָעָה.
יָדוֹ שָׁלַח בִּקְדוֹשֵׁי אֵל, כַּסְפּוֹ נָתַן לְהַכְרִית זִכְרָם.
כִּרְאוֹת מָרְדֳּכַי כִּי־יָצָא קֶצֶף וְדָתֵי הָמָן נִתְּנוּ בְשׁוּשָׁן.
לָבַשׁ שַׂק וְקָשַׁר מִסְפֵּד וְגָזַר צוֹם וַיֵּשֶׁב עַל הָאֵפֶר.
מִי זֶה יַעֲמוֹד לְכַפֵּר שְׁגָגָה וְלִמְחוֹל חַטַּאת עֲוֹן אֲבוֹתֵינוּ.

נֵץ פָּרַח מְלוּלָב הֵן הֲדַסָּה עָמְדָה לְעוֹרֵר יְשֵׁנִים.

סָרִיסֶיהָ הִבְהִילוּ לְהָמָן לְהַשְׁקוֹתוֹ יֵין חֲמַת תַּנִּינִים.

עָמַד בְּעָשְׁרוֹ וְנָפַל בְּרִשְׁעוֹ עָשָׂה לוֹ עֵץ וְנִתְלָה עָלָיו.

פִּיהֶם פָּתְחוּ כָּל יוֹשְׁבֵי תֵבֵל, כִּי פוּר הָמָן נֶהְפַּךְ לְפוּרֵנוּ.

צַדִּיק נֶחֱלַץ מִיַּד רָשָׁע, אוֹיֵב נִתַּן תַּחַת נַפְשׁוֹ.

קִיְּמוּ עֲלֵיהֶם לַעֲשׂוֹת פוּרִים וְלִשְׂמֹחַ בְּכָל שָׁנָה וְשָׁנָה.

רָאִיתָ אֶת תְּפִלַּת מָרְדְּכַי וְאֶסְתֵּר הָמָן וּבָנָיו עַל־הָעֵץ תָּלִיתָ.

On Purim morning say this following הָאֵל הַמּוֹשִׁיעַ:

שׁוֹשַׁנַּת יַעֲקֹב צָהֲלָה וְשָׂמֵחָה בִּרְאוֹתָם יַחַד תְּכֵלֶת מָרְדְּכַי תְּשׁוּעָתָם הָיִיתָ לָנֶצַח וְתִקְוָתָם בְּכָל דּוֹר וָדוֹר. לְהוֹדִיעַ שֶׁכָּל קֹוֶיךָ לֹא יֵבשׁוּ וְלֹא יִכָּלְמוּ לָנֶצַח כָּל הַחוֹסִים בָּךְ. אָרוּר הָמָן אֲשֶׁר בִּקֵּשׁ לְאַבְּדִי, בָּרוּךְ מָרְדְּכַי הַיְּהוּדִי, אֲרוּרָה זֶרֶשׁ אֵשֶׁת מַפְחִידִי, בְּרוּכָה אֶסְתֵּר בַּעֲדִי. וְגַם חַרְבוֹנָה זָכוּר לַטּוֹב.

On Saturday night מוֹצָאֵי שַׁבָּת:

וִיהִי נֹעַם יְיָ אֱלֹהֵינוּ עָלֵינוּ, וּמַעֲשֵׂה יָדֵינוּ כּוֹנְנָה עָלֵינוּ, וּמַעֲשֵׂה יָדֵינוּ כּוֹנְנֵהוּ.

יֹשֵׁב בְּסֵתֶר עֶלְיוֹן בְּצֵל שַׁדַּי יִתְלוֹנָן. אֹמַר לַיְיָ מַחְסִי וּמְצוּדָתִי אֱלֹהַי אֶבְטַח בּוֹ. כִּי הוּא יַצִּילְךָ מִפַּח יָקוּשׁ מִדֶּבֶר הַוּוֹת, בְּאֶבְרָתוֹ יָסֶךְ לָךְ וְתַחַת כְּנָפָיו תֶּחְסֶה, צִנָּה וְסֹחֵרָה אֲמִתּוֹ. לֹא תִירָא מִפַּחַד לָיְלָה מֵחֵץ יָעוּף יוֹמָם מִדֶּבֶר בָּאֹפֶל יַהֲלֹךְ מִקֶּטֶב יָשׁוּד צָהֳרָיִם. יִפֹּל מִצִּדְּךָ אֶלֶף וּרְבָבָה מִימִינֶךָ, אֵלֶיךָ לֹא יִגָּשׁ רַק בְּעֵינֶיךָ תַבִּיט וְשִׁלֻּמַת רְשָׁעִים תִּרְאֶה. כִּי־אַתָּה יְיָ מַחְסִי עֶלְיוֹן שַׂמְתָּ מְעוֹנֶךָ, לֹא תְאֻנֶּה אֵלֶיךָ רָעָה וְנֶגַע לֹא יִקְרַב בְּאָהֳלֶךָ, כִּי מַלְאָכָיו יְצַוֶּה לָךְ לִשְׁמָרְךָ בְּכָל דְּרָכֶיךָ, עַל כַּפַּיִם יִשָּׂאוּנְךָ פֶּן תִּגֹּף בָּאֶבֶן רַגְלֶךָ, עַל שַׁחַל וָפֶתֶן תִּדְרֹךְ תִּרְמֹס כְּפִיר וְתַנִּין. כִּי בִי חָשַׁק וַאֲפַלְּטֵהוּ אֲשַׂגְּבֵהוּ כִּי יָדַע שְׁמִי יִקְרָאֵנִי וְאֶעֱנֵהוּ, עִמּוֹ אָנֹכִי בְצָרָה אֲחַלְּצֵהוּ וַאֲכַבְּדֵהוּ, אֹרֶךְ יָמִים אַשְׂבִּיעֵהוּ וְאַרְאֵהוּ בִּישׁוּעָתִי, אֹרֶךְ יָמִים אַשְׂבִּיעֵהוּ וְאַרְאֵהוּ בִּישׁוּעָתִי.

וְאַתָּה קָדוֹשׁ יוֹשֵׁב תְּהִלּוֹת יִשְׂרָאֵל וְקָרָא זֶה אֶל־זֶה וְאָמַר

קָדוֹשׁ קָדוֹשׁ קָדוֹשׁ יְיָ צְבָאוֹת מְלֹא כָל־הָאָרֶץ כְּבוֹדוֹ. וּמְקַבְּלִין
דֵּן מִן־דֵּן וְאָמְרִין קַדִּישׁ בִּשְׁמֵי מְרוֹמָא עִלָּאָה בֵּית שְׁכִינְתֵּהּ
קַדִּישׁ עַל־אַרְעָא עוֹבַד גְּבוּרְתֵּהּ קַדִּישׁ לְעָלַם וּלְעָלְמֵי עָלְמַיָּא.
יְיָ צְבָאוֹת מַלְיָא כָל אַרְעָא זִיו יְקָרֵהּ. וַתִּשָּׂאֵנִי רוּחַ וָאֶשְׁמַע
אַחֲרַי קוֹל רַעַשׁ גָּדוֹל בָּרוּךְ כְּבוֹד־יְיָ מִמְּקוֹמוֹ. וּנְטַלְתַּנִי רוּחָא
וְשִׁמְעֵת בַּתְרַי קָל זִיעַ סַגִּיא דִּמְשַׁבְּחִין וְאָמְרִין, בְּרִיךְ יְקָרָא דַיְיָ
מֵאֲתַר בֵּית שְׁכִינְתֵּהּ. יְיָ יִמְלֹךְ לְעֹלָם וָעֶד. יְיָ מַלְכוּתֵהּ קָאֵם
לְעָלַם וּלְעָלְמֵי עָלְמַיָּא. יְיָ אֱלֹהֵי אַבְרָהָם יִצְחָק וְיִשְׂרָאֵל
אֲבוֹתֵינוּ שָׁמְרָה־זֹּאת לְעוֹלָם לְיֵצֶר מַחְשְׁבוֹת לְבַב עַמֶּךָ וְהָכֵן
לְבָבָם אֵלֶיךָ. וְהוּא רַחוּם יְכַפֵּר עָוֹן וְלֹא־יַשְׁחִית וְהִרְבָּה לְהָשִׁיב
אַפּוֹ וְלֹא יָעִיר כָּל־חֲמָתוֹ. כִּי אַתָּה יְיָ טוֹב וְסַלָּח וְרַב־חֶסֶד לְכָל־
קֹרְאֶיךָ. צִדְקָתְךָ צֶדֶק לְעוֹלָם וְתוֹרָתְךָ אֱמֶת. תִּתֵּן אֱמֶת לְיַעֲקֹב
חֶסֶד לְאַבְרָהָם אֲשֶׁר־נִשְׁבַּעְתָּ לַאֲבוֹתֵינוּ מִימֵי קֶדֶם. בָּרוּךְ אֲדֹנָי
יוֹם יוֹם יַעֲמָס לָנוּ הָאֵל יְשׁוּעָתֵנוּ סֶלָה. יְיָ צְבָאוֹת עִמָּנוּ מִשְׂגָּב־
לָנוּ אֱלֹהֵי יַעֲקֹב סֶלָה. יְיָ צְבָאוֹת אַשְׁרֵי אָדָם בֹּטֵחַ בָּךְ. יְיָ
הוֹשִׁיעָה הַמֶּלֶךְ יַעֲנֵנוּ בְיוֹם־קָרְאֵנוּ. בָּרוּךְ אֱלֹהֵינוּ שֶׁבְּרָאָנוּ
לִכְבוֹדוֹ וְהִבְדִּילָנוּ מִן־הַתּוֹעִים וְנָתַן־לָנוּ תּוֹרַת אֱמֶת וְחַיֵּי עוֹלָם
נָטַע בְּתוֹכֵנוּ. הוּא יִפְתַּח לִבֵּנוּ בְּתוֹרָתוֹ וְיָשֵׂם בְּלִבֵּנוּ אַהֲבָתוֹ
וְיִרְאָתוֹ וְלַעֲשׂוֹת רְצוֹנוֹ וּלְעָבְדוֹ בְּלֵבָב שָׁלֵם לְמַעַן לֹא נִיגַע
לָרִיק וְלֹא נֵלֵד לַבֶּהָלָה. יְהִי רָצוֹן מִלְּפָנֶיךָ יְיָ אֱלֹהֵינוּ וֵאלֹהֵי
אֲבוֹתֵינוּ שֶׁנִּשְׁמֹר חֻקֶּיךָ בָּעוֹלָם הַזֶּה וְנִזְכֶּה וְנִחְיֶה וְנִרְאֶה וְנִירַשׁ
טוֹבָה וּבְרָכָה לִשְׁנֵי יְמוֹת הַמָּשִׁחַ וּלְחַיֵּי הָעוֹלָם הַבָּא. לְמַעַן
יְזַמֶּרְךָ כָבוֹד וְלֹא יִדֹּם יְיָ אֱלֹהַי לְעוֹלָם אוֹדֶךָּ. בָּרוּךְ הַגֶּבֶר אֲשֶׁר
יִבְטַח בַּיְיָ וְהָיָה יְיָ מִבְטַחוֹ. בִּטְחוּ בַיְיָ עֲדֵי־עַד כִּי בְּיָהּ יְיָ צוּר
עוֹלָמִים. וְיִבְטְחוּ בְךָ יוֹדְעֵי שְׁמֶךָ כִּי לֹא־עָזַבְתָּ דֹרְשֶׁיךָ יְיָ. יְיָ חָפֵץ
לְמַעַן צִדְקוֹ יַגְדִּיל תּוֹרָה וְיַאְדִּיר.

The חַזָּן:

יִתְגַּדַּל וְיִתְקַדַּשׁ שְׁמֵיהּ רַבָּא. בְּעָלְמָא דִּי בְרָא כִרְעוּתֵהּ וְיַמְלִיךְ
מַלְכוּתֵהּ, בְּחַיֵּיכוֹן וּבְיוֹמֵיכוֹן וּבְחַיֵּי דְכָל־בֵּית־יִשְׂרָאֵל בַּעֲגָלָא וּבִזְמַן קָרִיב
וְאִמְרוּ אָמֵן.

יְהֵא שְׁמֵהּ רַבָּא מְבָרַךְ לְעָלַם לְעָלְמֵי עָלְמַיָּא.

יִתְבָּרַךְ וְיִשְׁתַּבַּח וְיִתְפָּאַר וְיִתְרוֹמַם וְיִתְנַשֵּׂא וְיִתְהַדָּר וְיִתְעַלֶּה וְיִתְהַלָּל

שְׁמֵהּ דְּקֻדְשָׁא בְּרִיךְ הוּא. לְעֵלָּא מִן כָּל־בִּרְכָתָא וְשִׁירָתָא תֻּשְׁבְּחָתָא
וְנֶחֱמָתָא דַּאֲמִירָן בְּעָלְמָא וְאִמְרוּ אָמֵן:
יְהֵא שְׁלָמָא רַבָּא מִן שְׁמַיָּא, וְחַיִּים עָלֵינוּ וְעַל כָּל יִשְׂרָאֵל וְאִמְרוּ אָמֵן:
עוֹשֶׂה שָׁלוֹם בִּמְרוֹמָיו, הוּא יַעֲשֶׂה שָׁלוֹם עָלֵינוּ, וְעַל כָּל יִשְׂרָאֵל וְאִמְרוּ
אָמֵן:

עָלֵינוּ לְשַׁבֵּחַ לַאֲדוֹן הַכֹּל, לָתֵת גְּדֻלָּה לְיוֹצֵר בְּרֵאשִׁית, שֶׁלֹּא
עָשָׂנוּ כְּגוֹיֵי הָאֲרָצוֹת, וְלֹא שָׂמָנוּ כְּמִשְׁפְּחוֹת הָאֲדָמָה, שֶׁלֹּא
שָׂם חֶלְקֵנוּ כָּהֶם וְגוֹרָלֵנוּ כְּכָל הֲמוֹנָם, וַאֲנַחְנוּ כּוֹרְעִים
וּמִשְׁתַּחֲוִים לִפְנֵי מֶלֶךְ מַלְכֵי הַמְּלָכִים הַקָּדוֹשׁ בָּרוּךְ הוּא,
שֶׁהוּא נוֹטֶה שָׁמַיִם וְיוֹסֵד אָרֶץ, וּמוֹשַׁב יְקָרוֹ בַּשָּׁמַיִם מִמַּעַל,
וּשְׁכִינַת עֻזּוֹ בְּגָבְהֵי מְרוֹמִים הוּא אֱלֹהֵינוּ אֵין עוֹד. אֱמֶת מַלְכֵּנוּ
אֶפֶס זוּלָתוֹ, כַּכָּתוּב בְּתוֹרָתוֹ, וְיָדַעְתָּ הַיּוֹם וַהֲשֵׁבֹתָ אֶל־לְבָבֶךָ
כִּי יְיָ הוּא הָאֱלֹהִים בַּשָּׁמַיִם מִמַּעַל וְעַל־הָאָרֶץ מִתָּחַת, אֵין עוֹד:

עַל כֵּן נְקַוֶּה לְּךָ יְיָ אֱלֹהֵינוּ לִרְאוֹת מְהֵרָה בְּתִפְאֶרֶת עֻזֶּךָ,
לְהַעֲבִיר גִּלּוּלִים מִן הָאָרֶץ, וְהָאֱלִילִים כָּרוֹת יִכָּרֵתוּן לְתַקֵּן
עוֹלָם בְּמַלְכוּת שַׁדַּי. וְכָל־בְּנֵי בָשָׂר יִקְרְאוּ בִשְׁמֶךָ, לְהַפְנוֹת
אֵלֶיךָ כָּל־רִשְׁעֵי־אָרֶץ. יַכִּירוּ וְיֵדְעוּ כָּל־יוֹשְׁבֵי תֵבֵל, כִּי לְךָ
תִּכְרַע כָּל־בֶּרֶךְ, תִּשָּׁבַע כָּל־לָשׁוֹן. לְפָנֶיךָ יְיָ אֱלֹהֵינוּ יִכְרְעוּ
וְיִפֹּלוּ, וְלִכְבוֹד שִׁמְךָ יְקָר יִתֵּנוּ, וִיקַבְּלוּ כֻלָּם אֶת־עוֹל מַלְכוּתֶךָ,
וְתִמְלוֹךְ עֲלֵיהֶם מְהֵרָה לְעוֹלָם וָעֶד, כִּי הַמַּלְכוּת שֶׁלְּךָ הִיא,
וּלְעוֹלְמֵי עַד תִּמְלוֹךְ בְּכָבוֹד, כַּכָּתוּב בְּתוֹרָתֶךָ, יְיָ יִמְלֹךְ לְעֹלָם
וָעֶד: וְנֶאֱמַר וְהָיָה יְיָ לְמֶלֶךְ עַל־כָּל־הָאָרֶץ, בַּיּוֹם הַהוּא יִהְיֶה יְיָ
אֶחָד וּשְׁמוֹ אֶחָד:

Mourner's קַדִּישׁ:
יִתְגַּדַּל וְיִתְקַדַּשׁ שְׁמֵיהּ רַבָּא. בְּעָלְמָא דִּי בְרָא כִרְעוּתֵהּ וְיַמְלִיךְ
מַלְכוּתֵהּ, בְּחַיֵּיכוֹן וּבְיוֹמֵיכוֹן וּבְחַיֵּי דְכָל־בֵּית־יִשְׂרָאֵל בַּעֲגָלָא וּבִזְמַן קָרִיב
וְאִמְרוּ אָמֵן:
יְהֵא שְׁמֵהּ רַבָּא מְבָרַךְ לְעָלַם לְעָלְמֵי עָלְמַיָּא
יִתְבָּרַךְ וְיִשְׁתַּבַּח וְיִתְפָּאַר וְיִתְרוֹמַם וְיִתְנַשֵּׂא, וְיִתְהַדָּר וְיִתְעַלֶּה וְיִתְהַלָּל
שְׁמֵהּ דְּקֻדְשָׁא בְּרִיךְ הוּא. לְעֵלָּא מִן כָּל־בִּרְכָתָא וְשִׁירָתָא תֻּשְׁבְּחָתָא
וְנֶחֱמָתָא דַּאֲמִירָן בְּעָלְמָא וְאִמְרוּ אָמֵן:
יְהֵא שְׁלָמָא רַבָּא מִן שְׁמַיָּא, וְחַיִּים עָלֵינוּ וְעַל כָּל יִשְׂרָאֵל וְאִמְרוּ אָמֵן:
עוֹשֶׂה שָׁלוֹם בִּמְרוֹמָיו, הוּא יַעֲשֶׂה שָׁלוֹם עָלֵינוּ, וְעַל כָּל יִשְׂרָאֵל וְאִמְרוּ
אָמֵן: